AF531186

The Horses of the Royal Canadian Mounted Police

The NWMP Musical Ride from a painting by Frederic Remington, 1877.

The Horses of the Royal Canadian Mounted Police

A PICTORIAL HISTORY

William and Nora Kelly

1984
Doubleday Canada Limited, Toronto, Ontario
Doubleday & Company, Inc., Garden City, New York

Library of Congress Catalog Card Number 84-10344

First Edition

Production by Paula Chabanais Productions
Designed by Donald Fernley
Typesetting by ART-U Graphics Ltd.
Printed in Canada by D.W. Friesen & Sons Ltd.

Canadian Cataloguing in Publication Data
Kelly, William, 1911–
The horses of the Royal Canadian Mounted Police: a pictorial history

Includes index.
Bibliography: p. 283
ISBN 0–385–19544–3

1. Police horses–Canada. 2. Horses–Canada.
3. Royal Canadian Mounted Police–History.
I. Kelly, Nora (Nora Hickson). II. Title.

FC3216.9.H6K44 1984 363.2'0971 C84–098790–0
HV8157.K44 1984

Library of Congress Cataloging in Publication Data
Kelly, William, 1911–
The horses of the Royal Canadian Mounted Police.

Bibliography: p. 283
Includes index.
1. Police horses–Canada–History. 2. Royal Canadian Mounted Police–History. I. Kelly, Nora (Nora Hickson) II. Title.
HV7957.K44 1984 636.1'0886 84–10344
ISBN 0–385–19544–3

Also by William and Nora Kelly

The Men of the Mounted (Nora Kelly)
The Royal Canadian Mounted Police: A Century of History
(Nora and William Kelly)
Policing in Canada (William and Nora Kelly)

Contents

To the memory of the horses
of the North-West Mounted Police
and the Royal North-West Mounted Police,
and their riders.

The North-West Mounted Police—NWMP
1873 to 1904

The Royal North-West Mounted Police—RNWMP
1904 to 1920

The Royal Canadian Mounted Police—RCMP
1920—

Preface

Why a history of the horses of the Royal Canadian Mounted Police? Because although many books have told and retold the story of the men, the sometimes pitiable, sometimes magnificent saga of the part the horses have played in the history of the Force, and hence of Canada, has never been recorded.

Without their horses, the North-West Mounted Police could never have made their prodigious eight-hundred-mile trek in 1874 over the trackless, inhospitable Canadian prairies, from Manitoba to the foothills of the Rockies. Without their horses, those original Mounted Police, fewer than three hundred men, could never have patrolled the 300,000 square miles of unsettled prairie for which the NWMP had the responsibility of policing.

The early NWMP horses provided the transportation that enabled the police to eliminate the unscrupulous whiskey traders who took advantage of the Indians. Similarly, the horses enabled the police to tend to the welfare of the settlers who, in subsequent years, flocked to the prairies and, at first, lived in dangerous isolation. The horses ridden by the police and police scouts played an important part in helping the Canadian militia to put down the Riel Rebellion in 1885. Without their horses, the men of the Royal North-West Mounted Police could never have hacked trails through hundreds of miles of desolate northern Canadian wilderness or have kept the peace during the powder keg of the post-First World War industrial disputes.

Moreover, those early feats of the men were often accomplished not merely with, but also at the expense of, their horses. During the Great March West, for example, all 310 NWMP horses endured hunger, thirst, plagues of mosquitoes, overwhelming heat, hail, thunderstorms, snowstorms and constant fatigue. Scores of them died on the march, and the others never fully recovered from their exhausting experiences and from drinking alkaline water, often the only water available to them on the prairies. During the Herculean building of the 357-mile Peace–Yukon trail in 1905-07, dozens of RNWMP horses died, and before the surviving animals could return to their own detachments, they had to trek more than one thousand trail miles back to their starting point.

The present horses of the Force, the sleek, black beauties of the Musical Ride, appear to have nothing in common with the work animals of earlier years, but the story of their breeding and training by the RCMP also deserves to be told.

Why is this book on the history of RCMP horses written by these two particular co-authors? The senior author served with the Force for thirty-seven years, from 1933 as a constable to 1970 as a deputy commissioner. His first impression of the horses came when, as a twenty-two-year-old recruit at the Regina barracks, waiting for the formation of his recruit squad, he saw the Musical Ride perform at the Regina exhibition grounds. An aeroplane flew low and buzzed over the horses; they scattered, throwing many riders. Only one rider was unable to remount his horse, which got back into formation and performed as perfectly riderless as the other horses with riders did.

Recruit Bill Kelly, who from childhood had been interested in horses, acquired an admiration for the RCMP horses which he still retains. When the equitation part of his police training began, he discovered, to his chagrin, that at first it dealt only with the important practice of grooming horses and cleaning stables, saddlery and harness. As the course progressed he thoroughly enjoyed the riding instruction, but there he learned, again to his chagrin, that the instructors were much less protective of the recruits than of the horses.

After graduation, Constable Kelly served for three years on three northern Saskatchewan detachments which used horses. There he travelled by saddle horse or by team and democrat while investigating such things as theft of cattle or wheat, the sudden death of a trapper, fishing or shooting of game out of season, and the making of illicit alcohol. If, travelling by team, he came to the end of a trail through the bush, he tied up his team, unharnessed one horse, saddled it with the saddle he carried in the democrat, and rode on. He developed his greatest appreciation of Mounted Police horses, however, when his team, Kit and Bess, carried him safely out of reach of two maddened wolf-dogs that pursued his small sleigh for miles over a frozen lake.

The interest of the co-author in Mounted Police horses also goes back many years. Nora Hickson grew up in Saskatchewan, a few miles from the site of old Fort Battleford, established by the early NWMP. After she became Mrs. Bill Kelly in 1940, she began writing about the Force. Her first book, *The Men of the Mounted,* was published in 1949, and after husband Bill retired in 1970, they worked together on *The Royal Canadian Mounted Police: A Century of History,* published in 1973. *Policing in Canada,* another joint effort, followed in 1976.

Each of those three books was written from a compulsion to fill what we considered a gap, and we planned this book with the same goal. We both have long realized the vital part that the horses of the Force have played in the work of the organization. We also recognize that the horses, especially those of the NWMP and the RNWMP, have helped shape Canadian history, often at great sacrifice. This book is our tribute to them.

William H. Kelly
Nora Hickson Kelly

ACKNOWLEDGEMENTS

It is impossible to thank, by name, everyone who has assisted us during the preparation of this book. Instead, we wish to thank RCMP Commissioner R. H. Simmonds for permitting us to deal with any members of the Force who could assist us in any way. We particularly thank those members, who include: the Officer in Charge of the Public Relations Branch; the RCMP historian and other members of that branch; the Officer in Charge of RCMP Equitation and the Musical Ride, his riding staff, and the staff of the Pakenham breeding station; and the curator of the RCMP Museum at Regina and his staff. Without their assistance, this book could never have been published. We gratefully acknowledge permission to use material from issues of the RCMP *Quarterly*, and we thank the authors of articles and other materials in those issues. We are grateful for the many photographs provided by the Force for inclusion in this book. Unless otherwise specified, all photographs are from the RCMP archives in Ottawa. We also thank members and ex-members for their generosity in providing photographs and information. We have made every effort to trace and credit accurately all the photographs in *The Horses of the Royal Canadian Mounted Police.* If any source has been cited incorrectly, we would appreciate being notified, through our publisher, so that any future editions may be emended.

Mid-winter equitation training in full winter dress. Regina, circa 1955.

Old Buck in later years, the "Bagley Pony," used on the March West, one of the original horses purchased in 1873. (RCMP Museum, Regina)

1

The Birth of the Force

How the Force Came To Be

Today the Royal Canadian Mounted Police no longer use horses, except for the Musical Ride and other ceremonial occasions. When the original organization was established, as "a Mounted Police Force for the North-West Territories," however, horses were as vital to the work of the Force as were its human members.

At that time, in 1873, the Dominion of Canada was just six years old. Only seven areas of the country had become provinces, and were, as such, responsible for their own policing. These were: Ontario, Quebec, New Brunswick, Nova Scotia and Prince Edward Island in the east; the then-small Manitoba bordering western Ontario; and British Columbia in the far west. The rest of Canada existed as the unorganized North-West Territories, for which the government of the Dominion of Canada was responsible.

During the late 1860s and the early 1870s, the federal government received many reports of lawlessness in the vast central prairie region of the Territories. Although only sparsely populated by Indians, Métis, fur traders and missionaries, the area obviously and urgently needed a police force. From Fort Whoop-Up and other outlaw trading posts near the foothills of the Rocky Mountains, unscrupulous white traders—many of them Americans—plied the Indians with whiskey in exchange for furs, buffalo robes and horses. The Indians, who had never before experienced alcohol, ran wild. They stole horses and traded them for more whiskey. They burned the legitimate trading posts of the Hudson's Bay Company. They robbed, tortured and murdered at will, so that travellers dared not venture near the foothills without an armed escort. Yet no one in the North-West Territories had the legal power to stop the whiskey trade or even to arrest a murderer.

Before the newly formed Dominion of Canada purchased the vast northwest from the fur-trading Hudson's Bay Company, which had owned it through British charter, that company had successfully maintained law and order in areas under its influence. However, the company's influence had never penetrated the foothills of the Rockies near what later became part of the Canadian–American border.

As the Canadian government knew, unscrupulous traders from Montana, just across the border in the United States, had discovered that whiskey, rifles and ammunition brought more profit than did such legitimate trading goods as blankets, calico, beads and knives. Those traders had built their outlaw forts in the foothills territory before it belonged to Canada, and they were still operating from them. The Canadian government also knew that the American traders acted illegally when they freely imported trade goods into Canada. They not only broke the import and export laws of the two countries, but they also failed to pay Canadian customs duties.

In May 1873, with the forceful approval of Prime Minister Sir John A. Macdonald, who was also Minister of Justice, an enabling Bill provided for the establishing of "a Police Force in the North-West Territories", to number not more than three hundred. Because of the huge area of that unsettled territory, the police would be mounted—on "the hardy horse of the country". Sir John A. had recently studied the Royal Irish Constabulary, a famous mounted police force, and he hoped the members of his new police would become equally good riders and marksmen. Armed simply but effectively, they would patrol the frontier, collect customs, prevent whiskey trading with the Indians, and generally maintain law and order. In doing so, they would also make the vast western prairies more attractive to potential settlers.

By September 1873, the Canadian government still had not sent any police to the lawless area. Then the U.S. government reported to Canada that white hunters from Fort Benton, Montana, had murdered more than thirty Assiniboine Indians in a "horrible massacre" in the Cypress Hills, North-West Territories. The U.S. government regretted that it could not initiate any action because the crimes had been committed on British territory.

On September 25, the Canadian government reacted to the Cypress Hills Massacre by passing an order-in-council appointing nine commissioned officers to the "Mounted Police Force for the North-West Territories". Recruiting followed immediately, and the formation of the North-West Mounted Police was underway.

The federal government's plan for its new mounted police force probably seemed perfectly feasible to officials in Ottawa, the capital of the young country. In fact, the scope of the plan was audacious.

The whole Force was to assemble at a point in Manitoba to be decided on later, and then the men and their horses would march straight west about eight hundred miles to the foothills of the Rockies, where they would establish order. Next the police would be divided into three groups. One group of men and horses would remain in the foothills. Another group would march north more than two hundred miles to Fort Edmonton, a Hudson's Bay Company trading post. The third group of police and their mounts would march back east about seven hundred miles and establish Mounted Police headquarters, probably at Fort Ellice, a prominent Hudson's Bay Company post on the upper Assiniboine River near the border of Manitoba and the North-West Territories, and a converging point of important trails leading into the Territories. From these three points of a huge, elongated, east-west triangle, the approximately 300,000 square miles of Canadian prairies would be policed by a Force of not more than three hundred men on horseback.

MAKING READY FOR THE MARCH WEST

The first recruits for the newly organized "Mounted Police Force for the North-West Territories" signed on in eastern Canada in the autumn of 1873. News of the Cypress Hills massacre had made the Canadian government anxious to get its new police force to the Territories as soon as possible. So, after slightly more than 150 recruits were accepted, they set out immediately to travel the all-Canadian Dawson Route to Lower Fort Garry in Manitoba before freeze-up. There they would train during the winter, it was planned, and the next spring they would march westward, mounted and armed with rifles, approximately eight hundred miles over open prairie to the foothills of the Rockies.

Grouped into Divisions (commonly called "Troops") "A", "B" and "C", of about fifty men each, three contingents set out in October 1873 from Collingwood on Lake Huron and crossed the Great Lakes by steamer.

From Prince Arther's Landing (Port Arthur) on Lake Superior to the Manitoba prairies, all contingents travelled for some miles in wagons and carts, but mainly in small boats over the notorious Dawson route. This route included dozens of small lakes and rivers and almost fifty back-breaking portages, some as long as two miles.

West of Lake of the Woods the third contingent, a few days behind the others, endured an early winter blizzard, not unusual for that part of the country. It soaked their tents, then froze them so hard that they could not be unpacked for several days. In sub-zero weather the contingent made a twenty-mile march through deep snow. The men had not been provided with uniforms to wear en route, although each had been issued with a greatcoat which, even over their regular clothing, failed to keep out the bitter cold. Their boots froze solid, forcing some men to march with their feet wrapped in underwear and shirts.

At last even the third contingent arrived safely at Lower Fort Garry on the Red River, twenty miles north of Winnipeg. There arrangements had been made by the man Sir John A. Macdonald had appointed acting commissioner of the Mounted Police Force, Lieutenant Colonel W. Osborne Smith, then commander of the Canadian militia at Fort Garry.

From the time of his appointment in September, Smith had been very busy on behalf of the new Force. He had made arrangements for the government to lease from the Hudson's Bay Company the Stone Fort, in which the men could be accommodated. He had hastily arranged for the erection of stables nearby for fifty horses, with harness rooms and storage space for hay and oats. Even more important, he had purchased thirty-three horses.

Smith was very conscious of the needs of the Force in this regard. In his correspondence with the Dominion government on his appointment he had stated: "No time should be lost in getting [horses] so as to have them in thorough training for any movement in the spring. Canadian [meaning Ontario and Quebec] horses do not do well till after a year's acclimatization. Horses can be bought much lower now than in the spring."

He had also set standards for the police horses he was to purchase: "One hundred and twenty-five dollars to be the price, the Horse to be over Four and under Seven years.... To be Fourteen hands three inches high at least.... A proportion of mares will not be objected to. When stallions are brought for inspection and approved they will be accepted as they stand, or if required to be altered at your [the sellers'] risk." No doubt Smith was aware of Sir John A.'s stipulation that the Force should use "the hardy horse of the country".

Both the quality and the number of horses purchased by Smith fell far short of police requirements. Most of them were unbroken broncos. In acquiring them Smith had faced the same problem the Force was to face as long as it depended upon horses for patrol work in the west, that of finding a sufficient number of suitable horses for an organization that was to become more like a first-class cavalry unit than an ordinary rural mounted police force.

By the time the police arrived at Lower Fort Garry in late October, the usual early prairie winter had set in. Smith, aware of the responsibilities the NWMP would face the following spring, immediately ordered Inspector J. M. Walsh to lay out a 40-by-50 yard training ground in the vicinity of the fort. According to James Fullerton, a recruit who was later to write about his experiences, this "hippodrome" was lined with brush to cushion the landing of inexperienced riders when they fell or were thrown to the frozen ground.

Acting Commissioner Smith, upon learning that the recruits had not been properly sworn in, had them sworn in at the Old Fort on November 3rd, and each man was given a regimental number.

The permanent commissioner, thirty-two-year-old Lieutenant-Colonel George Arthur French, formerly commandant of the Canadian School of Gunnery at Kingston, Ontario, arrived from the east in mid-December. He took over from Smith and immediately instituted a riding schedule for all ranks. Constables rode from 9:00 to 10:00 A.M. and officers from 10:00 to 11:00 A.M. Sub-constables of the three Divisions rode for one hour each day, each Division having two afternoons a week during the time left after the usual parade and foot-drill periods.

Inspector J. M. Walsh, acting adjutant, took over the additional duties of acting veterinary surgeon and riding master. Staff Constable (Sergeant-Major) Sam Steele, known as the "stablemaster", was assigned to "break" the horses and to instruct the NCOs and constables in riding. (Incidentally, rank names for the first few years were very confusing, with NCOs rated as several ranks of constables, and the men as sub-constables. In 1879, however, the various classifications became those which the police with military backgrounds had used from the beginning: constable, corporal, sergeant, staff sergeant and sergeant-major. That same year the "Mounted Police Force for the North-West Territories" officially became the North-West Mounted Police.)

Steele was a tall, fair-haired young man, so embarrassingly slim-waisted that he wore a sash under his tunic to give him a less girlish figure. Nevertheless, in spite of bitter winter weather with frequent sub-zero temperatures, he worked unceasingly with his fewer than forty horses and more than three times as many NCOs and men. As he wrote later in his autobiography, *Forty Years in Canada,* he "drilled five rides a day the whole of the winter in an open manège, and the orders were that if the temperature was not lower than 36 degrees below zero [Farenheit], the riding and breaking should go on."

Breaking the broncos was difficult work, as most of them had never been handled. Even after they had been gentled enough to let recruits mount, they often threw their riders violently to the ground.

Making matters worse, many of the men had no riding experience. The recruiting posters had stated that every man must be able to ride, but recruiting had been done so hurriedly, and the Force had left so hastily for the west, that there had been no riding tests. The officers and a solid core of others were experienced horsemen with military training, but the new Force also contained former clerks, tradesmen, professors, gardeners, planters, sailors, students, surveyors and even a bartender.

In spite of the inexperience of so many of the men, Commissioner French was determined that the horses would be well cared for. As a young Irishman he had served briefly with the Royal Irish Constabulary and had learned about horses. His order book of 1873 stated: "Many of the NCOs and men, being under the impression that they are permitted to finish their stable work and return to barracks long before the stable hour expires, are labouring under a great mistake; for the future they will occupy the whole stable hour in grooming their horses with the exception of the time employed in feeding and watering."

In mid-December the North-West Mounted Police made its first patrol, searching for whiskey smugglers operating among Cree Indians on the west shore of Lake Winnipeg. The patrol, however, was not mounted. Instead, Inspector J. F. Macleod, a constable, and three sub-constables (one from each troop) used police horses to draw bobsleighs. They also took two dogteams hauling toboggans, loaded with tents, blankets, food, and snowshoes for the most difficult part of the patrol.

On the fourth day the police reached the traders' small shack, where they found ten gallons of liquor. Accounts differ, but the Force's first official historian, John Peter Turner, reported that the police spilled the liquor on the snow, arrested the six traders, and took them back to the Stone Fort for trial. The little party, including the six prisoners in the horse-drawn bobsleighs, arrived at the fort the day before Christmas.

Satisfaction in the Force's first successful patrol added zest to the monotonous routine of riding, breaking horses and drilling during the bitter cold weather. Sometimes dances also broke the monotony. On one occasion Staff Constable Steele and a comrade accepted an invitation to a ball in Winnipeg, twenty miles distant, and rode there in spite of a strong head wind and a temperature of 20 degrees below zero Fahrenheit. Steele's position as riding instructor allowed him to take the best horses for the forty-mile round trip. So he and his friend rode trained American trotters which the police had purchased in Iowa, U.S.A., from Colonel Shaddock, an American army officer from whom other horses were purchased later. Steele wrote that in spite of the weather, the ride was one of the warmest he had ever experienced. "The seat," he explained, "was a military one, which all soldiers practiced, every stride raising us several inches off the saddle and bringing us down with a bump which would have been fatal to anyone with a weak heart."

During the rest of the winter Steele continued to train horses and men. By mid-winter "horse exercise" was instituted, in which horses were taken for long and arduous rides, which hardened both horses and recruits in preparation for the long march the following summer. Basic cavalry manoeuvres also became part of the training. Riding drill was now organized into classes, with officers and constables in one class, and sub-constables divided into classes according to proficiency. In addition, each troop practised as a unit two afternoons a week. Steele wrote later that by spring the men "were very fine riders, laying the foundation of Canadian horsemanship in the wild and woolly west."

Meanwhile, Commissioner French had long since realized that in order to achieve his dream of "an immense, unbridled realm policed by a thoroughly organized and fully equipped body of troopers", he needed more men and horses. Early in 1874 he went to Ottawa to persuade the government to increase the strength of the Force to the maximum of three hundred and to allow him to purchase the necessary number of horses.

By this time the Conservative government of Sir John A. Macdonald had fallen and had been succeeded by a Liberal government. The new prime minister, the Hon. Alexander Mackenzie, was a strong advocate of prohibition and fervently hoped to suppress the whiskey traffic in the North-West Territories. In March 1874, his government authorized what French asked.

Thousands of men, many of them influenced by romantic ideas of scarlet-tunicked police galloping over the western prairies, applied to join the Mounted Police Force. Commissioner French personally supervised the choice of about two hundred mature, well-developed men, most of whom had some military service, and a few of whom had experience in the Royal Irish Constabulary. He had no difficulty in forming three good Division, "D", "E" and "F". The extra fifty men he planned to use as replacements for the anticipated drop-outs, invalids and dismissals among the original 150 men in the first three hastily recruited Divisions.

Commissioner French also personally supervised the purchase of approximately 250 horses suitable for saddle or carriage use, many of which had Standardbred blood. These he acquired mainly from farmers and horse dealers in the Toronto and Kingston areas of Ontario. The horses, of many different colours, were assembled with the men at the New Fort, Toronto, on the site of the present-day Canadian National Exhibition grounds. To avoid the prairie rainy season, the commissioner planned that they would remain at the New Fort, on the shore of Lake Ontario, during April and part of May. Meanwhile, horses and men would be trained in mounted drill.

Near the end of April 1874, the Canadian government appointed John L. Poett as the first veterinary surgeon to the North-West Mounted Police. Canada had few such qualified veterinarians in those days, and the position seemed made to order for the young Scotsman. He had graduated from the Edinburgh Veterinary College and had served as First Veterinary Surgeon to the Royal Horse Artillery, but he had also lived and practised in Canada for several years. The importance the NWMP placed on its horses is indicated by the fact that the salary of the veterinary surgeon was $1,400 a year, which was $200 more than the salary of the surgeon who attended the men.

Poett's first task was to inspect the horses assembled in Toronto, and to make sure they were fit for active duty. He could see at a glance that no matter what their colour they were exceptionally fine horses. They were all over 15.5 hands high, and with good conformation. However, he discovered that many were infected with catarrhal fever, a type of equine influenza that had swept southern Ontario in the autumn of 1872. The disease was not serious, and most of the afflicted horses seemed to recover quickly. The infection actually lingered, however, as later events would show.

The horses needed full health and strength to survive what was to come, although the first part of their journey west was no problem. They would not have to endure travelling over the rigorous Dawson Route, since the Canadian government had obtained permission from the U.S. government for the Mounted Police to travel through the United States, provided that the police wore civilian clothes, and that rifles, ammunition and officers' swords were packed in boxes. The plan was that the horses as well as the men should go by train from Toronto to Fargo, North Dakota, a journey of about 1,300 miles.

From Fargo, Divisions "D", "E" and "F" would march 160 miles north to Camp Dufferin, site of the present-day town of Emerson, Manitoba. There they would meet Divisions "A", "B" and "C", and from that point the whole Force would set out on its long march westward.

On June 6, 1874, two weeks later than Commissioner French had hoped, two special Grand Trunk Railway trains left Toronto, carrying the commissioner, 15 other officers, 201 constables and sub-constables and 244 splendid horses.

At Sarnia, Ontario, the trains picked up nine railway cars of farming equipment the police had purchased earlier because the men would have to be pioneers as well as police on the unsettled prairies. For ease of shipping, the wagons, mowing machines, hayrakes, ploughs and harrows had been taken apart and would later have to be re-assembled. After crossing into the United States at Detroit, Michigan, the special trains picked up two cars containing thirty-four more horses.

Embarkation of NWMP horses at Toronto, June 6, 1874. (Henri Julien sketch)

Poett's arrangements for shipping, feeding and watering the horses en route worked well, except perhaps for the second night out of Toronto. On June 7 the police stopped at the stockyards in Chicago, Illinois, so that the horses could feed in open corrals overnight. Literally thousands of pigs wallowed in sties near the horses' corrals, and for the two officers and thirty men who were assigned to guard the horses, it was a miserable night. It rained ceaselessly, and the pigs gave off an unbearable stench.

Although travelling by train for 1,300 miles was relatively comfortable for the men, the horses grew weary from having to stand for many hours at a time, always bracing themselves against the constant lurching of the trains. The lurching also resulted in some kicks and contusions that demanded Poett's attention. More difficult for the animals, however, was the lack of enough space to lie down. Although the horses had another day's rest after leaving Chicago, one horse, in a car with fifteen others, eventually became so tired that it did lie down. It was badly trampled. In spite of Poett's best efforts, it died within two hours and became the first of many casualties among the Mounted Police horses in their westward trek.

On the morning of June 12 the two Grand Trunk Railway trains arrived in Fargo, North Dakota. After disembarking the horses and attending to them, the police unloaded the freight cars. They planned on fitting the wagons together and using them immediately as transport for the 160-mile northward trek. To their dismay they found that not only the wagons, but the harness and even the saddles had been shipped in pieces. Moreover, the harness was of different makes, and the wagon parts had been distributed haphazardly along the line of freight cars. Before the men could assemble anything, they had to spread everything out over an open area of several acres, and then search here and there for bits and pieces that would fit together.

At four o'clock the next morning, in the first light of dawn, Commissioner French set his men to work in relays. The saddlers, working under the saddler-major, began to sort out the harness and saddlery, while the wheelers put the wagons together. Other men carried out the stores from the railway cars, and later loaded them onto the wagons.

To the surprise of the Fargo townspeople, the police accomplished most of their seemingly impossible task that same day. At five o'clock in the afternoon, "D" Division left Fargo with twenty-nine loaded wagons drawn by fifty-eight riding horses. Six miles out on the trail they made camp and waited for the others. At seven o'clock that evening, "E" Division left Fargo. The next day "F" Division followed with all but the heaviest stores, which would be shipped to Dufferin by Red River steamer.

As the wagons left Fargo, the first of many troubles beset the police and their horses. Many of the horses had never been hitched to vehicles. Some kicked and bucked, refusing to pull the wagons till the men soothed them and put their own shoulders to the wheels. Others galloped wildly over the prairie, their inexperienced drivers unable to stop them until troopers on horseback rounded them up.

Also during the first six miles of the northward trek along the cart trail that followed the left bank of the Red River, the Force lost its second horse. A grey mare, which Poett had treated in Toronto for a severe attack of laryngitis, suddenly became prostrated about four miles out of Fargo. It died almost immediately. The veterinary surgeon believed it had died from "acute congestion of the lungs brought on by over exertion and insufficient strength after [its] late illness".

That night in camp, horses and men endured the onslaught of great swarms of mosquitoes. The wakeful men could at least fight back by swatting and by using a foul-smelling concoction recommended at Dufferin, but the insects settled in layers on the defenseless animals. Henri Julien, a Montreal correspondent-artist for the *Canadian Illustrated News,* who was accompanying the police, reported half seriously that the fierce insects could tear a mosquito net to pieces or put out a fire. The next day, Sunday, French designated as a day of rest. The constant attack from mosquitoes day and night probably made men and horses glad to get moving on Monday morning, however, even though the bloodthirsty insects followed them.

As Divisions "D", "E" and "F" pushed on towards Dufferin, Commissioner French had good reason to regret that unavoidable two-week delay in leaving Toronto. The unusual mid-June heat of early summer drove the temperature into the nineties. The horses were not acclimatized, and many, especially those weakened from their catarrhal fever, suffered greatly from the intense heat. They also developed saddle and collar sores. Long daily marches, sometimes more than thirty miles, and the unaccustomed work of pulling wagons added more strain. Two weakened horses died from sunstroke.

French recognized the difficulties thrust on his horses, but he felt he must hurry for several reasons. As long as he and his men were on U.S. soil, where only U.S. law applied, he had no legal authority. He might also have wanted to hurry through the Sioux Indian territory he was crossing. No doubt he was also very aware that in little more than a week, from the summer solstice onward, the days would be getting shorter. The sooner he could get back to Canadian soil, and the sooner he could begin the march west, the better.

From the beginning of the 160-mile northward journey, French had considered the horses by making sure that the wagons were not too heavily loaded. On the other hand, he felt he could allow only five days to get from that first camp to Fort Dufferin, where the recently promoted Assistant Commissioner Macleod and Divisions "A", "B" and "C" would arrive from Lower Fort Garry ahead of him.

French's 1874 annual report to the government made light of his journey's difficulties, although Poett's appendix to the same report stated that the horses "suffered much", and that it "began to tell on the still enfeebled constitutions of some of them".

"On [June] the fifteenth," French wrote, "we made our regular start, doing about 27 miles; and as the wagons were lightly loaded (11 cwt being the maximum), some being empty, and having a number of spare horses, we kept up and exceeded this rate to the 19th...."

He did mention that the Force had so far lost "only" four horses. What he failed to mention was that the losses might have been greater, except that Macleod had sent twenty-five fresh western horses from Dufferin to meet him part way.

On the evening of June 19, the three Divisions from the east camped alongside the already settled "A", "B" and "C" Divisions at Fort Dufferin, Manitoba, a Hudson's Bay Company post with an adjoining small settlement just across the Canadian-American border from Fort Pembina, North Dakota. There the easterners picketed their horses in a make-shift corral of stakes and cables surrounded by a protective outer ring of loaded wagons, with only a single-passage opening left at one point. As they picketed them, they looked askance at the scrawny bronco ponies of "A", "B" and "C" Divisions, tethered some distance away at picket lines on the open prairie.

The next night, however, the broncos proved their worth. At ten o'clock a fierce thunderstorm suddenly broke on the police encampment. Incessant streaks of forked lightning lit up the sky and deafening thunder shook the earth, while high winds lashed hail and rain to a stinging velocity. The western ponies in their picket lines merely turned their backs to the weather. But the eastern horses were unaccustomed to prairie thunderstorms. They plunged about in their zareba of wagons, terrified by the lightning and the storm noises, especially by the fusillade-like flapping of the canvas wagon-covers that had been ripped open by the first strong gusts of wind.

The men were ordered to turn out, but they could only stand and watch as the fury of the storm increased. Staff Constable Steele, who was riding near the large corral, saw the whole incident. Lightning suddenly struck in among the eastern horses. They snapped their halter ropes and charged wildly through the circle of heavily loaded wagons, trampling several to kindling. Dashing through a row of tents, they headed for the gate of the large field in which the police were camped. Nothing could halt them. The six guards who tried were trampled underfoot, one with his scalp gashed and pulled over his forehead.

As the frenzied animals charged the gate they clambered over one another in horrible confusion, the screams of the injured rising above the howling cyclonic

Preparing for the March West at Fort Dufferin, June 1874. (Henri Julien sketch)

wind. Flashes of lightning lit the awful scene as the helpless police watched about 250 horses gallop out into the open, across the Pembina bridge and into North Dakota. Steele wrote later that the unforgettable night had a "weird and romantic complexion, typically suggestive of the wild west".

At daybreak the next morning, Steele, Sub-Inspector James Walker, Chief Constable J. B. Mitchell and others saddled western broncos and Steele's favourites, the Shaddock horses. They rode after the runaways, hoping to capture them before the Sioux got them. The police were painfully aware that if they lost many horses at this point, they could not even begin their westward march. At worst, it might have been the end of the North-West Mounted Police.

Even though the eastern horses were still tired from their 160-mile march from Fargo to Dufferin, they were so crazed with fright that by the time they halted from exhaustion, they had galloped between thirty and fifty miles into North Dakota. The western horses overtook most of them, and all but one of the rest were recaptured later. By the time Steele and his comrades had herded the runaways back to camp, they had ridden a hundred miles in twenty-four hours.

Fifteen-year-old trumpeter Frederick Bagley, determined to share in the adventure, had ridden with the older men. Like them he had spent a full day in the saddle. When his horse delivered him back to camp he was fast asleep, so exhausted that he had to be lifted down and put to bed.

During the next few days, many of the horses lay about scarcely moving. Some of the eastern horses were so unnerved by their terrifying experience that for the rest of the summer they were ready to stampede at any unusual noise. Poett noted other effects. For example, many of the eastern horses that had not quite recovered from various diseases, especially chest diseases, now had relapses. Some of the western horses used to recapture the others became so exhausted that as soon as they returned to camp they, too, were sent to the veterinary surgeon. And now some of the western animals, perhaps because of their exhaustion, contracted catarrhal fever from the eastern ones.

While the horses were resting, the police made what they thought were final preparations for the march west. Commissioner French rode back and forth over the sixty miles between Dufferin and Winnipeg attending to related matters. Men who knew anything about the North-West Territories warned French that he would be forced to turn back. Métis recently arrived from the west reported that the prairies were unusually dry and that sufficient water and pasturage for large numbers of animals would be hard to find. The best-informed Winnipeg man prophesied that French would lose 40 per cent of his horses and be lucky to be back by Christmas. It was one thing for a small party of men and carts to travel northwest over well-travelled trails to the established Hudson's Bay Company posts, through areas where they could find enough water and pasturage. It would be quite different for a large pioneer police force to head straight west into uncharted plains.

French, however, refused to be daunted. His men continued to sort uniforms, arms, saddlery and stores and to pack supplies in wagons and ox-carts. Officers bought cattle to be slaughtered en route and others for breeding purposes, and about a hundred oxen for transport and farming. Extra troops from Divisions "D", "E" and "F" were transferred to bring "A", "B" and "C" up to strength. Finally each Division was assigned horses of a distinctive colour, and every man was detailed to look after a particular horse.

Young Trumpeter Bagley coveted an unusual buckskin with a black streak along its back, although he knew that another man had chosen it first. When the horses were assigned, Bagley arranged to be "guarding" it. He got the animal and also the reputation of being a "danged hoss thief".

Now came the frustration. Even after the police would have been ready to move on, they had to wait for revolvers from England and other supplies slow in arriving. Many of the men were already dispirited from the heat, the mosquitoes, the unusually hard work, the news of Sioux scalpings just across the border, badly cooked food and rumours of dangers ahead. Defects in equipment had begun to appear. Although the saddlery was similar to what was supplied to the English cavalry of that time, it proved unsuitable for long patrols. The packing in the saddles loosened and gave the horses sore backs. The steel stirrups and buckles rusted easily and were difficult to keep clean.

One by one, thirty-one NCOs and men, some of them horseshoers, deserted and crossed over into the United States. A few others left when French offered to let them go without reproach.

Morale improved, however, when revolvers and other supplies arrived, and Commissioner French set July 6 as the starting date for the march west. Now there was another delay, but this one merely raised morale even higher. On the day set for departure, Commissioner French received a message from the commandant of the U.S. army post of Fort Pembina, saying that a band of Sioux had raided the

Stampede at Fort Dufferin, June 20, 1874. (Henri Julien sketch)

nearby settlement of St. Joseph (usually called St. Joe). The American commandant asked for the co-operation of the NWMP in cutting off the Indians if they tried to cross into Canada.

In their first mounted patrol a large section of the Force, fully armed, rode to the place where the Sioux were most likely to cross the border. The police saw no Sioux, and after a few hours they learned that the Indians had dispersed. Nevertheless, the men enjoyed the short-lived excitement of that mounted patrol. They rode back to the camp in high spirits, to make, during the next two days, what were indeed final preparations for the great March West.

The Great March West

Accompanied by bugle calls, cracking of whips and shouts of command, the astonishing two-mile-long cavalcade of North-West Mounted Police, which included 310 horses, pulled out of Dufferin toward evening on July 8, 1874, and headed into the late-afternoon sun for the foothills of the Rockies some eight hundred miles westward.

Division "A" took the lead, mounted on prancing dark bays. After "A" rumbled thirteen supply wagons covered by tarpaulins. The other five mounted Divisions marched behind, each followed by wagons, seventy-three in the whole cavalcade, drawn by horses of various colours. "B" rode dark brown horses, "C" had bright chestnuts, "D" were on greys and buckskins, "E" on blacks and "F" on light bays. The men's scarlet Norfolk jackets, white helmets and white gauntlets contrasted vividly with the drab prairie background, while the officers' colourful helmet plumes and gold embroidery added further splendour. Swords, brass buttons and brightly polished boots gleamed, while lance pennons fluttered in the breeze.

The 275 officers and men of the North-West Mounted were pioneers as well as police. During their great march, and later wherever they settled, they would have to protect and provide for themselves. Two nine-pounder field guns, two mortars and artillery ammunition wagons augmented "C" Division. At the rear of the procession came 114 ox-drawn Red River carts, two-wheeled carts made by the Métis completely of wood, with no proper greasing system, so they squeaked and creaked continuously as they moved. After the Red River carts came a large herd of cattle for slaughter; cows and calves; clanking mowing machines, ploughs and harrows; portable forges and field kitchens. Onlookers shook their heads as balky horses created confusion, cattle bawled and Métis drivers urged sullen and plodding oxen forward with flamboyant curses.

The "pull-out" or "Hudson's Bay start" of July 8 allowed the police to make sure that they had forgotten nothing important and that they were not too heavily loaded. After three miles they made camp by a small lake and checked everything. The next day Commissioner French sent two wagonloads of syrup and an insubordinate officer back to Dufferin, where the syrup was exchanged for oats, and the officer was left behind.

That first night out, some eastern horses stampeded. No specific reason is given in diaries or historical records, but almost any unaccustomed sound was enough to frighten the still nervous eastern horses. As usual, the police had put the horses in the centre of their encampment, in an enclosure made with a large cable and stakes. They used the wagons to make an outer enclosure, leaving passages at strategic points for sentries to be stationed. Frightened horses jumped the cables and dashed about until they found the passages, then galloped through them to the open prairie.

Next morning the police recovered all the horses, along with fifty oxen that had strayed away. In considering the incident, the police could see that perhaps the guards could not have prevented the stampede, but they certainly should have been able to prevent the oxen from straying. Obviously they needed a better guard system.

During the next five months Commissioner French and others kept diaries. John Peter Turner organized them later into a composite, vividly descriptive narrative in *The North-West Mounted Police.*

On the afternoon of July 9 the march continued. Men and horses were tortured by clouds of mosquitoes, one horse died and three broken-down wagons were left behind. On July 10, the mowing machines cut hay along the way, but the horses had to be sent across the Canadian-American border to the Pembina River in U.S. territory for water. On July 11, the men had no dinner at noon, but the horses were watered at a creek, and then the cavalcade pushed on for another six hours. When they camped late that evening, the nearest water was said to be fifteen miles away, so both men and animals did without any. During those first few days they made an average of less than twelve miles per day.

On July 12 young trumpeter Bagley, who with his buckskin pony was officially part of "D" Division, sounded reveille at 3:00 A.M. The men had no breakfast, and neither horses nor men had any water. They started marching at 5:00 A.M., again beset by mosquitoes. Later in the day they endured a heavy thunderstorm with hail, and then an enormous swarm of grasshoppers, one of many swarms plaguing Manitoba that year, blackened the air to the height of several hundred feet. The ravenous insects devoured all grass, flowers and leaves, attacked the paint and wood of the wagons and carbines, and penetrated the blanket rolls. Worst of all for the horses, the insects covered the drinking pools like a thick scum.

The next day the cavalcade got away at 3:00 A.M. Now the carts and wagons began to break down, causing many delays. The men tried to make up lost time by travelling until 8:00 P.M., when they camped at Calf Mountain, fifty-nine miles from Dufferin. Some of the horses, unaccustomed to the work required of them, showed signs of exhaustion. Even at that late hour, however, after seventeen long hours of travel, Commissioner French ordered the men to cut hay with the mowers before turning in.

On July 14, the cavalcade had great difficulty getting the wagons across the steep-banked Pembina River, which now flowed through Canadian territory in the path of the march. By the time they camped at 9:00 P.M., many horses were completely exhausted. Some Métis drivers and their oxen did not arrive in camp until midnight.

J. P. Turner's composite account of the march as it continued gave details from various diaries of the difficulties the police encountered. "July 15: Started at 6:00 A.M.... Distance covered 26 miles. July 16: Started at 4:00 A.M. and travelled twelve miles before breakfast.... Buffalo trails and wallows on all sides. July 17: Left at 3:00 A.M. and twelve miles without water.... Many wagons and carts far behind. July 18: Broke camp at 4:00 A.M.... The oat supply almost gone.... Two horses were left behind, unfit for further travel. Rain all night; mosquitoes bad."

By July 19, after only twelve days on the trail, many horses were too exhausted to go on, so for two days the dusty, travel-weary troops camped at their first

Cutting hay in the early days of the March West, 1874. (Henri Julien sketch)

crossing point of the meandering Souris River, where wood, water, and grass were abundant. All oxen and carts reached camp by nightfall of the first day, but two more horses were left behind, and two more died. At the Souris camp wheelers repaired wagons and carts, saddlers repaired saddlery and harness, blacksmiths shod horses at their portable forges, and all the men enjoyed the luxury of bathing and washing their clothes.

As the cavalcade resumed its journey, the horses continued to suffer. Most of those being used for team work were actually saddle horses. When they developed sore shoulders from ill-fitting harness, they had to be replaced by other saddle horses, which in turn developed sore shoulders. Making matters worse, most of the police used as teamsters had little or no experience in driving horses and were unable to help them in difficult situations.

The veterinary surgeon was in constant demand not only to try to treat harness galls, but also to treat horses suffering from other ailments. Often the only water available was from alkaline prairie sloughs. Horses died from acute attacks of dysentery. Many others developed diarrhoea, then became so exhausted and emaciated that they had to be abandoned or tended individually by sub-constables behind the column. One young member, alarmed when his invalid charge lagged far behind the column, shot it. On overtaking the others he explained breathlessly that five blood-thirsty Sioux had attacked him and shot his horse. Commissioner French did not believe him, but there was no time to investigate.

Occasional hail storms drove the still nervous eastern horses to stampede. Numerous prairie fires destroyed pasturage. The eastern horses became so debilitated that the men had to dismount and walk every alternate mile. Even the western horses suffered from the lack of good grass and water, the swarms of mosquitoes, and the intense heat which sometimes reached 100 degrees Fahrenheit.

By July 22, fourteen days out of Dufferin, horses and oxen, overcome by hunger and fatigue, straggled behind the main cavalcade to a distance of several miles. The next day more weak horses were left behind and another died. Fortunately, some temporary relief was at hand. Just beyond Roche Percée on the banks of the Souris River, in what is now southeastern Saskatchewan, the cavalcade found ample pasturage and fresh water and even coal, which the men used to boil water for bathing and washing clothes. There, 270 miles and sixteen days from Dufferin, Commissioner French called a halt for several days. At first many horses were so fatigued that when they lay down they could not get up without help. A few days later, the benefit the horses had derived from resting was offset by a urinary disease contracted from eating a broad-leafed plant. Many of them became ill, and one horse died of the disease which Veterinary Surgeon J. L. Poett reported as "a mild form of hamaturea [sic] or bloody urine".

The desperate condition of the horses forced Commissioner French to hold a consultation with his officers. They reviewed the government's proposal that the whole Force should march to the foothills of the Rockies, after which one group of police would remain there, a second group would march north to Fort Edmonton, and a third would return east to establish NWMP headquarters at Fort Ellice, about one hundred miles north-northeast of where they were presently camped near Roche Percée.

The commissioner and his officers considered the fact that they had accomplished about one-third of the journey to the Rockies, and that they would probably have to travel the remaining two-thirds over territory even more inhospitable than that over which they had already travelled. French and his officers agreed that, burdened by failing horses, dysentery-weakened men, and weary cattle, they could not accomplish even the first phase, the march to the Rockies, before winter set in, let alone the government's entire plan.

They decided that Inspector W. D. Jarvis should take the greater part of "A" Division to Fort Edmonton by way of Fort Ellice, while the rest of the Force marched westward. Most of the healthy horses and men of "A" Division would be transferred to other Divisions, and in their places Jarvis would receive the sickest horses and the youngest and weakest men. He would drop off the sick men and horses at Fort Ellice and then proceed north-westward to Fort Edmonton by way of the well-travelled Saskatchewan–Fort Edmonton cart trail, making a journey of almost eight hundred miles from Roche Percée.

After five days at Roche Percée, Commissioner French and the main contingent continued their journey westward to the foothills of the Rockies.

Two days later, on August 1, Jarvis and his depleted Division "A" of thirty-one men set out for Fort Ellice, with the sick men driving the wagons and thirteen Métis driving the carts. In addition to fifty-five sick horses he had five reasonably healthy horses, seventy-four oxen and cattle, fifty-seven ox-carts, twenty-six wagons, fifty-two cows and forty-five calves. There were also agricultural implements and general stores not deemed essential to the main body of the Force, one item of the latter being 25,000 pounds of flour.

At first, although the police changed horses twice each morning and afternoon, Jarvis and his contingent made only eight to ten miles each day. The footsore cows and calves lay down every few yards and had to be coaxed to their feet and prodded on. Horses collapsed, and four had to be abandoned, to recover if possible by themselves, once free of strain, and be retrieved later. At one point the exhausted horses could not pull the wagons over hills, and oxen had to replace them.

Inspector Jarvis was a man with a colourful vocabulary. When he was near any team having difficulty getting up a hill, he would often resort to shouting a string of rather earthy phrases of "encouragement" at the struggling team. One morning he was "encouraging" the team of an Irishman who had been brought up by a maiden aunt and so was not used to such vulgarity. The Irishman had the habit of noting in his diary any strong language he heard. As Jarvis passed, he sprang from the driver's seat, dropped to one knee, and wrote furiously in his little book. Nearby men laughed uproariously, but fortunately the inspector had already gone on to "encourage" other teams and was out of sight and earshot.

Camp on the banks of the Souris River, west of La Roche Percée, July 24, 1874. (Henri Julien sketch)

There were few such instances of comic relief for the Force on its great trek west. On the muddy bank of Calumet Creek, a few miles short of their destination, the men had to pull out five horses that had collapsed and were mired in the mud. Later, six horses came out from Fort Ellice to help Jarvis's contingent travel the last few miles to the fort, but even so, one more horse collapsed and died on arrival there.

Jarvis had taken twelve days to cover one hundred miles. The exhausted party remained at Fort Ellice for six days so that the animals Jarvis would take on farther could rest. Then he designated which animals and men should remain: the very sick men, some exhausted and sick horses, most of the cows and calves, and a large quantity of supplies. Nevertheless, when he left Fort Ellice on August 18, 1874, his column was quite substantial. It included two officers, twenty-one NCOs and constables, thirty horses, fifty-three ox-carts and thirteen Métis drivers, twelve wagons, and thirty head of cattle.

Although Jarvis was now travelling along the main cart trail from Fort Winnipeg to Forts Carlton, Pitt and Edmonton, the size of his column still created difficulties. Making matters worse, a week of hot dry weather was followed by rains which made the trails muddy and greasy. Then the weather turned cold but the rains continued. Horses still suffered from the effects of drinking alkaline water, and one died from dysentery.

In early September the weather turned so cold that ice formed overnight on the sloughs. On September 8, Jarvis and his column took all day to cross the South Saskatchewan River, even with the aid of a cable ferry already established there. The next day they pressed onward through torrential rain and hail, which culminated in a terrific thunderstorm. Two days later, on reaching Fort Carlton, still three hundred miles from Fort Edmonton, some of the horses were almost dead from exhaustion.

"If they were not government property, but my own," Jarvis remarked, "I would shoot the worst."

Fortunately, the Hudson's Bay Company post at Fort Carlton provided indoor stabling. For five days the horses were shielded from the sleet and the bitter cold northeasterly wind. While they rested, the remainder of the column laboriously crossed the nearby North Saskatchewan River by scow ferry.

Throughout the journey thus far, Jarvis had met many small parties of travellers, freighters, traders, missionaries and Métis hunters, many of whom were going east to Winnipeg in anticipation of winter. At Carlton he met a Roman Catholic priest who, while travelling from the south a few weeks earlier, had visited Commissioner French's westward bound column. The priest relayed to Jarvis the disheartening news that French's horses were in no better condition than his own and were dying in large numbers.

On September 20, Jarvis's horses were the last of his column to be ferried across the North Saskatchewan River, to join the larger part which had crossed five days earlier. The next day the entire party moved on again. Its parade state was much the same as when the column had left Fort Ellice, reduced by two horses, one ox, three cows, two wagons and nine carts.

The cart trail Jarvis and his contingent were following was difficult going at the best of times. A few miles out of Fort Carlton it became cluttered with roots and stones, which repeatedly tripped up the horses and oxen. As if this were not enough of a setback, recent downpours had flooded out long stretches of the trail, further reducing the party's rate of progress and intensifying the men's frustration.

Hauling the guns through the Dirt Hills, 1874. (Henri Julien sketch)

As the column plodded on, the men were able to augment their rations from the abundant wild ducks and geese flying south, but the horses' rations dwindled. Sharp frost had spoiled the pasturage. The supply of oats had run out before the column reached Fort Carlton, and although Jarvis had purchased barley from the Hudson's Bay Company there, many of the weakened horses could not digest the barley. They collapsed from hunger and fatigue, and the men had to raise them to their feet by sliding poles under them. At night the cold stiffened them so critically that the men had to get up several times to rub them down, losing sleep themselves and becoming exhausted, too, in the process.

On October 19, Jarvis and his pitiful procession straggled into the Hudson's Bay Post at Victoria, about seven hundred miles from Roche Percée. There they left behind all the cows and calves and eleven oxen, arranging with the trader to care for them during the winter. By this time the horses and the rest of the animals were little more than living skeletons, but loads were redistributed and a day or two later the reduced column pushed on.

Men went ahead to build corduroy roads over muddy stretches, and bridges over streams, all with logs cut from nearby woods. Where the deepest mudholes became sloughs, the men unloaded the wagons and hauled them across by hand. Then they carried the supplies over on horseback, reloaded the wagons and pushed on. Even with that help from the men, many horses kept falling in their tracks and had to be lifted to their feet. Other horses were kept going by men who walked beside them and incessantly urged them on, holding them to their tasks with both hands—one at the head, the other at the shoulder.

At Sturgeon Creek, on October 26, not far from Fort Edmonton, it seemed that the exhausted animals and men might never reach their destination. Some of the horses, unable to proceed, were left behind in tents with specially chosen men to care for them. Then, in a desperate effort to survive, the rest of the animals and men crept forward for twenty continuous hours. Historian Turner gives details taken from the October 26 entries in the various diaries:

> The trail grew worse, sloughs across it every few hundred years; men and animals struggled knee-deep in black mud. Time and again the wagons had to be unloaded and dragged out by hand. On every side were small ponds covered with thin ice, which proved to be a menace. The horses and oxen, feverish and thirsty, would rush to the ponds, crash through and wait to be hauled out with ropes. Some were so exhausted they had to be held up by the head while the ropes were being attached.

At five o'clock the next morning, only four miles from Fort Edmonton, the column paused for a three-hour rest. The men pitched some tents and built two rows of fires, then washed, dried and rubbed down the horses. When the animals were turned out to graze for a short time, one became almost hopelessly mired and was saved only when a number of men, floundering in mud and water to their armpits, went to its rescue with ropes.

Just then Inspector Jarvis, who had ridden ahead, returned from Edmonton with the welcome news that he had obtained good winter quarters from the Hudson's Bay Company. Turner continues: "By great effort, Edmonton was reached over a fairly dry trail. Although exhausted, the horses pricked up their ears and made feeble attempts to trot towards the building."

During the next few days the police went back to help the animals who had lagged behind, and on November 2 the last stragglers reached Fort Edmonton, nearly 1,200 trail miles from Dufferin. Jarvis, in his first report to the Canadian government, commented, "The attention paid by Constable Labelle (farrier sergeant) to the horses saved many of them."

While Inspector Jarvis and his party were wending their tortuous way to Fort Edmonton, Commissioner French and his five Divisions, plus the remainder of Jarvis's "A" Division, freed of invalids and cattle, continued their march from Roche Percée, 270 miles west of Dufferin. As they left on the evening of July 29, their destination was, in general, the foothills of the Rockies some five hundred miles distant. More specifically, they aimed for the junction of the Bow and Belly (South Saskatchewan) rivers. There, the commissioner had been led to believe, he would find the infamous Fort Whoop-Up and the outlaw whiskey traders whose notoriety had been the ultimate catalyst for the formation of his police force. There, too, he had been told, he would find plenty of rich grazing land, suitable to support a strong police post.

French's contingent, like Jarvis's, suffered constant hardships along the way. But whereas Jarvis was faced with rain, sloughs and rivers, French had to contend with intense heat, thick clouds of mosquitoes, parched prairie and a general lack of good water and pasturage. The police suspected that the latter had been caused by the Indians setting prairie fires to impede their progress.

The intense heat of the prairie forced French and his men to travel morning and evening so that the horses could rest during the mid-day heat. In spite of the few days spent recuperating at Roche Percée, weary horses soon lagged far behind the main column, which itself was strung out for four or five miles. Although exhausted, the eastern horses were still nervous and stampeded one night after rockets were fired as a signal to a missing man who had wandered too far in search of ducks. On August 7, when the temperature reached a sizzling 91 degrees Fahrenheit, the weakened horses could not pull the guns across the Dirt Hills, estimated to be about a thousand feet above the plains, and had to be replaced by oxen.

During the next few days, in the region of Old Wives Lake, some 150 miles from Roche Percée, alkaline water aggravated the diarrhoea already prevalent among the horses and men. Sub-Inspector Cecil Denny noted in his diary, "Water scouring the horses.... Horses looking fearful.... A few more days of this and we shall not have a horse left." Veterinary Surgeon Poett stepped up the horses' treatment of large doses of flour and starch and added doses of carbolic acid, which partially controlled the ailment. By this time, however, the lack of oats for a considerable time had done almost irreparable damage to the horses' health. Even after Assistant Commissioner Macleod obtained 15,000 pounds of oats from the Boundary Commission stores, forty miles to the south, the police witnessed little improvement in the condition of the horses. The new supply of oats allowed a ration of only six pounds per day per horse. This was scarcely more than one-third of the seventeen pounds per day allowed the horses of the Department of Public Works in Winnipeg, where the horses also had ample hay and good water and very light work. The day after the oats arrived, Commissioner French was forced to leave twenty-six invalid horses and seven sick men at a place they called Cripple Camp.

On August 21 the cavalcade entered the last great buffalo range, which created new problems. Buffalo had trampled the few water holes into gumbo paste. Also, the ponderous herds had destroyed the pasturage, so that the horses' feed now consisted of a reduced ration of four pounds of oats daily and wild sage. The police blamed the sage for the urinary troubles which now plagued the horses, some of them fatally. As if this were not enough, while the column moved through the buffalo range, unidentified insects stung the male horses on their sheaths, causing swelling and pain. During the few days preceding August 23, by which time French was forced to send horses back to Cripple Camp with some regularity, nine horses collapsed from exhaustion.

On the night of August 24, in sight of the Cypress Hills, about 590 miles from Dufferin according to French's odometer fastened to a wheel of a vehicle, the cavalcade stopped to allow the men to reshoe horses and oxen and to repair equipment. In the course of this four-day halt, several Métis visited the camp and told hair-raising stories of Fort Whoop-up. French tried to buy some Indian ponies from them, but the outrageous price of $150 each was more than he was prepared to pay.

The police cavalcade set out again on August 29, but at the four-mile point they unexpectedly came on a fresh-water slough with plenty of good grass to augment the horses' oats, and with geese, ducks and antelope to augment the men's meagre food supply. There they decided to make camp. During their welcome two-day rest, Assistant Commissioner Macleod returned from his second trip to a Boundary Commission depot, this time with twenty-seven ox-cart loads of oats he had previously purchased.

Somewhat fortified and refreshed, animals and men marched on again. Soon they came upon great herds of buffalo travelling south to avoid the winter. For days the NWMP column travelled westward precariously through the moving herds, sometimes forced to line up transport wagons to head off stampedes of the ponderous creatures.

Cripple Camp. (Henri Julien sketch)

The subsequent scarcity of water and grass weakened the already weary horses. Each day more horses died, while exhausted and dying oxen lay strewn in the wake of the plodding cavalcade. One bitter cold and rainy night in early September, five horses dropped dead and three others almost collapsed. After that the commissioner ordered every officer and man to give up one blanket to a horse and to double up with a comrade to keep warm. Even so, some animals still wasted away and died. The march was becoming a disaster.

"I am beginning to feel very much alarmed for the safety of the Force," the commissioner wrote in his diary.

The police cavalcade crawled along with ever-increasing difficulty as cold rains fell. Horses continued to get sick and die. The police often made night camp on bare ground with no water or grass for miles around. In his diary, the commissioner wrote of this period, "Horses starving, oats alone just keeping them up." Then the horses began to have spasms in the face and neck, similar to those caused by the dreaded tetanus. A number of them died within twenty minutes after the spasms started. The veterinary surgeon blamed the attacks on the alternating heat and cold during the march which intensified the deplorable physical condition of the horses.

As Commissioner French sought the junction of the Bow and Belly (South Saskatchewan) rivers, which the scouts had told him was only a few miles ahead, and at which point he expected to find Fort Whoop-up, he ordered the horses turned loose in a well-grassed coulee. There, protected from a wet northeasterly wind, they could forage for themselves. When the men drove the horses out of the coulee to resume the march, however, five, little more than skeletons, were too weak to climb out and had to be left behind, some to fend for themselves in that sheltered place, although any obviously near death would be shot. Three others climbed out only with assistance from the men. The commissioner re-issued orders for the men to protect the horses with their own blankets. By this time, between the Cypress Hills and the junction of the Bow and Belly rivers, and over a journey of one-hundred and fifty miles, twenty-five horses and twelve hardy Red River oxen had died from the effects of cold and hunger.

On September 11, when the police reached the forks of the Bow and Belly rivers, they discovered, much to their disappointment, that the place contained neither Fort Whoop-up nor any rich grazing land. It was obvious to them that it would be futile to establish a police post there. Furthermore, French's scouts reported the alarming news that for thirty miles to the west there was neither grass nor trail, and if they continued in that direction they would again face thousands of buffalo migrating southward.

The only possible route was south to the well-wooded Sweet Grass Hills, some sixty miles away near the U.S. border. There the men could rest. Meanwhile, Commissioner French could go to Fort Benton, Montana, to buy supplies and to contact the Canadian government in Ottawa by telegraph. Later, refreshed and re-supplied, Divisions "B", "C" and "F" could continue west, and Divisions "D" and "E" could return east to establish NWMP headquarters.

Before breaking camp, French ordered Superintendent Walsh to take a contingent of seventy men, fifty-seven horses and some wagons and ox-carts directly north to Edmonton, and so avoid the extra travel of going first to the foothills. Soon, however, a scouting party reported to French that conditions to the north were no better than to the west. Commissioner French sent a courier to order the return of the north-bound contingent, and by the time it caught up with the main cavalcade, six of its horses and some oxen had already died.

Meanwhile, after a rest of three days, French's column of emaciated horses and oxen and tattered men set out for the Sweet Grass Hills. This was the most arduous stage of the whole journey, partly because of the appalling condition of the animals and men, and partly because the early winter had set in. On the first day out, two horses died, making a total of nine horses dead and five oxen abandoned within a mere thirty-six-hour stretch. By now the men were walking most of the time to spare the horses. Some had walked so far that their boots had fallen apart and they had to wrap their feet in sacks.

By mid-September, ice covered the prairie ponds. The men feared that an early snow would cover the dried buffalo chips, thereby depriving them of fuel. Worse still, a severe cold spell would kill the weakened animals and the men would have no means of transport whatsoever. But the ragged command plodded forward on sheer nerve, while horses and oxen staggered woodenly forward or dropped out along the trail. And always, except for the three conspicuous peaks of the Sweet Grass Hills in the distance, the same unbroken horizon stretched out before them. Lacking even mediocre pasturage on the ground trampled by the migrating buffalo, the pitiable horses struggled on, sometimes in penetrating rain, sometimes in sleet and snow. Sub-Inspector Denny wrote in his diary, "Can't go much farther."

On September 17, after travelling eight miles before breakfast, the column encountered a cold, wet gale. The men drew up the wagons to form a corral and draped tents to the windward side to protect the horses, blanketed and huddled inside. After the gale subsided men and animals plodded on, stiff legged, for another seven miles before camping for the night.

The next day spirits revived when the exhausted men had their first view of the glittering snow-capped Rockies, one hundred miles to the west. French and his party had ridden ahead to pick a camp site, and scouts brought back word that a camp with ample grass and water was being established a few miles ahead. According to Turner, as the column crept forward, the men shouldered the wheels, "stumbling and lurching, swearing and cheering," heartened by the news. Later that day, in driving sleet and snow and weakened by cold and hunger, the first of the trembling horses and tattered men of the eight-mile strung-out cavalcade reached the camp which would soon be known as Dead Horse Coulee.

NWMP crossing the Belly River, September 14, 1874. (Henri Julien sketch)

Back on the trail, the other men and animals staggered slowly on, only the men knowing that a camp with good water and grass was just a few miles ahead. Ex-Sub-Constable E. H. Maunsell, presumably the last survivor of the great march west, writing in the Winter 1983 issue of the *RCMP Quarterly*, had this to say about the last couple of days before reaching Dead Horse Coulee:

> About the twentieth of September, we experienced a severe snowstorm, and this day's march put me in mind of a picture I once saw of the retreat of Napoleon's army from Moscow: I was driving a Red River cart following the trail that the lead wagon had made in the snow. Now and then I would pass a wagon, the team of which was too played out to continue and was, therefore, waiting for the rear-guard to give it assistance.
>
> We also had a number of saddle horses which were so weak that they could not be induced to travel without being led. We used to tie seven or eight of these together in a line and a man would lead each string. If one of these fell, sometimes the whole line would tumble—like a lot of nine-pins.
>
> Because of this storm, the buffalo started moving south. The visibility, however, was extremely limited and, as a result, we were overrun quite frequently by bands of buffalo which did not seem to notice us in the thick snow.

At long last, all safe in the Sweet Grass Hills, about 850 trail miles from Dufferin according to French's odometer, the exhausted contingent rested. Divisions "B", "C" and "F" made plans to continue westward to set up a police post in the vicinity of the whiskey traders, while Divisions "D" and "E" prepared to return east to establish NWMP headquarters at Fort Ellice. French selected the best horses and oxen for "D" and "E", in anticipation of hundreds of miles more of gruelling march, and assigned all uneccesary stores and equipment to "B", "C" and "F".

A few days later, in preparation for continuing the march, the commissioner, Assistant Commissioner Macleod and eight men, plus several Métis drivers with empty ox-carts set out for Fort Benton, Montana, some 160 miles to the southeast. Inspector W. Winder was left in charge at Dead Horse Coulee. At Benton, the police's large purchase of oats, provisions, socks, gloves and moccasins was no surprise to the trading companies. Although the police had watched in vain for any sign of the notorious and powerful Blackfeet, those Indians had actually been stalking them for weeks and had subsequently spread the news of the red-coated pony-soldiers "thick as ants on a hill".

While at Benton, Commissioner French learned from Ottawa that when he

In sight of the Sweet Grass Hills. (Henri Julien sketch)

returned east he was to establish headquarters not at Fort Ellice, but about a hundred miles north of it, at Livingston on the Swan River, where contractors were already erecting police buildings. Also while at Benton he learned from the I.G. Baker Trading Company that Fort Whoop-Up was at the forks of the Belly and St. Mary's rivers. This point lay about seventy miles northwest of the Sweet Grass Hills and was easily reached by way of the Benton trail a few miles west of where the police Divisions were camped.

French left Benton ahead of Macleod to join Divisions "D" and "E", which were already on their way back east heading for the new location of NWMP headquarters at Swan River.

As Macleod and the others left Benton to return to the North-West Territories, they were accompanied by Jerry Potts, a half Blood Indian, half Scots plainsman with an uncanny sense of direction, even in country he scarcely knew. Commissioner French had engaged him as a scout and interpreter, chiefly to guide the police to Fort Whoop-Up, but he subsequently served the NWMP for twenty-two years. Potts now led Macleod and his party back to the Sweet Grass Hills.

Macleod sent word to Inspector Winder to meet him with the remaining men, horses, other animals and equipment, by travelling from Dead Horse Coulee, due west to the Benton trail. On October 2, Winder arrived as instructed. The next day Macleod arrived from Benton. Then, led by Jerry Potts, the diminished cavalcade went on to Fort Whoop-up.

At last three Divisions of the NWMP were in the heart of the untamed west. But Potts soon dispelled their expectations of daring whiskey traders and wild Indians. Most of the trading outfits, he said, had left for winter quarters in Missouri when they had learned that the Force was approaching. And the Blackfeet, in opulence after the season's trading, were not inclined to fight, except perhaps against their hereditary enemies, the Crees and the Assiniboines.

On October 9, Potts led Macleod and his men to the high ground overlooking the notorious fortress between the Belly and the St. Mary's rivers. There was no sign of life below, where the pallisaded, bastioned Fort Whoop-Up was flying a commercial flag which the men mistakenly thought was the Stars and Stripes. Nevertheless, Macleod ordered the two nine-pounder guns and the two mortars to be placed in strategic positions. Then, with rifles loaded and ready, Macleod's horsemen moved toward the fort. The men expected at any moment to receive an order to dismount and deploy.

"But", wrote historian Turner, "Macleod rode straight ahead, Potts at his side. There were murmurs of amazement as the assistant commissioner dismounted and strode toward the open main gate. Entering and going to the nearest building within the enclosure, he rapped on the door."

After Macleod's continued knocking, the door was opened by an uncouth, grey-haired man. Dave Akers nonchalantly invited the police to "come right in" and make themselves at home. All the whiskey traders had left the place long ago, he said, and the northern manager of the I.G. Baker Company was using the old fort as his own base. The manager was away, but the visitors were very welcome.

It was an anticlimax. Actually, long before Macleod and his men drew near the ill-reputed fort, a party of buffalo hunters had warned the traders that a large party of horsemen wearing red coats was approaching. The style of trading had been altered accordingly, and a thorough police search of the building revealed no liquor.

From Whoop-Up, Jerry Potts led Divisions "B", "C" and "F" to a place on the Old Man's River which he advised would be suitable for a permanent police post. There at ten o'clock on the morning of October 13, about nine hundred trail miles from Dufferin, Macleod ordered the troops to make camp.

"If you want to write home," a staff constable announced, "now is your chance. Your address is c/o North-West Mounted Police, Camp McLeod, North-West Territories, via Benton, Montana." Then, letters written, the men began chopping down cottonwood trees with which to build Fort Macleod.

By this time Commissioner French and Divisions "D" and "E" had marched several hundred miles back eastward, headed for the forks of the Swan and Snake rivers, spurred on by the commissioner's fear that an early winter would overtake the weary troops dressed mostly in threadbare summer clothing. At Cripple Camp they had picked up the former invalids, both horses and men, by then completely recovered, and in spite of continuing difficulties they neared the Swan River toward the end of October.

When the commissioner rode ahead to Livingston, however, to inspect the new Swan River barracks about which Ottawa had notified him, he was utterly dismayed. He found unfinished buildings strung out for a thousand feet on top of the biggest ridge of granite boulders in the district. The unseasoned wood had shrunk, and daylight filtered through the innumerable cracks. Not a tree protected the place from biting north winds, and there was neither accommodation nor equipment for all the men. Inspector A. Shurtliff, who had arrived from Fort Ellice, reported that half the hay which had been cut for winter use had been burned by prairie fires, as had all the hay the police had hoped to purchase from the Hudson's Bay Company.

French ordered the men to remain nearby at the Hudson's Bay Company post at Fort Pelly where there was good grass, while he and his senior officers held a board of inquiry. As a result, Division "E", the sick men, and all the weak animals remained to winter as best they could at Fort Pelly or at the Swan River barracks.

On October 24 the commissioner and the rest marched on again, heading for Winnipeg, where French presumed he could conveniently winter his men and animals. By this time the prairie was covered with wind-driven snow, but "D" Division and the strongest horses and oxen marched steadfastly on by way of Fort Ellice. Even some of these horses became so exhausted after leaving Fort Ellice that six had to be left behind. By the time French and his party arrived in Winnipeg on

November 7, one man had marched dismounted for so many miles since leaving Dufferin in July that he had worn out two pairs of boots and twelve pairs of moccasins.

French was very bitter about the Swan River barracks scandal, especially when he heard that the Canadian government had paid the contractors $30,000, a huge sum in 1874, while the NWMP had been forced to practise the strictest economy. His cutting remarks made him so unpopular at Winnipeg that the authorities there decided no accommodation was available for French and his party. Leaving his sick horses with Veterinary Surgeon Poett, French and the rest of his party went on to winter at Dufferin, sixty-five miles to the south. He arrived there at the end of November, in weather of 30 degrees below zero Fahrenheit.

"D" Division was back at the starting point of the march west. Since leaving Fargo, North Dakota, the previous June, it had travelled 1,959 miles according to French's odometer, an average of about nineteen miles a day. This mileage did not even include French's three hundred-mile round trip between Dead Horse Coulee, in the Sweet Grass Hills, and Fort Benton.

Many of "D" Division's horses and oxen, like those of the other Divisions, had died during the march, in all, 83 horses of the 310 of the original six Divisions. The sacrifices of this two thousand-mile marathon continued long after it was over, for many other horses died later from the effects of the gruelling march. The horses and men of all six Divisions had gone hungry, had drunk filtered mud, and had grown desperately weak from diarrhoea and dysentry. They had made the great march, at first stifled by the dust and ashes of prairie fires, in temperatures reaching 100 degrees Fahrenheit in the shade. All the Divisions had endured bitterly cold weather and early winter storms, and "D" Division had capped off the enterprise by trudging through snowdrifts at temperatures around 30 degrees below zero Fahrenheit.

Although the NWMP had not accomplished precisely what the government had proposed, they had placed groups of police in the foothills of the Rockies, at Fort Edmonton, and at Swan River where the headquarters of the Force was still under construction. Moreover, the march itself, the longest on record of a force carrying its own supplies, represented a unique achievement. As in other facets of the pioneering experience and the taming, generally, of an unsettled land, this feat could not have been accomplished without the equine contribution, the integral role played by the NWMP horses. In the early years of the Force, the horses were, almost equally with the men, a most essential element.

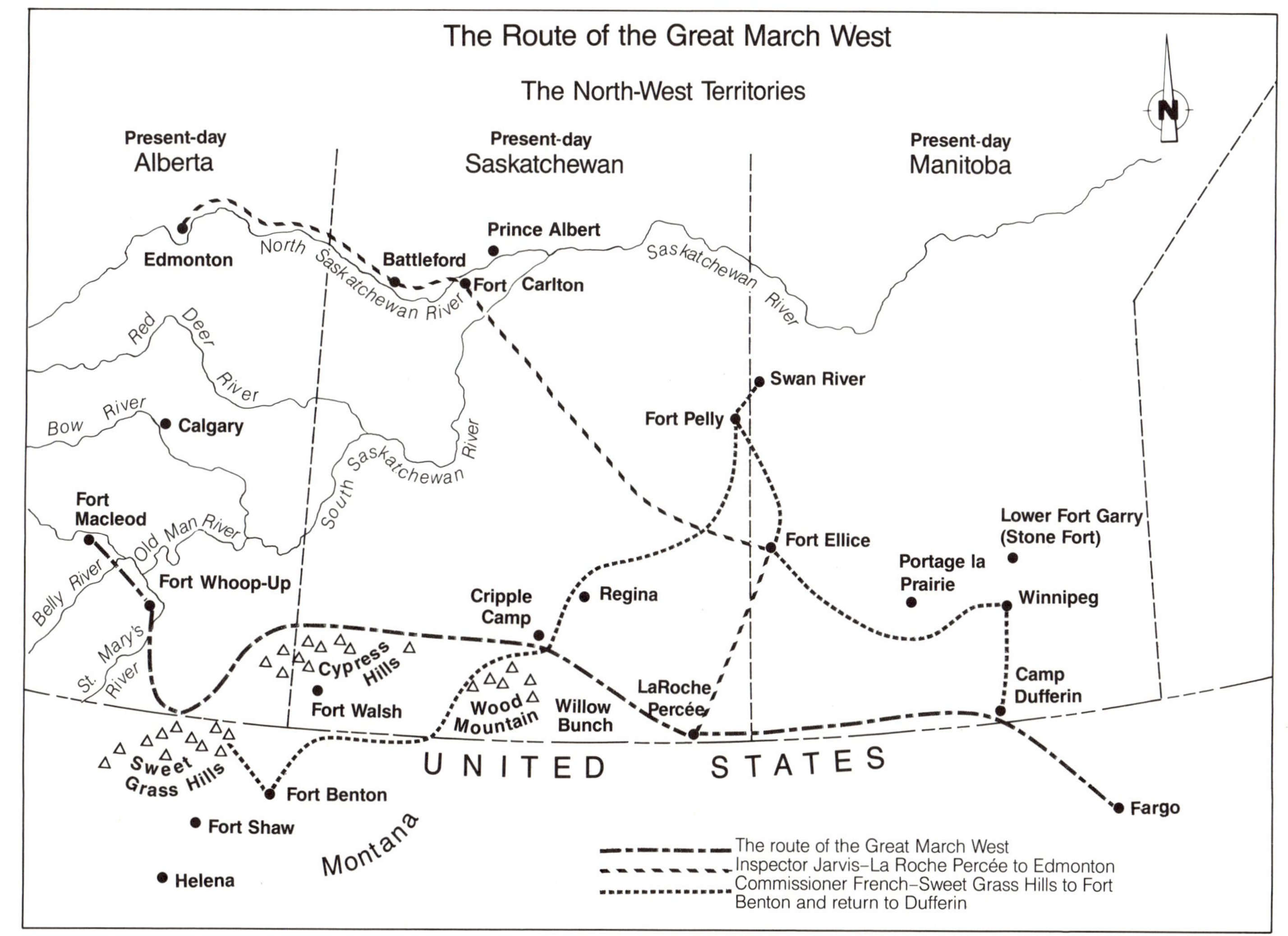

The Route of the Great March West
The North-West Territories
Present-day Alberta
Present-day Saskatchewan
Present-day Manitoba
N
Edmonton
North Saskatchewan River
Battleford
Prince Albert
Fort Carlton
Saskatchewan River
Red Deer River
Bow River
Calgary
South Saskatchewan River
Swan River
Fort Pelly
Fort Macleod
Old Man River
Belly River
Fort Whoop-Up
St. Mary's River
Fort Ellice
Lower Fort Garry (Stone Fort)
Portage la Prairie
Winnipeg
Regina
Cripple Camp
Cypress Hills
Fort Walsh
Wood Mountain
Willow Bunch
LaRoche Percée
Camp Dufferin
Sweet Grass Hills
Fort Benton
UNITED STATES
Fargo
Fort Shaw
Helena
Montana
The route of the Great March West
Inspector Jarvis–La Roche Percée to Edmonton
Commissioner French–Sweet Grass Hills to Fort Benton and return to Dufferin

A mounted patrol in 1878, near Fort Walsh.

2

Bringing Law and Order to the Canadian Frontier

Early Patrol and Escort Duties

As Divisions "B", "C" and "F" set up Camp Macleod and began building Fort Macleod at the place on the Old Man's River to which Jerry Potts had led them, Assistant Commissioner Macleod realized that his troubles were far from over. Weighing most heavily on his mind was that his horses, which Commissioner French had left with Macleod when he set out with the strongest animals for his return trek eastward to establish headquarters, were in a deplorable condition.

The assistant commissioner knew that the basic problem was the horses' "alkalied" condition. While he and Commissioner French were at Fort Benton, old-timers had told them that horses became seriously affected when forced to drink large quantities of alkaline water while travelling long distances across the prairies. None of them would recover normal health was the dire prophecy, and some would eventually die from the effects.

Even so, Macleod was expected to begin immediately to carry out the police duties for which the NWMP had been sent to the western frontier. He and his men were to prevent the smuggling of liquor and other goods from the United States, and also to prevent the exploitation of the Indians by unscrupulous traders. This work would require long patrols with horses ill and exhausted after their five-month march over the hostile prairies, whereas what they needed was a long period of rest and recuperation.

Most of the horses at Camp Macleod fulfilled the old-timers' prophecy. Even after getting better water, good feed and some rest, they failed to regain normal vitality, and some died. Horses apparently well enough to be used on patrol would collapse on the trail. In fact, when the first convicted prisoner, a whiskey trader, escaped, Macleod refused to allow his ill-conditioned horses to pursue him.

Soon after the arrival of the police at Camp Macleod in mid- October, extremely cold weather set in, which further debilitated the weakened horses. Toward the end of the month, a heavy snowstorm with bitter winds and a temperature of 10 degrees Fahrenheit threatened the very lives of the animals. Macleod ordered them herded into nearby woods and blanketed for extra protection. During this period the weather was so severe that it caused the death of thirty-three oxen on the ox-trains freighting supplies from Fort Benton to the trading posts in the Canadian foothills. This critical situation forced Macleod to order the building of stables before men's quarters, except those required by sick men.

Making matters worse, it seemed unlikely that the police could obtain enough hay to feed horses and cattle during the long winter. Soon after arriving at Camp Macleod, the assistant commissioner had hired men to cut hay, but he had obtained only twenty-five of the fifty to sixty tons he had expected. The only hay he could buy was of poor quality, and the eighteen tons he obtained near Camp Macleod cost $50 a ton, an exhorbitant price since good hay was selling in the Ottawa Valley in 1984, 110 years later, for $75 a ton. Macleod obtained another eighteen tons at $27 a ton from Fort Kipp, a trading post twenty miles to the east. Rather than haul the hay to Camp Macleod, he sent fourteen horses and thirteen men to Fort Kipp to remain there until the horses had used up the hay. This arrangement had the additional advantage of allowing the police to keep an eye on a Blood Indian camp, rumoured to be close to a cache of liquor.

The feed situation worsened when hay in the area from which Macleod expected a delivery was trampled into the ground by a herd of buffalo. He then realized that since he could not obtain enough hay in the vicinity of Camp Macleod for his animals, he must send them to where hay was available. On October 30, Inspector James Walsh and thirteen men, with eighty-one horses and thirty cattle and oxen, headed for Sun River, Montana Territory, some two hundred miles to the south. There, Macleod had learned, good grazing and water were available. He hoped that with these, plus twenty tons of oats he had purchased for the animals, by spring the weak horses would have recuperated sufficiently to be used on patrol work. Meanwhile, to replace some of those horses, Macleod would purchase some Indian ponies, which were accustomed to "pawing" for pasturage beneath the snow which already covered the ground.

The day Walsh left there was snow on the ground, but the next day a chinook took most of the snow away except in the coulees through which he had to travel. The weakest horses could not get through the snow and were abandoned. In all, fifteen horses died in the two weeks it took to get to Sun River. After arranging with a rancher to winter the animals and leaving a constable there to help the rancher, Walsh and the other men rode back to Camp Macleod.

By the time Walsh returned, Macleod realized that his hay supplies were not sufficient for the animals he had hoped to keep at Camp Macleod. He decided to keep only one team for each of the four Divisions and the Indian ponies he had recently purchased, and on December 15, 1874, Walsh and some men set out on a second trip to Sun River with the rest of the animals. By this time, Macleod had obtained permission from the Canadian government to purchase horses wherever they were available, so Walsh was authorized to see what he could find in the United States.

When Walsh and his men left for Sun River, the police had almost completed work on Fort Macleod, and a village had sprung up nearby. When they returned at Christmas with a string of unbroken broncos, the first of many such purchases, "bronco busting" became a feature of life at Fort Macleod, as it soon would do at other NWMP posts.

In spite of the limited number of horses now at Fort Macleod and the poor condition of most of them, the police had to make many patrols, one of which covered one hundred miles. Some patrols were made to take blankets and supplies to destitute Blackfoot, Blood and Piegan Indians camped in the Macleod district. On other patrols the police investigated liquor trafficking and complaints of horse stealing, the latter of which had not previously been considered a crime among the Indians.

In late December two particular patrols demonstrated the value of native horses. On the last day of the year, in bright sunshine, two constables who had spent Christmas at Fort Macleod set out on their native horses to patrol back to Fort Kipp. There by this time a police detachment had been established, about twenty miles east of Macleod. After the constables left, the Macleod police received word that Christmas mail had arrived at Fort Whoop-Up, twenty miles southeast of Kipp. Normally it would take a week for the mail to reach Fort Macleod, so Sub-Inspector Denny volunteered to fetch it from Whoop-Up, which had become a legitimate trading post since the arrival of the NWMP.

Denny set out to patrol to Whoop-Up in the afternoon, also riding a native horse. Suddenly at sunset a cold north wind sprang up, and within minutes he and his horse were being driven forward in a blinding snowstorm. All signs of the trail disappeared and Denny considered returning to Fort Macleod, but he could not face the fierce wind and beating snow. Before long he was completely lost. He tied the reins around his horse's neck, then sat huddled in his buffalo coat while for hours the animal made its own way through the storm. The sub-inspector had given up all hope of surviving when, to his surprise, the horse entered the gateway to Fort Kipp. The instinct of the native horse had undoubtedly saved Denny's life.

The two Fort Kipp constables were far less fortunate. By the following morning, when Denny left for Fort Whoop-Up, they still had not returned to their detachment. When he arrived back at Kipp to leave some of the mail, he learned that the constables' horses had returned without their riders. Later, Indian trackers found the constables, one dead and the other beyond aid. The police realized that the constables, too, might have survived if, like Denny, they had trusted their horses to carry them to safety.

During the following March and April, a long and hazardous patrol reinforced the lessons the police had learned from those two earlier patrols. It was undertaken because the Macleod police had received neither pay nor replacement uniforms from Ottawa since their arrival in the foothills area four months earlier. By this time the men were wearing a hodgepodge of tattered uniforms, civilian clothes, and Indian-type garments made from animal skins. Macleod complained to Ottawa by way of telegrams he had arranged to be sent from Fort Benton, but he had received no reply. At last, when he reported that eighteen men had deserted, the government instructed him to go to Helena, Montana, where he would find money deposited in a bank for payroll and supplies.

Macleod was also instructed to take preliminary steps for the arrest and eventual extradition of persons responsible for the Cypress Hills massacre, which in 1873 had given the Canadian government the final prod toward the creation of the NWMP. Accounts of the massacre had varied at first, but Abel Farwell, a respectable trader with a post in the lowland surrounded by hills, had later reported that he had watched the slaughter of the Assiniboine Indians, powerless to prevent it.

About two hundred Assiniboines, Farwell said, were camped near his post. Some fifteen wolf hunters from Fort Benton, Montana, arrived and camped nearby. The wolfers, who included not only Americans but also several French Canadians and at least three English Canadians, were out in pursuit of Cree Indians who had stolen some of their horses. The Assiniboines had nothing to do with the theft of the horses, but the white men got drunk and vowed to attack them anyway.

They also got the Indians drunk by giving them liquor. The next day, after more carousing, the wolfers opened fire on the unprepared Assiniboines. Farwell reported that they murdered more than thirty men, women and children, wounded many others, and forced all able-bodied Indians to flee to the hills.

Macleod knew the probability of late winter storms, a common feature of the climate, but he dared not delay until after the spring break-up. When he set out from Fort Macleod on the six-hundred-mile return journey to Helena, his party consisted of Sub-Inspector Denny, two constables, and guide-interpreter Jerry Potts. They took with them seven carefully chosen native horses which, unlike eastern horses, could forage for themselves even in the snow. Five of them they used as saddle horses, and the other two as pack horses to carry blankets, buffalo robes, boiled bacon, biscuits, tea and oats.

Weather conditions were good for the forty miles to Fort Whoop-Up, where Macleod and his party stayed overnight. Next morning, in a cloudy sky, they saw a "sun dog", a patch of sunlight refracted on ice crystals which, in western Canada, foretells bad weather, but Macleod, anxious to get to Helena, pushed on. During the day the little party came to open prairie, and that night in bitter cold they camped at a place devoid of shelter. There was no pasture for the horses, so they were fed oats. The cold intensified as a north-westerly wind sprang up, and the shivering men took turns to ensure that the hobbled horses stayed near the camp. But a snowstorm whipped over the open prairie and hid everything from view, and the horses wandered away. A constable managed to find them, but by then he was lost. Sub-Inspector Denny went out next, found the constable and the horses, and guided them back to camp.

In the morning, although the storm had not abated, the little party set out again. After travelling through the blizzard all day, they camped in the shallow valley of the Milk River, where the only shelter available for men and horses was an overhanging "cut bank". With not a shrub or tree in sight, the men obtained fuel from the wood of an old wagon frozen in the river. As the cold grew more intense and the wind howled incessantly, a herd of buffalo also sought shelter under the cut bank. The police feared their horses would become lost among the milling herd, and they fought to keep the buffalo away from them. At the same time, as the storm increased in violence, the police also had to concentrate on controlling the build-up of snow sweeping over them from above. Fortunately for Macleod and his party, the native horses did not panic, as eastern horses surely would have done.

The storm continued to shriek over them all that first night, all the next day and

Helping half-frozen Constable Ryan remount during Assistant Commissioner James Macleod's late winter patrol from Fort Macleod to Helena, Montana, 1874-75. (Painting by A. B. Stapleton)

through the second night. Sleep was impossible. By now the five men were frostbitten, Denny being the worst, with a frozen foot. As dawn broke after the second night in the cut-bank camp, the storm continued, so on the advice of Potts they stayed there. They made a dug-out by digging into the hard-packed snowbanks, which gave them better shelter for their horses, their supplies and themselves. For another day and another night they huddled there while the storm raged overhead. The men had little left to eat but cold bacon, and although they had sparingly doled out the oats to the horses, there were few left.

On the morning of the third day it stopped snowing, but the temperature had dropped to 55 degrees below zero Fahrenheit. Potts advised moving on thirty miles south to Rocky Springs, where there were several empty huts. The patrol continued, but only after the men had walked the stiffened horses for a while to make sure that they could travel.

Macleod and his party immediately encountered yet another serious problem. The strong wind whipped up the loose snow so that the riders could not see beyond their horses' ears, and only Jerry Potts kept his sense of direction. The men called to each other from time to time to make sure they were all together. When one constable lagged far behind and failed to respond to a call, the others went back for him. They found him sitting in the snow holding his horse's reins, too cold and stiff to remount. He begged them to leave him there, but they helped him remount and the party moved on.

It began to snow again. Even the usually unperturbable and talkative Jerry Potts was silent as he rode doggedly forward into the blinding snow, concentrating on keeping his direction. The police knew that their lives depended on Potts and his horse. Denny went completely snow-blind, and all the rest suffered to some extent, but Potts kept going. The men sagged in their saddles as the utterly exhausted horses moved stiffly foreward. Suddenly Potts' horse halted; the patrol had arrived at Rocky Springs. The men made camp, then they and the horses ate the last of their rations.

The next morning broke clear and windless. Potts was now in familiar territory, and after a couple of hours' slow travel, Macleod and his party reached the Marias River and a small trading post supervised by a unit of the U.S. Cavalry. In a short time the hospitality of this frontier military outpost had thawed out the unexpected guests who at first, looking little like the scarlet riders of the plains, had been taken for whiskey traders. Under the guidance of the Cavalry the police and their horses made their way to Fort Shaw in the Sun River Valley, the headquarters of the area cavalry, where Denny was left behind to have a frozen toe amputated and to recover from his snow-blindness.

From Fort Shaw the police rode on without difficulty to Helena. During several busy weeks Macleod obtained money for supplies and $30,000 in cash to pay his men. In connection with the Cypress Hills massacre of the thirty Assiniboine Indians by the white wolf hunters from Fort Benton, he retained counsel and had them make application for the extradition of the killers.

On his return journey to Fort Macleod, his party included a few conscience-stricken deserters who had decided they wanted to stay in the Force after all. Except for difficulties in crossing swollen rivers, the men and horses made the return journey without incident. Later Macleod made several more of the six-hundred-mile return trips to Helena, but none was more difficult than the first one. His choice of native horses for that journey had undoubtedly made the difference between success and tragic failure.

By the time Macleod returned to Fort Macleod, the police realized that apart from the condition of the horses it was impractical to use that fort as a base for the patrolling of the Cypress Hills, 160 miles or more to the east. They also realized that there was more police work in that area than they had first thought. In May 1875, "B" Division, under the command of Inspector James Walsh and led by Jerry Potts, headed for the Cypress Hills massacre grounds on the headwaters of Battle Creek. Three weeks later the men began hewing logs to build Fort Walsh almost on the exact spot where, two years earlier, the wolf hunters had murdered the Canadian Assiniboine Indians.

As a result of what Macleod had learned in Helena, Montana, about the Fort Benton murderers of those Indians, the Canadian government had appointed Lieutenant-Colonel A. G. Irvine, formerly commandant of the garrison of Red River, as an inspector of the NWMP. He had worked undercover for several months in Montana, accumulating more evidence and witnesses, and subsequently the Canadian government laid extradition charges against fourteen of the alleged murderers.

The American authorities arrested the only seven they could find, then two of them escaped custody, leaving only five to stand trial for extradition at Helena in July 1875, with Macleod and Irvine in attendance. Abel Farwell and other witnesses gave strong testimony, but the accused swore that they had been attacked by the Indians and had only defended themselves. During the hearings, crowds of drunken and threatening frontiersmen thronged the courtroom and the main street, ready to riot on behalf of their fellow Montanans. One defense lawyer shouted above the courtroom's din that before the accused were taken to Canada for trail, he and his friends would "wade knee deep in Canadian blood". Fortunately that was not necessary: in view of the conflicting testimony, the American commissioner in charge of the hearing refused to order extradition.

The five alleged murderers were freed, at which point one of the exuberant and well-lubricated accused charged Macleod with false arrest. The assistant commissioner was in turn arrested and placed in custody. He was soon released, however, on the basis of having acted "strictly under the orders of his own government and with the approval of the Government of the United States". Macleod, Irvine, and the rest of their dispirited party returned to Fort Macleod. The still-fatigued horses, as well as the men, had made that six-hundred-mile round trip in vain.

Not only the horses under Assistant Commissioner Macleod's command gave cause for concern, but so also did those under Commissioner French's command at Swan River headquarters, and the horses at Fort Saskatchewan, where Inspector Jarvis and his "A" Division had built a fort soon after their arrival at Fort

Constable James Schofield in full-dress uniform, 1878. (Glenbow Archives, Calgary)

NWMP members and Indians in the Cypress Hills, circa 1879. Note the youthfulness of some members, the ill-fitting uniforms and the pony-like horses. (RCMP Museum, Regina)

Edmonton in the late autumn of 1874. When Veterinary Surgeon Poett reported at the end of 1875 specifically on the Swan River horses his comments applied equally to the other NWMP horses.

According to Poett, the poor condition of the animals during the summer and autumn of 1875, their first in the west after the Great March, predisposed them to sickness and disease. "The percentage degree of sickness and of weak and debilitated horses," he said, "has been extraordinarily great among so few a number of horses." Moreover, it was difficult to improve the condition of the horses while they were denied a sufficient amount of grain, were fed on non-nutritious hay, and were kept continually on patrol. It would be much easier on the horses, Poett suggested, if the police used some solely for saddle work and others for team work, rather than using the same horses for both duties.

Meanwhile, in spite of the poor conditions of the horses, in the summer of 1875 the NWMP had to make an unusually long and arduous patrol when they escorted Major-General E. Selby Smyth, head of the Canadian Militia, on an inspection tour of the main Mounted Police posts established by then. As a first step, the police met him at Winnipeg and escorted him three hundred miles to NWMP headquarters at Swan River, from which point he would begin his tour.

Soon after Selby Smyth arrived, the police received a message informing them that the Métis on "the Saskatchewan" had formed an independent government, headed by Gabriel Dumont (later to become Louis Riel's commander-in-chief during the 1885 Riel Rebellion). Hence Commissioner French personally led the first relay escort of fifty mounted men, which set out from Swan River for Fort Carlton on the North Saskatchewan River, three hundred miles away. En route, however, as the escort crossed the ferry operated by Dumont himself on the South Saskatchewan, French learned that the Métis had merely organized an association common to Métis settlements and hunting brigades.

At Fort Carlton, before French returned with his men to Swan River, he handed over the escort duties to Inspector Jarvis, who had brought a new escort from Fort Saskatchewan, three hundred miles away. Jarvis then escorted Smyth over the most difficult relay of the tour, using mainly the same horses he had taken west the year before. This four-hundred-mile section of the tour included painfully rough trails. By the time the Jarvis escort completed its relay at the Red Deer River crossing north of Calgary, many horses suffered from hoof problems, some others were crippled, and all were exhausted.

Assistant Commissioner Macleod and his escort party planned to take over from Inspector Jarvis at the Tail Creek crossing of the Red Deer. They arrived ahead of time and spent the next few days preparing for the major-general's inspection. Rigid drill was held, horses were groomed, accoutrements burnished and wagons and camp equipment put in first-class condition. Then Macleod received a message from Fort Saskatchewan notifying him that the major-general would be crossing the Red Deer at a different place from where it had been arranged.

Now Macleod had to take his well-polished escort at a fast clip over fifty miles of rough, thickly-wooded country, which lacked even the semblance of a trail and was dotted with swamps and creeks. Mosquitoes rose in clouds around the riders, who made smudge fires at each stop, with the horses crowding around them as anxiously as the men. There was very little "polish" left to Macleod's escort after fifty miles of mud and tangled woods, but when they met up with Jarvis, they found that the official party had fared no better. Many of Jarvis's horses were travel weary, a number had serious hoof trouble, and others were crippled. The condition of both the horses and the terrain had forced a slow pace, which did little to improve the major-general's frame of mind.

Rather fortunately, after such a strenuous and extremely uncomfortable journey, the petulant major-general was in no mood for more than a cursory inspection, hastily organized. Soon Inspector Jarvis left for Fort Saskatchewan, and Macleod escorted the official visitor southward about two hundred miles to Fort Macleod by way of Fort Calgary, then under construction by the police.

By the time the major-general arrived at Fort Macleod, the assistant commissioner had learned the reason for the inspection tour. Sir John A. Macdonald's Conservative party was now the Opposition Party in Parliament, and he and his supporting newspapers had severely criticized the Liberal government for the NWMP's early organizational and other problems, including Commissioner French's continuing problems at Swan River headquarters. Selby Smyth had been sent to investigate the Opposition Party's charges. Later he reported favourably on the Force, and the issue was dropped in Parliament.

Although the inspection tour ended at Fort Macleod, the police escort continued. It next escorted the major-general two hundred miles to Fort Shaw, Montana, so that he could make an official visit to the commandant of the U.S. Cavalry post there. After the return journey to Fort Macleod, the police escorted him westward about a hundred miles, to within twelve miles of Wilde Horse (later Fort Steele) in the Rockies. From that point Major-General Selby Smyth and his private party made their way to New Westminster, British Columbia, while the police returned to Fort Macleod.

No doubt all parties concerned were relieved when this arduous exercise ended. The escort itself had involved about 1,500 miles of travel. In addition, by the time all the men and horses had returned to their respective posts, the distance travelled by the various relays totalled well over 3,000 miles.

A patrol in the autumn of 1875, one that finally brought a few of those involved in the Cypress Hills massacre to trial, illustrated just how strenuous a task it was to enforce the law in such a vast territory. The NWMP had failed to have the suspected killers extradited from the United States. But when three of them crossed into Canada on their own, the police at Fort Macleod and Fort Walsh were alerted, and they arrested them. Inspector Irvine then set out to escort the prisoners eight hundred miles across the vast plains to distant Winnipeg to stand trial. His party also included Abel Farwell, another witness, and a guide, Pierre Léveillé, a huge Métis reportedly so strong that if his horse got stuck in the mud, he simply lifted it by its tail and propelled it forward.

Irvine now benefitted from the experience of the NWMP on the march west the previous year. He wisely chose to take an easier southern route on this patrol, and because his party was small, he was able to find pasturage and water for the horses. He remained in Winnipeg for the trial, at which conflicting evidence resulted in the acquittal of the accused. After the trial, he and his reduced party, which included the witnesses and the guide, left Winnipeg immediately to get back to Fort Macleod in time to celebrate Christmas there. No doubt they felt much in need of some cheer after such a harrowing and ultimately fruitless journey. This 1,600-mile patrol was only the first of many such marathon patrols which had to be made from time to time until an adequate judicial system, including a network of local gaols, was established in the Canadian prairie region.

The NWMP horses would have been hard pressed to make even the necessary patrols connected with normal law-enforcement duties. The burden was made even greater because they had to continue making long patrols to escort officials of various federal government departments, including those looking into the government's newfound interests in the Territories. In the summer of 1876, for example, the NWMP provided an escort for the three Indian Treaty commissioners and their staff when they went to Forts Carlton and Pitt to negotiate and sign Treaty No. 6, in which certain Indians, mostly Plains and Wood Crees, deeded 120,000 square miles of territory to the Canadian government. In exchange the Indians would have land reserved for themselves, and schools would be provided, as would farm equipment, oxen, and seed for growing potatoes, oats, barley and wheat.

Inspector James Walker and fifty mounted men met the commissioners at Duck Lake, about twenty-five trail miles from Carlton. The police remained at Carlton during the days of the negotiations, then escorted the commissioners to Fort Pitt, about 160 miles westward, and then, after the treaty had been signed, back to Fort Carlton.

The escort of four hundred miles was not particularly onerous, but the auxiliary patrol mileage necessary for the success of the project, as often happened in such cases, far exceeded those of the escort. In fact, auxiliary patrols made by police from outlying areas going to help keep the peace where necessary during treaty proceedings totalled more than 1,200 miles. For example, Inspector Walker and his men journeyed almost three hundred miles from Swan River headquarters to Duck Lake and, later, another three hundred miles back to headquarters. Inspector Jarvis and a party of mounted men travelled nearly six hundred miles from Fort Saskatchewan to Fort Carlton and back in order to help with the policing at Carlton and Pitt. Other police travelled many miles in escorting the commissioners part way on their outward journey from Winnipeg, and then more miles when the commissioners returned to that city.

Meanwhile, an unusual patrol had begun as a result of a change within the Force itself. The former Assistant Commissioner Macleod had replaced Commissioner French and had been permitted to transfer NWMP headquarters from Swan River to Fort Macleod. From the latter point Macleod could more readily supervise the additional police he wanted near the U.S. border in case Sioux Indians, then fighting the U.S. Cavalry, fled across the international border into Canada.

About the middle of July, Macleod and a small party of men left Fort Macleod for Swan River, a distance of 750 prairie miles. Within twenty-four hours of his arrival there he had organized the transfer and was leading a second march west back to Fort Macleod. His column included oxen, other cattle, wagons loaded with equipment, and the mounted troops of "D" and "E" Divisions which had accompanied Commissioner French on his return from the Sweet Grass Hills in the autumn of 1874.

Instead of Macleod taking the shortest route back to Fort Macleod he journeyed westward by way of Forts Carlton and Pitt to attend the negotiations then underway in connection with Treaty No. 6. Later, when Macleod's cavalcade left Fort Pitt and travelled southward toward Fort Walsh en route to Fort Macleod, it encountered many of the same difficulties faced two years earlier by French's cavalcade on the original March West. On reaching the South Saskatchewan River, the police found the water very deep and about a quarter of a mile wide. Again and again the strong current drove the horses back to shore. The guide swore that only a miracle would persuade the animals to cross the river.

Two constables performed the miracle. Slipping off their clothes and mounting two of the more docile horses, they rode into the river. A few yards from shore they slipped from their seats. Swimming close to the horses' heads they coaxed and guided the animals through the strong currents. One constable finished the frigid crossing clinging to his horse's tail. The other horses, apparently satisfied that the feat could be accomplished, followed without much persuasion.

Getting supplies and equipment across presented another problem. The men improvised a raft of two wagon beds lashed together, with wagon sheets drawn underneath to prevent leakage. At each crossing these rafts were swept downstream a mile or so, and the NWMP horses, pulling from along the banks like barge horses, had to tow them back upstream to be unloaded. But in three days of ceaseless toil the horses and men completed the crossing and marched on southward.

At Fort Walsh the horses and men of "E" Division ended their trek, having travelled nearly a thousand miles from Swan River. After a week's rest, "D" Division rode on 160 miles westward to Fort Macleod. By the time they arrived there in late October, they had travelled nearly 1,200 miles. The horses and men of Macleod's party, which had also made the 750-mile outward journey, had travelled nearly two thousand miles in all, slightly more than Commissioner French and his horses had gone two years earlier, excluding his auxiliary mileage.

Now, however, conditions were vastly different. Macleod's column was much smaller than French's, and the police's two years' experience in prairie travel had taught them which routes were the easiest to take. French, on the other hand, had been forced to travel over hundreds of miles of inhospitable prairie that lacked good pasturage and water, partly because he knew of no better alternative at the time, but also because the Canadian government had stipulated the general route he must take. In any case, French's greatest difficulty came from the size of his cavalcade and its needs. Although the police still had to make long, tiring patrols, neither men nor horses were now forced to endure the devastating hardships suffered on the March West.

The transfer in 1876 of NWMP headquarters from Swan River to Fort Macleod, which resulted in "D" and "E" Divisions' moving to the southern prairies, came none too soon. Ever since the Custer massacre in June of that year, when at the battle of the Little Bighorn General Custer made his last stand in the American campaign against the Sioux, those Indians had been so effectively harassed by the U.S. Cavalry that in the late autumn they began to cross into Canada seeking refuge.

By the end of December a large group camping near Wood Mountain in the Cypress Hills included 500 braves, 1,000 women, 1,400 children and 3,500 horses. When Sitting Bull, leader of the Sioux, arrived near Fort Walsh in May 1877, with 135 lodges, it brought the number of Sioux in Canada to about 4,000. This aggravated an already dangerous situation and forced the NWMP to maintain constant mounted patrols over large areas. The strain on the horses was sometimes unbearable, and some of them collapsed.

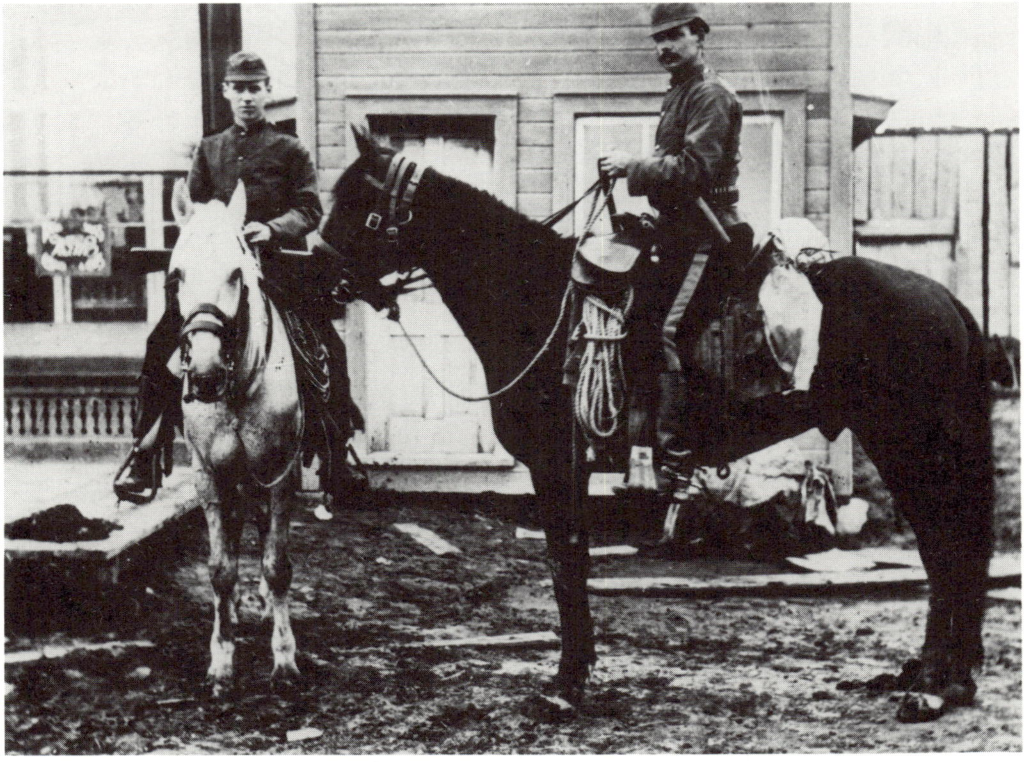

Two NWMP members on patrol, circa early 1880s. The rarely photographed "deer-stalker" patrol caps were issued to members for a short time. Halter ropes and picket ropes were carried by all members on patrols. (RCMP Museum, Regina)

Meanwhile the police had to continue their routine patrols in connection with other law-enforcement duties such as preventing smuggling over the border, investigating horse stealing and clashes among the Indians, and making preventive patrols to keep the peace on Indian reserves. At the same time they had to provide horses for special escorts and other non-routine duties. For example, in September 1877, in connection with the signing of Treaty No. 7 at Blackfoot Crossing, between the Canadian government and the Blackfoot Indians, a large body of police and their horses was needed for escort duty and also to maintain law and order among the five thousand Canadian Indians present. The police contingent included 108 officers and men out of a total Force strength of 329, and 119 horses out of a total of 315. Thus the remaining police had fewer than two hundred horses, none of them in prime condition, to patrol tens of thousands of miles over the vast prairies.

For the next several years, until the Sioux began to return to the United States to reserves set aside for them, the NWMP strained their limited resources in men and horses to control the often recalcitrant American Indians. The police not only had to attend to their material needs but also to maintain peace between the Sioux and Canadian Indians and to help the Sioux maintain peace among themselves.

Police horses had to travel countless miles as their riders investigated the Sioux' frequent theft of horses—sometimes even of police horses. On one occasion at Wood End, Sitting Bull's braves stole several NWMP horses from the herd tended by a lone policeman powerless to stop them. Later a sub-inspector and a small escort rode to Sitting Bull's camp and demanded the horses. Sitting Bull, who was mounted on a fine horse, hinted scornfully that the police could do nothing to get their horses back.

"I would take even the horse you are riding if I thought it stolen," the sub-inspector declared.

"It is," Sitting Bull challenged.

The officer unobtrusively sidled his horse closer to the chief's. Suddenly leaning over, he lifted Sitting Bull from his saddle, grabbed his horse's bridle, and pulled the animal aside. As the Indians stared dumbfounded, the officer's men closed in to protect him. Then the police party, with Sitting Bull's horse in tow, galloped to their fort. The Sioux planned to attack the fort that night, but did not carry out their plan.

During those same years of Sioux problems, the NWMP had to keep up with the increasing patrol work demanded of the numerous police posts now dotting the prairies. In addition to the difficulties created for the horses by the greater number of miles they had to travel, the continued scarcity of good pasturage and water also adversely affected their health. Exhaustion and disease continued to take their toll. The absence of replacement stock forced healthy horses to work continuously, so that they in turn succumbed to sickness and disease. For almost two decades after the NWMP's arrival in the west, it never had enough horses to allow for rest periods for overworked animals.

The Force not only needed more horses, but it also needed horses of better quality. For this reason it continued to bring in horses from Ontario (Canada, it was called), although everyone knew that the eastern horses did not withstand the rigours of patrol work as well as the western broncos. The eastern horses did, however, look like those of a quasi-military mounted unit.

Since 1875, Assistant Commissioner Macleod had tried to make the best use of his too few horses by using them as teams instead of as saddle horses for patrol work. He had learned that two wagons, each drawn by four horses, could carry twelve men and everything they required for a month. This released not only four saddle horses for other duties, but also the pack horses needed by some saddle-horse patrols to carry feed and equipment. Moreover, he claimed, wagons and teams could travel farther in a day than saddle horses and could be taken to most places on the prairies. In 1876, after explaining the situation to the government, he obtained official permission to use wagons to carry half his men on patrol.

The use of wagons, however, did not solve all Macleod's horse problems. As work loads changed from one Division to another, horses had to be transferred to where they were needed. They had repeatedly to be taken from men who had developed an interest in caring for them, and placed in the hands of strangers.

In 1878, in an effort to overcome the difficulties in obtaining enough suitable horses, Commissioner Macleod established a police breeding farm at Pincher Creek, about thirty miles west of Fort Macleod. That same year he estimated that he needed 450 horses, not including spares, to do the necessary patrol work. Instead, he had 352 horses, of which only 200 were fit for patrol work. Of the others, 60 two-year-olds and 52 brood mares were at the breeding farm, and the remaining 40 were about to be cast (discarded).

In spite of the Force's efforts to breed its own horses, it still had to purchase a good number each year. In 1881, for example, it purchased 133 remounts, 60 of them from Ontario. The other 73, from western ranches, Commissioner A.G. Irvine described as "the finest ever driven in the country". By this time western ranchers were breeding more horses, so the Force was less dependent on horses from Ontario and the United States, and the Ontario horses were used mainly for team work or on the drill square. With more and better horses available, in 1882 the Force gave up the idea of breeding its own horses, at least for the time being, and leased the breeding farm to a local ranching company.

Over the years, diseases among the police horses so plagued the NWMP that it operated camps where sick and exhausted horses received special attention. Even so, many horses succumbed to disease. For example, from 1881 to 1890, 167 horses died, including some at Battleford, Macleod and Lethbridge that died of typhoid. Others among the 167 were some of the Ontario horses, purchased in 1883, that contracted the contagious glanders disease. Although at that time there was no law in the west making it mandatory to destroy horses suffering from glanders, the Force, as usual, destroyed the infected horses rather than risk spreading the disease. That same year, on the recommendation of the Force, the North-West Territories Council passed an ordinance requiring that every horse suffering from glanders must be destroyed.

The police always had difficulty providing enough healthy horses for general regular work, so the special escorts were an added burden, usually creating great hardships for the horses and taking men away from their regular duties. In these early days of the west, however, no ceremonial occasion was thought complete unless it included a colourful mounted escort of the NWMP. Such an escort welcomed every visiting dignitary, and if he travelled beyond the railroad it remained in attendance, partly for ceremonial reasons and partly to ensure his safety. Even the distances the horses sometimes had to travel to the place where the escort duties would begin entailed hundreds of exhausting miles over rough trails. The NWMP escort in 1881 for the Marquis of Lorne, then Governor General of Canada, illustrates the exhaustive effort involved in appropriately escorting these early VIPs on their tours of the Canadian west.

Early in 1881 the Canadian government notified Commissioner A. G. Irvine at NWMP headquarters at Fort Walsh of the need for an escort to accompany the governor general on a lengthy tour of the North-West Territories during the following summer. The tour would be made to demonstrate the concern which Queen Victoria ("The Great White Mother") and the Canadian government felt for the settlers and Indians on the great western plains.

The governor general would travel by train to Portage La Prairie, Manitoba, where by that time the construction of the cross-Canada railway would have reached. From that point he would travel by the river steamer *Assiniboine* to Fort Ellice, where an escort of North-West Mounted Police would meet him. Relays of NWMP escorts would then accompany him through the Territories, by way of Forts Qu'Appelle, Carlton and Battleford, to Calgary. From Calgary the Marquis of Lorne would re-cross the vast prairies on his return to Winnipeg.

Commissioner Irvine's plan was that an escort formed at NWMP headquarters at Fort Walsh would go to Fort Ellice by way of Fort Qu'Appelle. Superintendent W. M. Herchmer, stationed at Battleford, would be in charge of all proceedings, and with a supporting party he would meet the escort at Qu'Appelle and travel with it to Fort Ellice. Inspector P.R. Neale, based in the Justice Department in Ottawa, would go to Winnipeg to purchase additional horses and wagons, and three ambulances (of the type usually supplied to officers commanding troops in the field so that they could travel in more comfort than by riding in the saddle or by wagon), in which the governor general's party would travel, and he would deliver all these to Herchmer at Fort Ellice. Meanwhile, police from convenient posts would cache provisions and other supplies, including oats for the horses, along the proposed 1,200-mile route.

In accord with Irvine's plan, on July 13 Herchmer left Battleford for Qu'Appelle, 280 miles to the southeast. His party included one NCO, seven constables and fourteen horses. At Carlton, one hundred miles along the way, Herchmer's troubles began when he met three constables on patrol to pay Treaty money to Indians, in such annual payments per Indian as had been agreed by Treaty. Their horses had become so exhausted that they were unserviceable, and Herchmer had to give them four of his horses so that they could continue the patrol. Also at Carlton he learned that oats he had ordered delivered there had been sent on to Battleford, so he had to borrow oats from the Hudson's Bay Company, promising to replace them later. On July 21, eight days out of Battleford, Herchmer arrived at Qu'Appelle.

Meanwhile, on July 14, Sergeant-Major Thomas Lake and the governor general's escort party of three staff sergeants, three corporals, sixteen constables, thirty-one horses and three wagons had left Fort Walsh on their 315-mile journey northeast to Qu'Appelle. Lake immediately ran into trouble when one horse went lame and had to be sent back. One night, about one hundred miles out of Fort Walsh, all his horses stampeded, presumably alarmed by some unfamiliar sight or sound, and his men failed to find fourteen of them. Because his journey took longer than expected he ran out of rations for men and horses. He sent a messenger to inform Herchmer of his difficulties, and received a four-horse wagon loaded with supplies, which enabled him to arrive at Qu'Appelle on July 26.

After a delay of five days to allow Lake's exhausted horses to rest, on July 31 the combined parties set out for Fort Ellice, about 140 trail miles to the east. Because of Lake's lost horses, Herchmer had been forced to use many team horses for saddle purposes. His column now included seven NCOs, thirty-two constables and fifty horses. En route Herchmer received a message from the Justice Department in Ottawa telling him to go to Portage La Prairie to take over the horses and equipment that Inspector Neale had purchased in Winnipeg. He continued on to Fort Ellice to leave some men, horses and supplies and then went on to Portage La Prairie, some 140 miles farther east.

Meanwhile Neale had marched the sixty miles from Winnipeg to Portage La Prairie with thirty-nine horses, twelve wagons and three ambulances. He and his party of hired teamsters had scarcely settled in when a sudden thunderstorm with terrific winds enveloped the camp. In a few moments the wind swept away the tents, bedding and wagon covers. Luckily, Neale's men had not turned out the horses and they were able to shelter them in nearby stables. A few days later as a teamster was exercising a four-horse team, a vicious cow charged the team and gored one of the horses, and the team bolted. Soon order was restored, and life in the camp returned to normal.

Herchmer arrived at Neale's camp on August 7 and took possession of the horses, nineteen of which were unbroken remounts, and the wagons and ambulances. He remained overnight and the next day at the request of the Indian Department he took charge of an additional eight horses and four wagons. Two of the wagons would carry the extra baggage of the governor general's party. The other two were loaded with gifts which the governor general would distribute to the Indians he met on his journey. By the time Herchmer's party returned to Fort Ellice on August 12, his original horses had travelled more than 550 miles, even before beginning the escort duties.

On his arrival there he learned that a horse, named Custer by the police, had died of dysentry. The horse had been seized by Inspector Walsh from a Sioux Indian who had brought it to Canada after capturing it at the Battle of the Little Bighorn in the United States in 1876. The U.S. Cavalry, rather than have Walsh return the horse to them, had asked him to keep it, and the police had named it Custer because it had presumably served with General Custer's troops in that battle.

The day after Herchmer's arrival at Fort Ellice he headed the twenty-man mounted escort which met the governor general, the Marquis of Lorne, as he disembarked from the river steamer *Assiniboine* to the notes of the Royal Salute sounded by a NWMP mounted trumpeter. The governor general reviewed the escort and then retired for the night at the home of the Hudsons' Bay Company factor. Meanwhile, the four-horse police team hauling the baggage of the governor general and his party from the *Assiniboine* ran away, overturning the wagon and breaking the teamster's collar bone.

The next day there was some delay in leaving Fort Ellice until the Marquis of Lorne had held an Indian Council, as he would do at every major stopping place on his journey. When at last the cavalcade set out at 3:00 P.M., it consisted of eighty-four horses, nineteen wagons, three ambulances and forty-six men in addition to the governor general and his personal entourage. This latter included his private physician, a clergyman, a military secretary, two military aides, an artist, two newspaper correspondents, a chef and six servants. Also travelling with him was an assistant commissioner representing the Indian Department.

After the first day the cavalcade followed a standard travel procedure. The trumpeter blew reveille at 3:00 A.M. and the cavalcade started at 6:00 A.M. It stopped for breakfast at 10:00 A.M. and for dinner at 3:00 P.M. At night the party usually camped on the open plains, except when they reached a Hudson's Bay Company post, where they observed more ordinary meal times. Meanwhile the police not only acted as escorts but also as servants of the governor general's party. At each stop they had to pitch tents, unpack large amounts of baggage and equipment, and later repack the baggage and equipment and take down the tents, in addition to performing many other chores.

The size of the cavalcade caused it to travel slowly. Other problems arose from the fact that thirty-six of the horses were young remounts, not used to the work expected of them. Moreover, they quickly became exhausted in the heat of the hot prairie sun. Nevertheless on August 17, after four long, slow days of travel, the cavalcade arrived at Fort Qu'Appelle, where Inspector Sam Steele headed a guard of honour.

At Qu'Appelle the Marquis of Lorne held his second Indian Council. Indians in colourful dress, and young mounted warriors in paint and feathers gathered from miles around to stare at the son-in-law of "The Great White Mother", Queen Victoria. By this time the governor general's tiresome four-day, 140-mile journey from Fort Ellice to Qu'Appelle had made him apprehensive of the long journey ahead. At Qu'Appelle he decided not to return to Winnipeg over the Canadian plains. Instead he would go from Calgary south to Fort Macleod, then on to Fort Shaw and Helena in Montana. There he would be within easy reach of an American railroad on which he could return to Winnipeg.

After two days at Qu'Appelle the long cavalcade began its nearly two-hundred mile journey northwest to Carlton, en route to Calgary. Six days later, on August 25, it arrived at Batoche on the South Saskatchewan River, about thirty miles southeast of Carlton, which was situated on the banks of the North Saskatchewan. The police used a scow ferry operated by Gabriel Dumont to take their vehicles across the wide South Saskatchewan. But at each crossing the scow landed a long distance down river from where it should have landed, and the horses had to haul it back up river, barge style, into place for unloading. Although the horses crossed the river by swimming, the whole crossing took four hours. That evening the vice-regal visitor and his large escort arrived at Carlton, where men and animals were accommodated in the Hudsons' Bay Company fort.

The next morning, after the usual Indian Council, the governor general and his party boarded the river steamer *Northcote* to travel north-eastward downriver to the settlement of Prince Albert. Later they would take the river steamer *Lily* to Battleford. Meanwhile the NWMP escort trekked westward one hundred miles to Battleford to meet the governor general there a few days later. When Herchmer and his column arrived there on August 29, he was relieved to find that Commissioner Irvine had sent fresh horses from Fort Walsh, some two hundred miles to the southwest, to replace some of his men's exhausted mounts.

When the governor general arrived at Battleford at 6:00 A.M. on August 30, the NWMP met and escorted him to the home of David Laird, lieutenant-governor of the North-West Territories, of which Battleford was then the capital. That same day the governor general held an Indian Council, and the next day he visited the NWMP barracks.

After two days at Battleford the cavalcade moved on toward Calgary, some three hundred often trail-less miles to the southwest. The cavalcade now consisted of fifty mounted men, and twelve four-horse wagons driven by members of the Force. One of the guides was a Cree Indian chief named Poundmaker, an advocate of peace in whom the police had great faith but who, against his will, four years later, rebelled against Canadian authority during the Riel Rebellion of 1885. After the cavalcade left the Battleford area it often travelled through virgin territory with ample water but with no woods to provide shelter or fuel. A welcome break in the monotony came after a week on the trail, when a guide sighted a herd of buffalo.

Herchmer proclaimed a hunt in honour of the Marquis of Lorne, and three buffalo were killed.

By this time the weather had turned so cold that hoar frost covered the tents in the mornings. Travel had been slower than expected, and oats for the horses and general supplies were running low. Then came a delay when Herchmer's column had to pause while taking three thousand pounds of oats from the wagons which Herchmer had sent on ahead, but which had been delayed en route. Then one of Herchmer's wagons, overloaded with oats, broke an axle, and this delayed him even more.

When Herchmer neared the point at which he had planned to cross the Red Deer River, about one hundred miles north of Calgary, he was informed that the banks were too steep. He then had to take his column southeast along the river bank many miles before finding a suitable crossing. This point was fifty miles north of Blackfoot Crossing on the Bow River, sixty miles east of Calgary, his destination. The extra travel had caused him to use more provisions, already in short supply, so he decided to go to Blackfoot Crossing where he knew he could obtain supplies.

Meanwhile the September weather had not only remained cold, but it had also turned wet. The governor general's party found travelling uncomfortable as the horses dragged their vehicles through muddy trails. Some of the horses cast their shoes and had to be abandoned. The police kept a lookout for them, and the following year found them, one by one, about a hundred miles away.

In spite of all difficulties, Herchmer made relatively good time over the 260 miles from Battleford and reached Blackfoot Crossing after nine days' travel. His change of river crossing, however, had created problems for the police elsewhere. Oats and other supplies sent to meet him at the planned crossing point on the Red Deer River had to be replaced with new supplies from Calgary.

On September 10, the day after the Marquis of Lorne had arrived at Blackfoot Crossing, masses of Indians in their most colourful dress gathered to greet their unexpected and important visitor. Among them were the chiefs of the Blackfoot Confederacy, including the great Crowfoot who had become a firm friend of the NWMP, all in their robes of state. In honour of the occasion, later called "the last great council of the west" and "the last open council in the Canadian west free from pre-arranged formalities", the governor general and his party donned their official uniforms.

Hurried preparations were made for an Indian Council and a pow-wow. Before the council began, young Indian warriors in paint and feathers gave their visitors a rousing welcome. As they galloped, yelling, screaming and shooting, past the governor general, who was seated before his personal tent, the welcome was a little too rousing for one member of his party. Turning to a member of the NWMP he asked, "Are your guns loaded?"

The governor general, attended by scarlet-coated policemen, held council with the Indian chiefs in front of a tent erected for the occasion. Among the assurances of loyalty he received from them was a special message from Crowfoot, who wanted him to know that his people owed their lives to the protection and assistance they had received from the NWMP.

Later that day the cavalcade continued on to Calgary, where it arrived on September 12, 750 miles from Fort Ellice. The usual council and pow-wow took place, but the highlight of the visit was an unexpected cattle drive through the small town, as cowboys drove thousands of cattle en route to a ranch at nearby Cochrane.

When the cavalcade set out for Fort Macleod on September 15, it included ninety-nine horses, seven having been left behind to recuperate from their strenuous journey. En route, however, in a relay system possible in that area, Herchmer received sixteen more horses and a supply of oats sent out from that post. When the column arrived at Fort Macleod on September 17, the governor general was welcomed by Commissioner Irvine, who had ridden over from Fort Walsh headquarters some 160 miles to the east.

On September 19, Superintendent L. N. F. Crozier took over the escort command from Superintendent Herchmer, so that the latter and his small party could get back to Battleford before the winter set in. Herchmer wrote later:

> I am pleased to be able to add that our percentage in loss in horses was small, taking into consideration the length of the trip, the loads carried and the pace travelled, bearing in mind also that the majority of the horses were remounts, supplied this year, these remounts having gone through many trying ordeals before reaching the Territories. To employ a remount at hard work immediately after its arrival in the country is unfair; in our own case, however, circumstances demanded it of us. The old police horses, too, had, in nearly every case, been working hard up to the last moment....
>
> Speaking generally, we had, owing to large amount of transport, two horses to a man. I believe it is unprecedented that not a horse was incapacitated from work by sore back or shoulders. I attribute this entirely to the great care and attention by Staff Sergeant and Saddler Major Horner.

On September 20 the escort cavalcade under Superintendent Crozier set out for Fort Shaw, Montana, the site of a U.S. Cavalry post two hundred miles to the south. En route the governor general visited the NWMP breeding farm at Pincher Creek, which at this time was still operated directly by the Force, thirty miles west of Macleod. Meanwhile Commissioner Irvine and the governor general's military aide rode on ahead to alert the commandant at Fort Shaw that the Marquis of Lorne intended to pay him a visit. They made fast time, covering the two hundred miles from Macleod in three days.

The commandant immediately sent out a mounted escort to meet the governor general and his escort, who were travelling slowly behind. Two days out, the American escort met Crozier's cavalcade and camped with it for the night. During the night the American horses stampeded, so the NWMP escort and the governor general went on to Fort Shaw without them. On September 28, eight days out of Macleod, the governor general and his NWMP escort arrived at Fort Shaw.

The U.S. Cavalry band welcomed the governor general with "Hail to the Chief" and "God Save the Queen", while the fort's guns boomed out a seventeen-gun salute. This was too much for the police team drawing the governor general's ambulance, and it bolted. The teamster let the horses run themselves out by going round and round several times, then pulled up safely to the officers' quarters, where the commandant was waiting. The governor general alighted quite unperturbed.

The next morning as he said farewell to his NWMP escort, the Marquis of Lorne thanked the officer, NCOs and constables. He expressed his entire satisfaction at the manner in which they had carried out their duties, often under very difficult circumstances. Then, accompanied by the U.S. Cavalry escort, and for a few miles by the NWMP escort, the governor general left Fort Shaw for Helena and Dillon, from which latter point he would travel on the Utah Northern Railroad en route to Winnipeg.

By the time the escort reached Fort Shaw, the governor general had been escorted about 1,100 miles over a period of forty-five days. Now the men and horses had to return to their respective posts. En route they encountered bitterly cold weather, early snowstorms and unseasonable blizzards. The horses suffered considerably and several, completely exhausted, were left at ranches along the way, to be picked up the following spring. Some of the escort, members of "B" Division, Qu'Appelle, stayed at Fort Macleod for the winter rather than attempt the hazardous journey across the plains, and those from Fort Walsh also remained there until the weather abated. Eventually all the men and horses arrived back at their posts, but many of the horses were in very poor condition.

The escort party that started from NWMP headquarters at Fort Walsh covered more than 1,900 miles in all the installments of its journey. Other members of the NWMP and their horses travelled thousands of additional miles in connection with the governor general's tour while making auxiliary patrols to service the cavalcade and then returning to their posts. The total mileage covered by the Marquis of Lorne's tour is truly astounding, particularly since most of it was over rough prairie trails and some of it over territory without trails.

The extent to which the NWMP was able to stretch its still modest human and equine resources is equally remarkable, since at the time of the tour there was a great demand on men and horses for general patrol work related to the Force's law-enforcement duties. At one time or another more than half the horses of the NWMP were in use, and toward the end of the tour the cavalcade included 115 horses, more than one-third of the 308 then in the Force. Also, more than a quarter of the Force's 293 men were continuously employed on duties connected with the tour. In fact, except for the March West in 1874, the Force's escort of the Marquis of Lorne through the North-West Territories was the most difficult and demanding task in its history.

In reporting on the tour to the Canadian government, Commissioner Irvine drew attention to the great benefits accruing from it to the country.

> The interest shown by His Excellency in everything concerning the prosperity and welfare of the settlers has left a lasting impression on them. He at all times took every opportunity of visiting their homes and conversing with them on their personal welfare and their plans for the future. He gleaned from all the information that could be obtained in reference to their opinions as to the prospects and natural resources of the country. The personal interest shown by His Excellency in the settlers will, I am aware, ever be remembered with feelings of loyalty and pride.
>
> Among the Indians too, His Excellency's visit has been productive of much good. As the direct representative of Her Majesty the Queen, His Excellency's presence in their midst, and the trouble and care taken to enquire into their wants, has had the effect of strongly impressing the Indians with the kindly devotion of the Great Mother towards her red subjects.

During the first half of the 1880s, the Canadian Pacific Railway had extended its track beyond Manitoba into the North-West Territories and across the prairies. As the head of steel pushed into the mountains, so did the NWMP, so that even in British Columbia they policed the area flanking the federal railway right of way. Some police, including the famous Inspector Sam Steele, went ahead of actual construction with contractors and supplies, riding along mountain trails cut in solid rock hundreds of feet above swirling rivers.

On one occasion, high above the Kicking Horse Pass, Steele's mount, a prairie horse unused to mountains, was terrified of the rocky cliff towering above him and kept edging toward the brink. At a very narrow part of the winding trail a construction worker suddenly appeared from the opposite direction carrying a big bundle of blankets. The horse whirled about, backing perilously near the edge. Steele sprang off and threw himself flat on the road. The animal's hind legs slipped over the edge, but Steele kept a firm hold on its bridle and head collar. Another policeman hurried to help, and together the two men dragged the trembling horse to safety.

Once the railway had traversed the prairies, settlers followed in earnest, so whereas the Force's main concern before 1880 had been with the Indians, it now centred on the settlers. As settlement of the Territories gradually increased, so did police patrols to check on the settlers' welfare. Although the police could make patrols along the main railway line by train instead of having to use saddle horses, settlements soon stretched out from the main line and the use of horse patrols became more extensive.

After branch lines of the railway were laid, the police took full advantage of them. In some places they even had their own railway handcars, so that they could travel on the railway whenever necessary. One resourceful constable, pursuing an escaped prisoner, built a platform on his handcar to convey his nervous bronco over a high trestle bridge across the South Saskatchewan River. While on railway patrol generally, though, if the police had to travel beyond the end of steel, they would usually hire horses at the rails' end. Even after the coming of the railway, however, the Force maintained its former strength of horses for patrolling sparsely settled areas.

The railway was also responsible for visits to the west by governors general, those from the mid-1880s being much less onerous for the police and their horses than that of the Marquis of Lorne in 1881. When the next governor general, the Marquis of Landsdowne, visited the west in 1885, he was able to travel across the prairies by rail. The NWMP provided mounted escorts only at large centres and

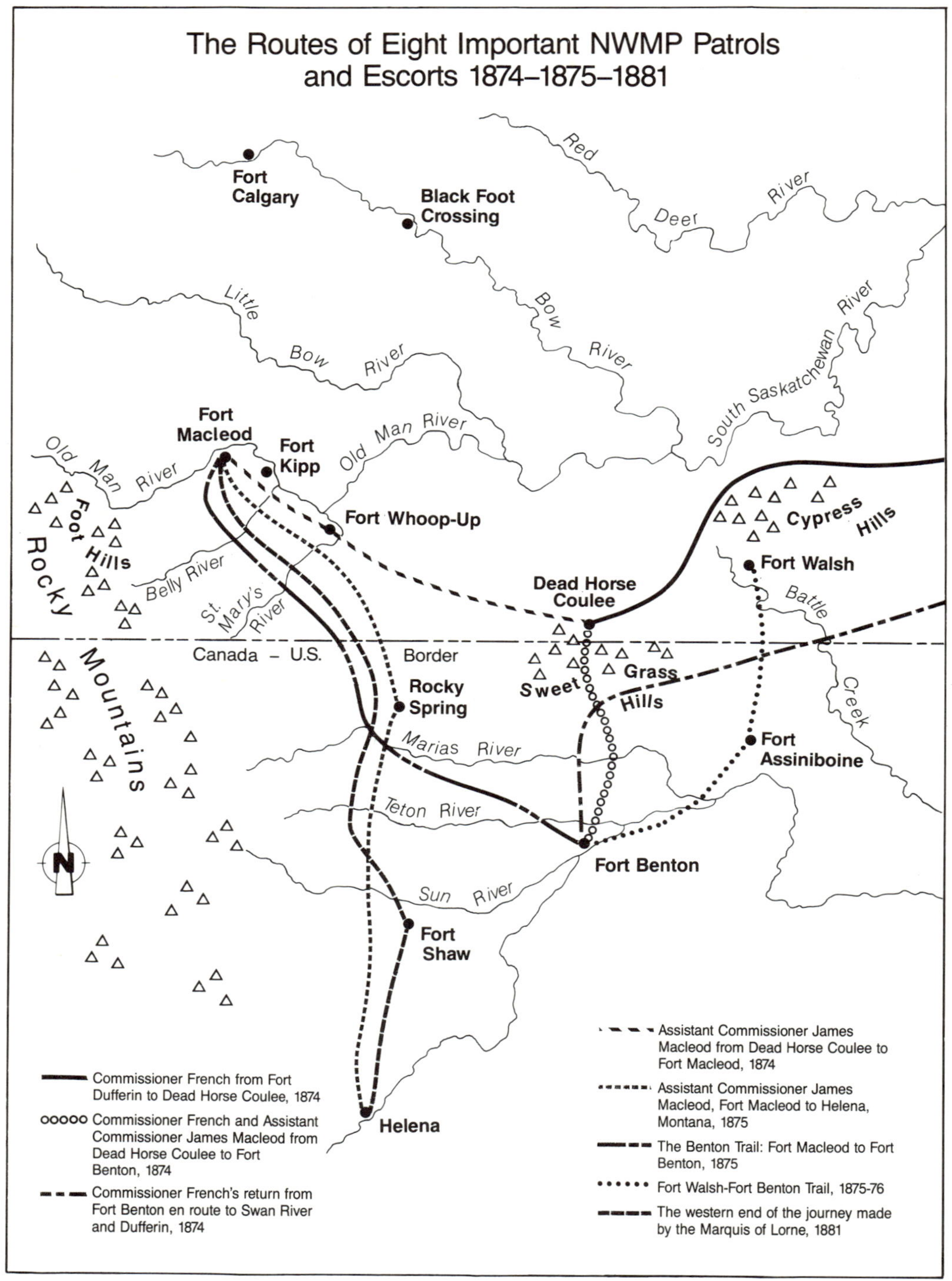
The Routes of Eight Important NWMP Patrols and Escorts 1874–1875–1881
Fort Calgary
Black Foot Crossing
Red Deer River
Little Bow River
Bow River
South Saskatchewan River
Fort Macleod
Fort Kipp
Old Man River
Old Man River
Foot Hills
Rocky Mountains
Belly River
St. Mary's River
Fort Whoop-Up
Dead Horse Coulee
Cypress Hills
Fort Walsh
Battle Creek
Canada - U.S. Border
Rocky Spring
Sweet Grass Hills
Marias River
Fort Assiniboine
Teton River
Fort Benton
Sun River
Fort Shaw
Helena
N
Commissioner French from Fort Dufferin to Dead Horse Coulee, 1874
Commissioner French and Assistant Commissioner James Macleod from Dead Horse Coulee to Fort Benton, 1874
Commissioner French's return from Fort Benton en route to Swan River and Dufferin, 1874
Assistant Commissioner James Macleod from Dead Horse Coulee to Fort Macleod, 1874
Assistant Commissioner James Macleod, Fort Macleod to Helena, Montana, 1875
The Benton Trail: Fort Macleod to Fort Benton, 1875
Fort Walsh-Fort Benton Trail, 1875-76
The western end of the journey made by the Marquis of Lorne, 1881

during travel other than by rail, such as when he went by trail from Indian Head to Fort Qu'Appelle about fifty miles away, and the Force provided him with a hundred-man mounted escort.

WAR ON THE HOME FRONT: THE NORTH-WEST REBELLION

For the men and horses of the NWMP, 1885 was a busy period, notably because of the Riel Rebellion and its aftermath. As police at the northern posts of Prince Albert, Battleford and Fort Pitt had explained in vain to the Canadian government, the Métis in that area, descendants of French hunters and Indians, had understandable grievances which undoubtedly should be redressed. The Métis wanted to retain their long, narrow homesteads fronting the Saskatchewan River, French-Canadian style, but government surveyors were re-mapping the land in square sections and quarter-sections and threatening them with eviction. The insensitive government's only answer to the Métis' pleas had been to strengthen the existing police posts and to establish another at Fort Carlton, which was, like the other three, on the north branch of the Saskatchewan. The Indians, too, had serious problems. For years hunger and poverty had plagued them on their reservations, yet in 1884 the heartless government, in spite of police reports, had reduced their limited ration quota.

In early March 1885, Superintendent N. L. F. Crozier at Fort Carlton notified the Canadian government of an imminent uprising. Louis Riel, leader of the Red River Rebellion of 1869 to 1870, who had returned from exile in the United States, was on the scene ready to lead a second rebellion.

On receiving government orders to reinforce Crozier's detachment, Commissioner Irvine immediately set out from Regina headquarters, in the bitter cold of a prairie winter, with a sleigh column of ninety men and sixty-six horses, with mounted men front and rear guarding the many sleighloads of supplies. Although some of the men suffered severely frostbitten faces and snow-blindness, and the horses had tremendous difficulty breathing in the icy air, Irvine's column hurried on northward for 291 exhausting miles, reaching Prince Albert after seven agonizing days.

Before Irvine and his sleigh column pushed on to Fort Carlton, about fifty miles upriver, Crozier and a party of fifty-six Mounted Police and forty-three Prince Albert volunteers (local townsmen and farmers) had tried to retrieve supplies and ammunition left behind by a trader who had abandoned his store at Duck Lake, not far south of Carlton. Crozier and his mounted men were intercepted by about 350 Métis and Indians led, with the approval of Riel, by Gabriel Dumont. The Métis, many of them sniping from behind a wooded ridge and a log building, tried to outflank the police and volunteers, who were manoeuvring their horses with great difficulty in the deep, encrusted snow. Crozier's party, far outnumbered, with twelve men killed and twelve wounded, and with five horses dead and several disabled, had to retreat to Fort Carlton.

When Commissioner Irvine and his sleigh column arrived at Carlton later that day, everyone agreed that Prince Albert, well-established, and the only white settlement in the area, was the logical centre of defence. Fort Carlton, on the other hand, was merely a Hudson's Bay Company post and was on the river's edge below a three-hundred-foot hill, which made it especially vulnerable to attack from above.

After dark, in preparation for evacuating Carlton, men saddled and harnessed horses, loaded sleighs with supplies, and sank surplus material through holes cut in the river ice to keep it from the rebels. They also stuffed hay into mattresses for the wounded men who would travel in the sleighs. After leaving Carlton at 4:00 A.M., the straggling two-mile column, which took two hours to climb the steep hill outside the fort, marched toward Prince Albert, where, after prodigious effort on the part of the horses, it arrived late that night.

Meanwhile the government was organizing military relief. Toward the end of March it wired a message to Commissioner Irvine over the Dominion Telegraph

NWMP troop en route to Battleford from Regina during the Riel Rebellion, 1885.

Line which had been extended in 1878 from Port Arthur, on Lake Superior, to Battleford: "Major-General Commanding Militia proceeds forthwith.... On his arrival, in military operations when acting with militia, take orders from him." Before Major-General Frederick Middleton arrived in the troubled area, however, the massacre of Frog Lake occurred, about thirty-five miles northwest of Fort Pitt.

Inspector Frances Dickens (son of the novelist Charles Dickens), in charge at Fort Pitt, had tried in vain to persuade the Indian agent at Frog Lake either that the settlers of the district should go to Fort Pitt for protection, or else that the agent should accept a substantial guard of Mounted Police. Early in April, a band of Cree Chief Big Bear's war-painted braves killed the Indian agent and seven other men, and took the other whites prisoner.

Twelve days later, during peace negotiations near Fort Pitt, between the Crees and a Hudson's Bay factor, constables Cowan and Loasby and a special constable inadvertently rode near the parlay camp. The Indians fired on them and the three men galloped toward the fort amid a hail of bullets from Indians in close pursuit. Cowan's terrified horse began to buck. Cowan swung from the saddle and ran for the fort, but was shot dead. Loasby kept on galloping, a stream of blood flowing from a serious thigh wound. Then his horse, shot in the neck, fell, and Loasby rolled with him. A Cree, in hot pursuit, rode him down and shot him, then galloped away, leaving him for dead. Later, however, Loasby managed to crawl toward the fort, was taken in, and lived. The special constable was captured by the Indians, but his life was spared.

NWMP border patrol during the Riel Rebellion, 1885. (Glenbow Archives, Calgary)

Inspector Dickens knew that the only thing he could do was to retreat from Fort Pitt to Battleford, where he could join the fight against Riel's ally, Cree Chief Poundmaker. That night, under cover of a severe snowstorm, the two dozen police stole out of the fort and crowded into a makeshift scow they had foresightedly made on the banks of the Saskatchewan River during the previous few days. For seven wretched days, their clothes freezing to their skin as they constantly bailed water from the leaking scow, they sailed one hundred miles down the ice-choked river, camping on shore at night in the open, and at last arriving safely at Battleford. No available record tells what happened to the police horses from Fort Pitt, but they certainly did not travel with Dickens and his men.

Meanwhile, two parallel columns of Canadian militia, each reinforced by a substantial body of Mounted Police, were marching north from the Canadian Pacific railway line, and from that point onwards, General Middleton was in full command. On arriving in the troubled area, his column, the main one, clashed unsuccessfully with the rebels at Fish Creek and was forced to halt and await reinforcements. The western column, under Lieutenant-Colonel W. D. Otter, reached Battleford, then set out to attack Poundmaker at Cutknife Hill about thirty miles farther west. Almost one-third of the attacking force were seventy-five NWMP under Superintendents W. M. Herchmer and Percy R. Neale (one of the Old Originals who had signed on at Lower Fort Garry in 1874). The police and their horses occupied the most dangerous positions throughout, acting as advance, rear and flank guards. When Otter's clash with the rebels proved no more successful than Middleton's, and he ordered a retreat to Battleford, the police and their horses again took up positions on the exposed parts of the column.

While clashes had occurred elsewhere, Major-General T. B. Strange and the Alberta Field Force had advanced from Calgary and Edmonton toward the area of conflict. The presence of this force moving through the western part of the prairies was chiefly responsible for saving that region from Indian warfare, with two contingents under Mounted Police officers getting much of the credit.

Inspector Sam Steele's mounted contingent was made up of the twenty-five NWMP who had served with him in the Rockies, part of a cavalry regiment, and a third corps, mostly settlers and cowpunchers, known as Steele's Scouts, which Major-General Strange called "the eyes and ears" of his command.

Inspector A. Bowen Perry's contingent comprised a corps of twenty-four Mounted Police from Fort Macleod, an infantry unit and a transport section. When they reached the Red Deer River, they found it high in flood, with a strong current, and with the ferry smashed to bits by the pounding water. Perry's men built a raft, then tied the horses' picket ropes together to make a 1,200-foot cable, which, after many misadventures, they used with the raft as a ferry for the men and supplies. The horses, however, swam across the swollen river.

On May 12, General Middleton won a decisive victory by capturing the Métis' headquarters at Batoche. Several days later Riel surrendered to a scout, but Gabriel Dumont escaped to Montana. Poundmaker gave himself up to prevent more bloodshed, and later, on July 2, Big Bear was captured by three NWMP constables.

The rebellion was over. It had never reached the full-scale war Riel had planned, one involving all the Métis and English half-breeds and about 20,000 Indians. The English half-breeds had sympathized but had refused to fight. The Blackfoot Indians in the south had also refused to fight, partly because they could see how readily the CPR had transferred Canadian troops to the west, and partly because the government, in alarmed haste, had also used the railway to send them huge supplies of food. Riel actually had only about five hundred Métis and one thousand Indians, a force which had not been able to make a strong enough stand to persuade the government to order any change in surveying the land, which continued to be mapped in square sections and quarter-sections. Riel and eight Indians were eventually hanged, and Poundmaker, Big Bear and eighteen Métis received various prison sentences.

POST-REBELLION POLICING

The duties of the Force after the rebellion were more onerous than ever. Men had to ride countless miles to gather evidence and witnesses for the trials of the rebel leaders, and the police in the north had to patrol more intensively than before, to guard against further Métis and Indian disturbances. Police in the south had to instigate a new campaign against thriving whiskey traders and smugglers who had taken advantage of the understaffed southern detachments to get back into business. To handle this extra work and that arising from the rapidly growing population of the vast prairies, by the end of 1885 the strength of the Force was almost doubled, reaching over one thousand, with a corresponding increase in the number of horses.

The year after the rebellion, 1886, reports from the various Divisions (not all of them directly involved in the rebellion) on the condition of their horses indicated that many of those hurriedly purchased the previous year had proved unsuitable.

The best report came from Fort Macleod, where all the horses were in good health, except that "corns were common owing to the stony nature of the ground which called for a great deal of extra shoeing". Battleford emphasized the general "unfitness" of its horses. At Maple Creek they were only in average condition. Prince Albert had lost some from hard work, exposure and bad forage. As the police realized, the poor condition of the horses was due largely to the extraordinary demands made of them during the rebellion. In 1886, two hundred of the Force's 845 horses had to be discarded and sold.

During that same year, however, the patrol work of the NWMP increased considerably. The police found it vitally necessary to supervise those militant Indians who had formerly believed the police to be invincible, but who had seen them sometimes unsuccessful during the rebellion, and who now were eager to demonstrate Indian strength.

The rebellion had also indicated the need for more training in mounted drill so that the police could maintain a higher degree of military preparedness in case of future Indian uprisings. In 1886 a special training camp was established on the banks of the Bow River, four miles east of Calgary. Leaving only enough men to take care of the barracks, "E" Division moved from Calgary to the training site, fully equipped to live for six weeks under canvas. Another fifty policemen and their horses arrived at the camp from Fort Saskatchewan. All received a thorough course of mounted and dismounted drill, rifle and revolver practice and special training in the care and management of horses.

Men and horses in other Divisions took similar training involving "mounted infantry" drill and the care of horses. The intensity of the training depended on the type of officer in charge. At Battleford the vigorous Superintendent Sam Steele reported, perhaps with exaggeration, "I kept them at it until there was no part of it they could not do well. The Divisions...at squadron and regimental drill could take their high jumps in line or column of troops. They could swim their horses across rivers with ease, and find their way in winter or summer without guide or compass to any place for hundreds of miles around."

A further after-effect of the Riel Rebellion on the NWMP was the re-establishment of the position of veterinary surgeon. Strange as it seems, but probably as a means of economizing, the federal government had abolished that commissioned rank position in 1877, only three years after the NWMP marched west. Veterinary Surgeon Poett had no choice but to resign, after which the Force's veterinary work had been done by veterinary NCOs. In 1884 Poett had re-engaged

The first NWMP riding school, built at Regina in 1885-86.

One of the two nine-pounder guns taken on the March West, and used for many years afterwards for the training of gun teams at Fort Macleod, circa 1890. (RCMP Museum, Regina)

Various types of transportation at Maple Creek Detachment, N.W.T., including team of mules drawing buggy, circa 1890. (RCMP Museum, Regina)

A mounted troop in drill formation at "G" Division headquarters, Fort Saskatchewan, circa 1890.

The commanding officer's team and sleigh, Regina, circa 1890. (RCMP Museum, Regina)

Single horse-drawn toboggans, often used for winter patrol work, circa 1900. (RCMP Museum, Regina)

as a constable, and had soon been promoted to the senior NCO rank of veterinary staff sergeant.

The poor condition of the NWMP horses after the rebellion forced the government to re-establish the commissioned rank position of veterinary surgeon, but the new appointment did not got to Poett. It went to NCO Robert Riddell, a graduate of the Ontario Veterinary College, who was promoted to the rank of inspector. The following year the new position of assistant veterinary surgeon was established, and the appointment went to John Burnett, also a graduate of the Ontario college. In 1888 Riddell resigned and was succeeded by Burnett, whose position was taken over by Theodore Wroughton.

By the end of 1887, the NWMP had purchased enough horses not only to replace the two hundred discarded and sold in 1886, but also to increase its horse strength to 921. The Force then had 634 saddle horses, 246 team horses, 24 pack horses, 6 scout horses, 6 Indian ponies and 5 mules. Even so, Commissioner L. W. Herchmer reported the need to purchase one hundred additional horses "to be distributed among the Divisions and thus enable us to turn out the same number of horses which will become slightly stale, for a run which will make them of much longer service, while if kept at steady work they would, in all probability, collapse before next winter and be a total loss." He might better have said that he needed one hundred spares to give the horses he already had a much-needed rest.

Commissioner Herchmer had good reason to ask for more horses. Settlement of the prairie region continued to increase slowly, until by 1890 the population of the North-West Territories together with that of Manitoba was well over 200,000. This meant that mounted patrols to check on the welfare of settlers also increased. In the post-rebellion period a patrol system was devised to protect every settler in every police district, so that no settler was overlooked, no complaint uninvestigated.

Patrol work by this time totalled almost 900,000 miles each year, or about thirty-six times the circumference of the earth. The limited number of horses meant that each patrol horse was expected to patrol from 2,500 to 3,000 miles annually.

The patrols to protect the settlers were not the only strain on the horses. They often had to travel fifty miles a day in pursuit of horse thieves and other criminals. On patrols near the Canadian-American border, horses travelled even longer distances for several days at a time to apprehend criminals before they crossed the border to safety. In fact, the demand for horses for patrol work was so great that only in winter, when the work pace slackened, could they rest between patrols.

During such slack periods they were often let loose to forage for themselves on the range where, fortunately, they seemed to thrive.

Travelling conditions continued to aggravate the police's horse problems. One officer reported: "During the summer, forced to travel on the trails under a hot summer sun in clouds of dust and attacked by myriads of mosquitoes, compelled to feed on unsuitable pastures and climb steep ascents...[the horses] had been worn down considerably." Horses on winter patrols were forced to endure winter storms and temperatures as low as 50 degrees below zero Fahrenheit.

Police horses and their riders travelled many miles during the hot dry summers of the late 1880s watching for signs of prairie fires. As settlers became more numerous, so did the devastating prairie fires, and severe fines were imposed on any persons proved responsible. As incentives to aid the police, informants were awarded half of the fines if they could prove who was responsible for such fires.

On one occasion, as a policeman galloped toward a prairie fire he met the police hay contractor galloping in the opposite direction.

"One of my men has started a fire! For God's sake turn out as many as you can and put it out!" the contractor gasped without drawing rein.

The policemen organized the fire fighting. At his direction men ploughed fireguards, set back-fires and beat out flames with wet sacks. They had the fire well

NWMP escort for the Duke of Cornwall (later King George V) on his visit to Calgary in 1901. The duke is the solitary figure on the left between the two escorting groups of Mounted Police. (RCMP Museum, Regina)

under control when the contractor returned. He had been to the magistrate, confessed it was his fault through his man's carelessness, and paid the fine of $100. He had also reminded the magistrate that he was also the informant, and received $50 back.

During the same period, as in earlier years, NWMP needed not only more horses, but also better-quality ones. The police felt more hopeful as settlement of the Territories increased, for professional men and farmers also needed good-quality horses for saddle and light vehicle work.

Ranchers and horse breeders responded to the increased demand by breeding better horses through the use of imported stallions of such breeds as Thoroughbreds, Standardbreds, Morgans and Cleveland Bays. The police benefitted, but still found it difficult to obtain enough of the better horses.

In the early 1890s, both team and saddle horses still suffered from making long patrols over rough trails. In 1891, when Veterinary Staff Sergeant Poett drew attention to the condition of horses in the Maple Creek Division, his remarks probably applied equally to horses elsewhere in the Force.

Poett stated that the Maple Creek team horses suffered badly from collar galls, no matter what the teamsters did to try to prevent them. He recommended that the horses used for draught work be replaced by "one or two teams of four mules each,

Inspector Charles Constantine and a party of policemen on patrol near Fort Saskatchewan, circa 1902. (Glenbow Archives, Calgary)

A riding instructor at Regina wearing the instructor's badge above his corporal's stripes, circa 1910. (RCMP Museum, Regina)

RNWMP member on a Canada—U. S. border patrol in 1917.

RCMP mounted troop preparing to leave the Regina barracks for Government House, to escort the lieutenant-governor to the opening of the Saskatchewan legislature. circa 1930. Grey horses for trumpeters were dispensed with soon afterwards.

Staff Sergeant H. L. Bossange and his horse, both of whom were killed by lightning while on patrol at Spirit River, Alberta, in June 1919. (RCMP Museum, Regina)

good serviceable animals and well broken ... to be employed on special work such as the drawing of rations and forage, or of logs and lumber". Poett noted that fewer teams of mules would be required, since the mules could draw heavier loads. He also noted that the use of mules would eliminate the need for "the heavy horses savouring of the Clyde type" and "the tall, delicate unsubstantial broncos" then used as team horses.

In commenting on saddle horses, Poett recommended that the Force use "small well-put-up" horses, ranging from 15 to 15.2 hands high. He believed that horses of that size excelled in endurance those from 15.3 to 16 hands, and that the smaller ones were more sure-footed and less likely to stumble with their riders. Poett, who had nearly eighteen years experience with NWMP horses by then, also believed that bay and roan horses were less susceptible to lameness and disease than horses of any other colour.

Poett's comments on the bay and roan horses implied that the Force should use horses only of those colours. But as it could not get enough suitable horses of any colour, its horses, of necessity, included bays, blacks, greys, chestnuts and buckskins, and the height of the horses ranged from 14.3 to 17 hands.

When Commissioner A. B. Perry took command in 1900, he set the standard for NWMP horses at between 15.2 and 16 hands. But even then the Force could not always obtain good-quality horses within that range.

Perry was acutely aware of the strain that too many patrol duties over too great an area placed on his too few horses and men. The year after he became commissioner he re-organized the patrol system by detailing a certain number of men to special patrol duty. Unlike the men at the stationary police posts, these special patrols kept constantly on the move, thus covering the greatest possible number of homesteads, farms, ranches and settlements in the least possible time. Perry's new system was obviously more efficient, and probably it afforded some relief to some men, but the horses still had to travel amazing distances.

Fortunately, no other horse ever had to make as extensive a patrol as that of Sergeant J. C. W. Biggs, who in that same period pursued a horse thief from Moose Jaw across the international boundary into Montana. The sergeant and his horse were away from their post for 135 days during which they covered 2,700 miles, an average of twenty miles a day.

Whenever escorts and honour guards were needed, the police had to call upon men and horses stationed at distant places to perform those duties. When Lord

Stanley, Canada's sixth governor general, visited the North-West Territories in 1899, the nearly one-hundred-man mounted escort that welcomed him to Regina had been drawn from points as far away as Battleford and Prince Albert some two hundred miles distant. When he visited Lethbridge, Fort Macleod and Calgary a few days later, and when he visited Edmonton on his return from the west coast, men and horses for escort duty were drawn from all parts of what became Alberta in 1905.

Two years after Lord Stanley's visit, the Duke and Duchess of Cornwall (later King George V and Queen Mary) visited the west. At Regina, still a small frontier town, the NWMP mounted troop met them at the station and escorted them to Government House. The police also provided the carriage in which they rode. A Canadian government official travelling with the royal party wrote later: "Police carriages ploughed their way through a sea of black gruel.... and mud flew in every direction, not even Her Royal Highness's fur cape escaping contamination."

The next day the royal visitors arrived in Calgary by train. In Victoria Park the Duke of Cornwall reviewed 250 mounted members of the NWMP, a quarter of its strength at that time, under the command of Commissioner A. B. Perry. The same government official noted that the military experts in the Duke's party expressed surprise and delight at the unexpected brilliance. Drawing on his own impressions he wrote: "To the eye of the civilian the smart uniforms and fine carriage of the Mounted Police, joined to their mobility and high discipline, indicate a standard of military excellence not elsewhere attained in this country, and not easily surpassed in any other."

In 1905 the RNWMP ("Royal" had been added to the Force's name in 1904) provided large escorts for Earl Grey, Canada's governor general at that time, when he attended inaugural ceremonies relating to the formation of the provinces of Alberta and Saskatchewan. In succeeding years the Force continued to provide mounted escorts for visiting governors general, but none entailed the problems posed by the escorts of the earliest years.

In 1905, when the provinces of Alberta and Saskatchewan were formed from part of the North-West Territories, the change did not ease the policing responsibilities of the Royal North-West Mounted Police or the patrol work required of it. The Force continued to do the same federal work as before. And although the other police work had become the responsibility of the new provincial governments, the Force continued to do that, too, but under contract with the provinces.

During the fifteen years preceding 1910, the prairie region had experienced such a great influx of settlers that by that year the white population from the Red River to the Rockies was about one million. At first the police merely had to increase their patrols, mostly to check on the welfare of the growing number of settlers. Later, as more and more immigrants applied for naturalization, the federal responsibilities of the Force demanded that its men and horses make additional patrols to investigate the applicants.

Prairie fires continued to demand service from horses and riders. In the late summer of 1905, when Constable Conradi was having a mid-day meal with a rancher near Battleford, Saskatchewan, he saw a raging prairie fire sweeping across the horizon. He jumped up from the table, dashed to the barn for his horse and galloped to a homestead in the path of the fire. Thanks to the stamina of his horse, Conradi arrived in time to help plough a fireguard. After the fire jumped the fireguard, Conradi saved the lives of the homesteader's wife and children.

With the beginning of the First World War in August 1914, federal responsibilities of the RNWMP forced its men and horses to make patrols for routine checking of the 173,000 Germans and Austrians in Alberta and Saskatchewan who were considered enemy aliens. Also at that time the Force increased its mounted border patrols to prevent saboteurs from entering Canada. The horses, no less than the men, had to endure increasingly heavy work loads.

In spite of its added responsibilities, as the war progressed the strength of the Force decreased. Men refused to re-engage when their terms of service expired and others deserted to join the army. In April 1917, the Canadian government permitted the RNWMP to recruit, and more than seven hundred men enlisted, some of them police recruits.

Although from the year after the Riel Rebellion to the beginning of the First World War the strength of the Force had been held at more than 1,000 men, by September 1918 its usable manpower in Canada had fallen to 303, and the number of its horses to 597. By that time Alberta and Saskatchewan had formed their own provincial police forces, and it seemed that the RNWMP, and consequently its horses, were on the road to extinction.

At the same time there were indications that even if the Force itself continued to exist, its horses would eventually no longer be needed for patrol work. At Regina in 1915 the Force had purchased its first car, and since then had been using it to transport prisoners between the Regina barracks and the Regina jail.

Forthcoming events were different, however, from those anticipated. After the end of the war in November 1918, the Canadian government revitalized the Force by ordering it recruited to a strength of 1,200. Also at that time it decreed that the RNWMP would enforce all federal statutes in the four western provinces of Manitoba, Saskatchewan, Alberta and British Columbia. This took the Force for the first time into Manitoba and British Columbia, where provincial police forces in existence before the NWMP went west had formerly handled federal as well as provincial law-enforcement matters. To add to the vitality of the reconstructed Force, the government supplied it with additional mechanized transport, including two passenger cars, ten trucks and fifteen motorcycles. Although this first substantial mechanization of the Force did accurately forecast the eventual decline of the horse for patrol work, events of the following year led to a new use for RNWMP horses.

INDIAN PONIES AND PACK HORSES

When Indian scouts worked for the police they preferred their own ponies to any of the police-owned Indian ponies or horses the police could provide. Just as the scouts were of vital importance to the North-West Mounted Police from 1874 onward, so were their ponies.

Indian scouts accompanied police on patrol, acting as guides, interpreters, and often as peacemakers with chance-met hostile Indians, riding their small ponies alongside the police on larger horses. They also rode them when they went ahead of the police to "scout" various Indian bands and so provide the police with information to help them deal peacefully with those bands.

During the North-West Rebellion in 1885, although many Indians lined up with the Métis against the Canadian government and their agents, the police, a good number of Indian scouts and their ponies still worked for the police. After the rebellion, the Indian ponies continued to be useful when their owners again acted as "the eyes and ears of the Force" during police dealings with Indians.

The Indian ponies were descendents of the fine Arabian horses brought to the American continent by the Spanish conquistadores early in the sixteenth century. The Spanish employed Indians to look after their horses, and the Indians soon acquired riding skills and horses of their own.

Horses became an important part of Indian life, allowing the Indians to wander farther afield to hunt and also to battle with their enemies. But the beautiful Spanish horses were at a disadvantage because the Indians failed to acquire knowledge about their care and breeding. Over successive generations, because of the lack of proper food, the generally poor conditions of Indian life, and indiscriminate breeding, the fine Spanish horses gradually deterioriated into the Indian ponies of the nineteenth century.

Even so, the ponies used by their Indian owners in the service of the North-West Mounted Police showed signs of their Arabian ancestry in their fine heads and dished faces. On the other hand, their difficulties and deprivations had made them much tougher than the police horses brought from the east, and probably tougher than the western broncos. Indian ponies could withstand long days on patrol, winter or summer, and then, like broncos, forage for themselves. As they were native to the country, the extremes of climate had little effect on them. Such qualities made them invaluable to their Indian owners and, consequently, to the Mounted Police.

Without pack horses many of the patrols of the early days, either ordinary or extraordinary, could not have been accomplished, since pack horses carried food for the men and the saddle horses, and camping equipment. Later, when patrols were made by team and wagon, pack horses often accompanied them, too.

True pack horses were not just saddle horses used to carry supplies. The best of them were native to the range, and usually felt at home even in remote areas. They could carry heavier loads than saddle horses, could travel longer and faster with such loads, and at the end of a day's journey could forage for themselves. Unlike saddle horses, they did not panic in the vicinity of wild animals, although they often demonstrated an uncanny sense of danger.

As the west became more settled, and most ordinary patrols were made to places where settlers gladly provided the police with food and shelter for themselves and their horses, the NWMP had less need of pack horses.

Although the Mounted Police had used pack horses ever since they went west in 1874, they made their first notable use of such horses in 1887-88, in connection with the establishing of Fort Steele in the Kootenay District of southern British Columbia. Reports had reached Commissioner L. W. Herchmer that the Kootenay Indians objected to living on reserves set aside for them and were about to rebel. Superintendent Sam Steele was given the task of establishing a police post in the troubled area, which lay in the Rocky Mountains just west of the border between British Columbia and the North-West Territories.

In the summer of 1887, Steel and his whole "D" Division travelled the last part of their journey, from Golden, B.C., by train, then down the Kootenay River by river steamer. Finally they climbed into the mountains with the help of a large pack-horse train provided by R. Galbraith, a settler of the district. Steele chose a suitable site for what was later to be called Fort Steele, and as soon as his men had made camp, they set to work cutting logs for the buildings.

The Galbraith pack train continued to take in building and other supplies for the fort. But Steele soon saw the need of having his own pack horses, not only for packing in supplies, but also for helping to haul the building logs. He purchased a pack train of twenty-four fine ponies and three mules, with full pack equipment.

The NWMP pack horses proved useful for the year Steele and his men remained in the Kootenay District. As he wrote later: "This train proved to be a good investment, earning its value every month, costing nothing to forage, and teaching many men the art of packing." He showed his appreciation during the winter when, although almost all the other horses were out on herd with no oat allowance, the pack horses and mules were allowed a small quantity of oats daily.

By the summer of 1888, the police had made friends with the Indians and were convinced that they would remain peaceful. Fort Steele was no longer needed as a well-staffed police post, and Steel and "D" Division were ordered to leave it. They were to trek eastward to Fort Macleod, getting out of the Rockies by way of the Crow's Nest Pass, which Steele considered to be the "best" way out.

The journey out of the Rockies was much more difficult than the journey in. Much of the route zig-zagged up and down mountainsides and could be traversed only by saddle and pack horses. The wagons, old and in poor condition, were sold,

NWMP Indian scouts on their own ponies, circa 1894. The NWMP staff sergeant on the far left rides a horse not much bigger.

as were surplus stores, barracks furniture, and so on. Before the column set out, the pack horses helped by carrying oats and biscuits to caches at intervals of a day's march until they reached the point in the foothills of the Rockies at which police wagons with supplies could come to meet Steele and his party.

When "D" Division left Fort Steele on August 7, 1888, its column contained forty-eight saddle horses, ten team horses ridden by men of the Division, twenty-five police pack animals tended by three government-employed packers, plus fifty-four pack animals provided by R. Galbraith and tended by ten packers. Laboriously the scores of animals climbed up and down cliffs and skirted mountain streams and huge stands of evergreens. They crossed, single file, narrow bridges over canyons and waterfalls, one bridge a thousand feet above a rushing stream. At night men and animals camped at places to which the pack horses had earlier carried their loads of supplies.

At last, seven days out of Fort Steele, Division "D" and its entourage reached the summit of the Rocky Mountains. A few hours later the Crow's Nest Pass loomed ahead, and still later the column trekked through the Pass.

The following day, at Lower Old Man's Lake, police and wagons from Fort Macleod met the men and animals from Fort Steele. The police transferred the loads from the pack animals to the wagons. Galbraith and pack train set out for their return trip to the Kootenay District, while the police pack horses enjoyed a well-earned respite on flat land. That night the police horses, which had been confined in small areas in the mountains, seemed to sense that they were nearing

RCMP saddle and pack horses on game patrol in Brazeau Forest in the Jasper Park area of Alberta, 1938. (A. R. Foster)

RNWMP pack horses on the Peace-Yukon patrol of 1905-1907 following a side-hill trail dug out for them by the police. (RCMP Museum, Calgary)

their native plains. They became so excited that they stampeded. However, the police recovered them the next morning, and in less than an hour they were on their way to Fort Macleod.

In the early days of the Klondike gold rush in the mid 1890s, the only way the gold-hungry adventurers could get to the Yukon was to travel by boat up the Pacific coast to Skagway and Dyea in Alaska, then trek over the mountains into the Yukon. The Mounted Police who went to the Yukon had to take the same route, using hired pack horses from the coast to the goldfields area. Inspector Charles Constantine, in charge of the NWMP there, asked the Canadian government to investigate the possibility of an inland, all-Canadian route to the Yukon. The government then instructed the Mounted Police to patrol from Edmonton via the Peace River District to the Yukon, and to report on the practicability of such a route.

Inspector J. D. Moodie, who led the Edmonton–Peace–Yukon patrol which left Edmonton in early September 1897, chose the four constables and the six saddle horses for his party with great care. As he well knew, the train of twenty-four pack horses that carried his supplies was equally vital to the success of the patrol that set out to travel about 1,250 miles through unknown wilderness and across mountains, to the headwaters of the Pelly River in the Yukon.

During the first part of the journey, bulldog flies attacked the horses in such vindictive clouds that the police had to grease the animals to ease their torment. Still the heavily burdened pack horses plodded on, through muskeg and almost impenetrable stands of evergreens. Skilfully they picked their way over mile after mile of rotting stumps while the police often had to chop their way through a three-hundred-mile stretch of burnt and fallen timber. The pack horses didn't panic even when a forest fire blazed toward the patrol party and they were saved from horrible death only by a last-minute change of the wind. Several died from eating a poisonous weed, but the rest of them uncomplainingly accepted the extra burden of supplies moved from the dead horses.

At Fort St. John, partway into the Rockies, deep snow threatened to delay the patrol until spring, but Moodie hired dogteams and horse sleighs to ease the burden on the saddle and pack horses. Then he persuaded a local Indian to guide them through the drifted mountain passes, and they pushed on. During the winter, food supplies for the horses and dogs ran low. One by one the police had to kill the pack horses to feed the dogs, because at that point they needed the dogs more than they needed the horses. Then they pushed on farther into the mountains, month after month, during the rest of the winter, the following spring and the brief northern summer.

By the beginning of October 1889, the tattered, weather-beaten police arrived at Pelly River. They no longer had any saddle horses: either the police had killed them for dog food, or they had sickened and died. Moodie and his men were still using pack horses, but these had been hired en route from Indians. Every one of their original pack horses had been sacrificed so that the patrol could continue.

At the Pelly, the police returned the rented pack horses to their Indian owners. Then they cached their pack saddles and other surplus goods and set sail in a canvas canoe toward Fort Selkirk, downriver but northward. After innumerable hazardous experiences as the perilous northern winter set in, on October 24 they staggered into Fort Selkirk, where the Pelly River flows into the Yukon River. The police had travelled 1,600 miles, including side trips for supplies, to reach this point from which travellers could easily sail to the heart of the Klondike District.

"I should say the overland route [from Edmonton to the Yukon] would never be used in the face of the quick and easy one *via* Skagway," Inspector Moodie reported later. Even pack horses could not successfully travel so many hundreds of miles over such a hazardous route.

From 1905 to 1907, after the Canadian government had ignored Moodie's report and ordered the RNWMP to build "a passable trail from Peace River to the Yukon" over part of Moodie's former route, pack horses again played a vital role.

After Superintendent Charles Constantine and his trail-building party reached Fort St. John in northeastern British Columbia, pack horses plodded back and forth carrying supplies from there to points along the trail under construction. Like Moodie's pack horses, they carried their loads over mountain passes, down into valleys, across swampy lowlands and up and over more mountains. During the summer of 1906, when the police had to find the best route by which to connect Whitehorse, in the Yukon, with the work already done, pack horses carried all supplies during the six-hundred-mile patrol march the police made out of Whitehorse.

In the spring of 1907, by which time construction had progressed as far as Fort Grahame, pack horses carried supplies from Fort St. John to Fort Grahame. For the whole journey the horses were harassed by deep snow, torrents of spring rain, highwater that forced them to cross most of the rivers on rafts, and poor feed. During the summer the same pack horses trekked back and forth out of Fort Grahame to take those supplies farther along the trail under construction. Not surprisingly, while the RNWMP worked on the Peace–Yukon trail, many pack horses, weakened by overwork, sickened and died, and many others died from exhaustion.

As the years passed, and especially as cars and trucks came into use, the Mounted Police used pack horses only in the most remote areas. Police-owned pack horses were regularly used for the last time during 1939-40 in the Jasper National Park area of Alberta.

Constable A. R. Foster used two pack horses and one saddle horse as he made game preservation patrols in the park. He noticed that his pack horses were much more at home in the rough country of the park than his saddle horse, and that the pack horses sensed dangerous places more readily. He was surprised to learn that one pack horse even seemed to remember danger. Whenever the constable rode up to a certain rather shaky forestry bridge over a canyon which he occasionally had to cross, his saddle horse and one of the pack horses crossed it without hesitation. But the other pack horse always broke away and dashed down into the canyon, a distance of about a quarter of a mile. Then it climbed up through the heavy bush to meet the constable and the other horses, who always crossed the bridge safely. Foster was convinced that the pack horse must at one time have had a bad experience crossing that bridge, or one like it, and it never forgot the danger.

NORTHERN SERVICE

The first Mounted Police in the Yukon went there in advance of the Gold Rush of the late 1890s. They had no need of horses en route since they travelled by water, up the Pacific coast to the mouth of the Yukon River in Alaska, then up that river into the Canadian Yukon. A second, larger contingent of NWMP went north in the autumn of 1897, to reinforce the police already there under the command of Inspector Charles Constantine. These men, like the adventurers they went to police, disembarked at Skagway, Alaska. Then they hired pack horses to take their supplies over rain-drenched mountain trails knee-deep in mud, to a point from which they could reach the goldfields area by riverboat.

Even after the police were well established in the Yukon they couldn't make much use of saddle horses. In summer the mountainous terrain and the lack of trails led them to use boats on the Yukon River wherever possible, and in the winter they found dogteams more practical.

The Mounted Police did, however, use horses in varying numbers from year to

Dawson City's only two remaining horses leading the Discovery Day Parade on August 17, 1935. (W. E. L. McElhone)

The same two horses being used for a democrat patrol from Dawson City to the Klondyke, 1936. (W. E. L. McElhone)

The same team doing farm work, Dawson City, 1936. (W. E. L. McElhone)

year. Official records for the early years have no breakdown to indicate pack, team or saddle horses, but presumably most were pack horses, which the Force sold when they were no longer needed. In 1898, NWMP in the Yukon had 101 horses, all based at Tagish, a detachment on the Gold Rush trail which led from Skagway through the mountains. By 1899 the Gold Rush was over, and the Mounted Police had only seven horses, all based at Dawson. In 1900 there were nine at Dawson and twenty-five at Whitehorse.

Meanwhile, when the Gold Rush was at its height Inspector Constantine had stressed the need for an all-Canadian inland route to the Yukon. The government, acting on his advice, ordered the Mounted Police to make a huge patrol from Edmonton to the Yukon, and then report on the feasibility of such a route. Inspector J. D. Moodie and a few men made the Edmonton–Peace–Yukon patrol from Edmonton in September 1898, but all of their thirty horses either died en route or had to be sacrificed to be used as dog food.

In spite of the Moodie party's terrible experience and Moodie's negative report on the route they took, in 1905 the government ordered Inspector Constantine to build a passable trail from the Peace River to the Yukon, over the most difficult 750 miles of Moodie's route. Once again the horses were to play an integral role in a Herculean endeavour, and many would be sacrificed in the process.

On March 17, 1905, Constantine left Fort Saskatchewan, near Edmonton, in charge of a trail-building convoy which included another officer, thirty NCOs and men, and a long procession of laden sleighs with sixty horses. During March, April and May, horses and men wound their way northwest toward the Peace River and Fort St. John, while every warm spring day softened the river ice and made crossings more dangerous.

Crossing the Peace River, the cook wagon broke through the ice, and a horse died from shock and exposure. Then, on June 1, the cavalcade pulled into Fort St. John, and the police spent the next two weeks haying and erecting winter quarters for themselves and the horses.

On June 15, Constantine and his thirty-one men began to construct the Peace–Yukon trail, relying chiefly on axes and horses in the absence of road-building machinery. Painstakingly, using the horses whenever and wherever they could, the police cleared away standing timber and windfalls, graded steep inclines, and bridged streams. By September 25, when horses and men went into winter quarters, their combined efforts had resulted in ninety-four miles of trail, over mountain passes, down into valleys, across swampy lowlands, and up over more

Police horse teams supplementing dogteams in the drawing of police supplies in the Yukon. (RCMP Museum, Regina)

mountains. Constantine was satisfied that up to that point only two horses had died, and all his men were well.

During the winter, however, the horses began to show signs of strain. The river steamer had arrived at Fort St. John too late for supplies to be sent before freeze-up to the advance party along the trail. Horses laboriously pulled one-horse sleds to freight the most vital supplies over the difficult mountain trail between Fort St. John and the winter camp of the advance party. The animals became so exhausted that they couldn't get up in the mornings without help.

In May 1906, horses and police emerged from their winter quarters and set to work again on the Peace–Yukon trail. During the next four months of brief northern summer, animals and men worked on with increasing difficulty. Such torrents of rain fell that Constantine could not even make an inspection of the completed route. The rain also ruined a hay crop put up with much labour, signalling reduced rations for the horses the following winter.

In July it became necessary to find the best route by which to connect Whitehorse, in the Yukon, with the work already done. Then pack horses carried the supplies for a group of police who rode from Whitehorse south through the mountains on a six-hundred-mile patrol of discovery.

By September the Peace–Yukon trail party had constructed another 134 miles of trail, but some men had become so exhausted that they had to be relieved. The horses had paid an even greater price: thirteen of them had died.

On September 25 the trail party survivors re-entered winter quarters. This time nineteen horses and sixteen police lived at Fort Grahame, in buildings hastily erected by some of the men earlier in the month. The rest of the construction party, thirty-eight horses and nine men, trekked on to Peace River Landing because there wasn't enough hay at Fort Grahame. There wasn't any water at Fort Grahame, either, as all the sloughs were frozen solid. The nineteen horses there, like the men, drank water the police obtained by melting snow.

In the spring of 1907, when police and horses were about to tackle the Peace–Yukon trailbuilding for the third summer, they desperately needed supplies. Constantine organized a pack train at Fort St. John. Then the pack horses struggled with heavy loads of supplies from that point to Fort Grahame, constantly harassed during the 150-mile journey by deep snow, torrents of spring rain, and treacherous mountainsides. From Fort Grahame, police horses relayed the supplies to the working parties farther along the trail. Meanwhile the rest of the horses worked on trailbuilding. By the end of the third summer, horses and men had built another 129 miles of trail at a cost of 26 horse casualties.

Commissioner A. B. Perry went from Regina to inspect the trail, accompanied by a few other Mounted Police. It took him eighteen days to go from Regina to Fort St. John, travelling by train, wagon and saddle horse. He then rode along the 357 miles of completed Peace–Yukon trail: 208 miles from Fort St. John to Fort Grahame, 116 miles beyond that to Bear Lake and 33 miles beyond that to the working party. The commissioner marvelled at the work his men and horses had done under indescribably stark circumstances. He was relieved, too, that the rest of the trail would go through less difficult terrain. The worst was over.

In appreciation, Perry decreed that the winter of 1907-08 should be more comfortable for both men and horses. The surviving animals went to winter at Hazelton, with one NCO in charge. The rest of the men went "out" from the north to winter in civilization.

Neither horses nor men of the Constantine party ever again worked on the Peace–Yukon trail. With the goal of completing it within reach, the Canadian government decided that the venture was too much for the federal treasury alone to finance. Commissioner Perry received orders to try to persuade the B.C. government to share in certain expenses and work, since the trail would be of benefit to that province. Perry tried to persuade them to participate in an extension of the trail as far as the Stickine River, but he failed.

The project was abandoned. Sickness and fatigue had permanently injured the health of many men, including Constantine, and dozens of horses had died helping build a road to nowhere. Even then, the travail of the surviving horses had not ended. They still had to trek another one thousand trail miles from Hazelton before they arrived back at their starting point, Fort Saskatchewan.

Meanwhile, as police in the Yukon had established themselves at several small detachments as well as at the main ones, they continued to use some horses for summer patrols and for packing or hauling supplies. In 1905, when Constantine was beginning his Peace–Yukon trailbuilding, the RNWMP in the Yukon Territory were using forty-three horses based at Dawson and fifty-eight at Whitehorse.

By 1918 they had six team horses at Dawson, plus three saddle horses and five team horses elsewhere. In 1929, although they used only two saddle and four team horses, those animals travelled more than 16,000 miles. The following year those horses travelled more than 22,000 miles, but that was only about one-quarter of the mileage the police achieved by other means, including water, dogs, train, stage and motorcar.

The last police horses in the Yukon, two team horses at Dawson and one saddle horse at a smaller detachment in 1938, competed that year with three cars and one truck. Records from 1939 make no further mention of horses in the Yukon. Records have never shown that the Mounted Police used horses in the neighbouring Northwest Territories (not to be confused with the earlier North-West Territories).

3

Into the Modern Era

Overseas Duty: The RNWMP and the Russian Revolution

While the Royal North-West Mounted Police was moving into the modern era after the end of the First World War by using cars, trucks and motorcycles in its first substantial mechanization, 181 of its horses were being sent abroad on a unique mission. This most unlikely use of Mounted Police horses occurred in 1918-19, after the Canadian government had ordered a squadron of RNWMP and its horses to Siberia to help the White Russians who had been overthrown by the Bolsheviks in the October Revolution of 1917. Before that revolution, which took place during the third year of the First World War, armies under the control of the Czarist government had supported the Allies in the European war. After the revolution the new Soviet government signed a peace treaty with Germany and withdrew the Russian troops.

Canada and its allies had more substantial reasons than friendship for wanting to help the White Russians oppose the revolutionaries. For one thing, the withdrawal of the Russian troops allowed Germany to concentrate all its forces on the Western Front and to make important gains in France and Belgium. But if the Allies could help the White Russians to regain power, the Russians would presumably re-enter the war on the Eastern Front, and the Germans would be forced to divert some of their forces from France and Belgium. Also basic to the Allies' desire to help the White Russians was the fact that, since the revolution, conditions in Russia had become so chaotic that the oil and grain resources of the Russian Ukraine could easily fall under German domination. If the White Russians could overthrow the Bolsheviks, however, they could also protect the Ukraine from the Germans.

RNWMP trooper on duty in Vladivostock, 1919.
(RCMP Museum, Regina)

In August 1918, as part of the larger plan made by the Allied command, the Canadian government ordered Commissioner A. Bowen Perry to recruit a squadron of cavalry. It would serve with a five-thousand-man Canadian Expeditionary Force which would be sent to Siberia, from which region they could help the White Russians. At RNWMP headquarters in Regina, Commissioner Perry immediately recruited a cavalry unit known as "B" Squadron, RNWMP, Canadian Expeditionary Force, Siberia. ("A" Squadron, RNWMP, had been formed earlier that year for service in France, but that squadron had used horses supplied from England.) The six officers, 184 other ranks, and 181 horses of "B" Squadron received mounted military training for duty in Siberia.

Only six days before the RNWMP contingent was to leave Canada the war in Europe ended, on November 11, 1918. But Canada, like other Allied countries, continued to implement the original plan. Hence on November 17, after a small advance party had already left, the rest of the contingent sailed from Vancouver, B.C., westward over the Pacific Ocean toward Siberia.

The 4,500-mile trip across the Pacific presented difficulties for the horses, especially during several storms which kept the men in charge constantly alert for their safety. Ventilation was also a problem, especially for the horses taking their turn at being stabled belowdecks. Nevertheless, only three horses were lost en route, from pneumonia. The records fail to mention whether one of the three was the horse that had leaped overboard into fifty feet of water as it was being loaded in Vancouver, and had been rescued uninjured with the help of "western cowpuncher recruits" and the ship's derrick.

After twenty-eight days at sea, the horses of "B" Squadron arrived at Vladivostock, a port on the east coast of Siberia controlled by the White Russians. By the time they arrived, the Canadian government had already realized that the only way its Expeditionary Force could help the White Russians would be to take part in a full-scale war. Canada was certainly not willing to do that.

So for six months the horses and men of "B" Squadron did no fighting, but remained peaceably in Vladivostock along with a host of British, French, Italian, American, Japanese, Serbian and other Allied troops. The RNWMP spent most of their time putting themselves and their horses through various kinds of mounted drills and other mounted exercises. Also, because the Bolsheviks were destroying parts of the Trans-Siberian Railway in an effort to prevent supplies from the port of Vladivostock reaching the White Russians, "B" Squadron made mounted patrols over parts of the railway leading out of the city.

On May 1, 1919, to break the monotony, the squadron organized a gymkhana on the Vladivostock race course. General Horvarth, the Russian commander-in-chief, took the salute as horses and men performed a Musical Ride and other mounted events before a cosmopolitan audience of ten thousand people. After the festivities, performers and audience alike were startled by an explosion. A man had thrown a bomb at the general as he was leaving the race course. The general escaped unharmed, but several nearby people were injured. Members of "B" Squadron overpowered the Bolshevik who had thrown the bomb, and also his accomplices.

Meanwhile the Canadian government had announced that the Canadian Expeditionary Force would gradually be withdrawn from Siberia. By mid-May "B" Squadron was preparing to return to Canada. The men were shocked to learn, however, that most of the horses were to be left behind. Not only had they grown fond of the animals during those months away from home, but some of the men had ridden these same horses on detachment duties back on the prairies. They grieved to know that the animals would be shipped by rail to the city of Yekaterinburg, headquarters of the White Russians more than four thousand miles away in the Ural Mountains. Then the horses, some of the best in the RNWMP, would be used to reinforce the White Russian Cavalry. The men's only consolation was that after the horses were handed over to Captain Smith, the British Army officer in charge of the supply train leaving for Yekaterinburg, they would be accompanied by Farrier Sergeant J. E. Margetts and also, at first, by five other members of the squadron.

On May 18, 1919, the trainload of horses and other military supplies left First River Station just outside Vladivostock. With the consent of the Chinese government, the train headed west over the original (shorter) route of the Trans-Siberian Railway through northern China. White Russians acted as guards for the train, but Captain Smith felt he could not rely on them to care for the horses as well, so although the original plan was for Farrier Sergeant Margetts' five comrades to turn back at Harbin, Manchuria, all six members of "B" Squadron accompanied the horses all the way to Yekaterinburg.

As the train pushed farther west over its Trans-Siberian route, it travelled through territory over which the White Russians had little control beyond the railway right-of-way. The train and its passengers, both human and animal, were in particular danger at the stops necessary for the horses to be fed and watered. Also, in spite of many such stops, two horses died from train fever from being cooped up in close quarters for a long time.

RNWMP Squadron on the barracks square, Vladivostock, Siberia, 1919.

On June 4, after the Bolsheviks had made several attempts to stop the train during the first two and a half weeks of its journey, they were finally successful in dynamiting it. Nineteen of the boxcars were smashed to bits. Two Russian soldiers and fifteen horses were killed, and twenty-four Russians were severely wounded. Many other horses were trapped inside overturned boxcars or entangled in the wreckage. Some were so severely injured that they had to be destroyed. Czechoslovak soldiers stationed in nearby woods came to help fight off the Bolsheviks, who retreated but kept on firing.

Meanwhile, twenty to thirty horses had broken loose from the overturned boxcars. They stampeded into the woods. Four of Margetts' men and a number of Russians mounted uninjured horses and endured the fire of the retreating Bolsheviks as they galloped after the runaways. After several miles the riders overtook them and herded them back to the safety of the train before nightfall.

After several days, what was left of the train was able to move on. Almost two weeks later, on June 25, Margetts and the other Mounted Policemen delivered their depleted stock of RNWMP horses to the White Russians at Yekaterinburg. During the thirty-eight days since leaving Vladivostock, while travelling more than four thousand miles, the horses had completed what was claimed to be the longest official journey ever made by horses on military service.

When the six members of the Force returned to Vladivostock, they learned that the rest of "B" Squadron had sailed for Canada. They in turn set sail for home. When the main party arrived back in Regina, on July 7, they were greeted by bad news. Only a few days after Margetts and his comrades had delivered the horses to the White Russians, the Bolsheviks had captured Yekaterinburg and also, presumably, the RNWMP horses.

STRIKE DUTY IN WINNIPEG

Suddenly and unexpectedly in 1919, the RNWMP found a new use for its horses in riot and strike duties. The first troop of RNWMP horses to perform riot duty was used in June of that year during the general strike in Winnipeg, where the RNWMP were now stationed in connection with performing federal police duties in Manitoba.

The strikers had good reason to be dissatisfied with poor working conditions, low wages and prices inflated after the First World War. But from mid-May, when a general strike included about thirty thousand essential workers such as firemen, light and power operators, telegraph and telephone operators, streetcar workers, garbage men, postal workers, milk and bread delivery men, and newspaper workers, the Winnipeg authorities had good reason for alarm.

Winnipeg citizens on the whole sympathized with the strikers, but as the need arose, thousands of citizens began acting as volunteer firemen, postal workers and so on. Then strikers began to use violence against citizens. The city police were in sympathy with the strikers, however, and declined to interfere. The abuse of citizens reached an alarming level. When the strikers scheduled a huge parade for the afternoon of Saturday, June 18, in spite of the fact that the Winnipeg authorities had forbidden it because they feared it would lead to violence and bloodshed, the authorities asked the RNWMP to provide a mounted troop to help keep order.

What the authorities knew, but the general public did not, was that a group of revolutionaries had infiltrated the strikers in the hope of eventually overthrowing the Canadian government. The more violence the revolutionaries could instigate, the more the authorities would have to respond with force, and thus the more chance the revolutionaries would have of persuading strikers in Winnipeg and elsewhere to join their revolutionary plans. There was much more at stake in Winnipeg that Saturday afternoon than merely the prevention of a forbidden parade.

At noon on Saturday about fifty carefully groomed, prancing horses of the RNWMP trotted out of barracks and carried their scarlet-coated riders to the heart of the city. Behind the horses came thirty-six other Mounted Policemen in motor trucks. Tens of thousands of strikers, many of them armed, milled about the streets or stood on rooftops, booing and jeering. Then strikers on the rooftops showered the horses and their riders with tin cans, bottles and bricks. Strikers on foot closed in, jabbing the horses' flanks with pocket knives and broken glass.

As the violence continued, Inspector W. C. Proby, in charge of the mounted troop, ordered his men to charge through the crowd. Then they wheeled about and charged again. Strikers with revolvers now fired at the Mounted Policemen. Others beat them with sticks and rocks and tried to pull them off their horses. Men on roofs hurled down great chunks of cement at horses and riders. One striker struck Proby from behind, and another aimed a revolver at him. Proby's life was probably saved by a corporal who felled the second striker just as he prepared to fire.

Then part of the mob turned on a stalled streetcar. They rocked it, trying to upset it and the motorman along with it, while others set fire to it. Proby ordered his troop to the rescue. As the mounted men rode forward, the strikers managed to tear a piece from the side of the streetcar. They hurled it among the horses and three fell.

RNWMP mounted troop on duty during the Winnipeg Strike, 1919. (RCMP Museum, Regina)

"Kill the bloody yellow legs!" shouted the strikers, and they moved in a body toward the horses and their uniformed riders.

"Draw pistols!" Proby ordered in desperation.

The police shot their first volley into the air as a warning, but it had no effect. A striker dragged a constable from his horse and clubbed him severely, while several other strikers did the same with other riders. The horse of Inspector F. J. Mead, the second officer with the mounted troop, fell, throwing his rider, but Mead regained the saddle before the strikers got him. By this time almost all the horses and men were injured or wounded. At last the battered police fired at the strikers in self defence, aiming only to wound. Several strikers were wounded and one was killed.

Now the strikers realized that the men on horseback were fully determined to enforce law and order, and gradually they withdrew. The mounted troop of bruised and bleeding horses and riders returned to barracks, accompanied by the trucks of police who on foot had defended their mounted comrades to the best of their ability.

A few days later the Winnipeg strike was called off, and sympathetic strikes in other Canadian cities were cancelled simultaneously. The horses of the RNWMP had helped directly in restoring order in Winnipeg. Indirectly they had also helped to defeat the plans of the revolutionaries, who were later convicted of seditious conspiracy against the Canadian government.

The Winnipeg experience made the federal and provincial governments aware of the value of properly trained mounted police in controlling industrial demonstrations. The sympathetic strikes that had broken out in other cities made them also aware that they must expect future industrial disputes, not only in western cities but also in other parts of Canada. The only provinces in which the Mounted Police enforced federal laws at that time were the four western provinces of Manitoba, Saskatchewan, Alberta and British Columbia, which meant that only in those provinces were they available and sufficiently empowered to assist local authorities, on request, in keeping the peace. Now the federal government and the other five provincial governments agreed that the Mounted Police should enforce federal laws in those provinces, too. The Force would also retain full police authority in the Yukon, the Northwest Territories (as distinct from the original vast North-West Territories which included the prairies), and the Arctic Islands. In November 1919, the federal government passed an Act amending the North-West Mounted Police Act, thus giving the Mounted Police jurisdiction in federal law enforcement in the whole of Canada.

THE DECLINE OF THE HORSE FOR POLICE WORK

In February 1920, the Royal North-West Mounted Police became the Royal Canadian Mounted Police. Its headquarters was moved from Regina to Ottawa, the national capital. A 160-man mounted squad was also moved to Ottawa, to be based at the newly established "N" Division at Rockcliffe, near Ottawa, but billetted at first at Lansdowne Park, the Ottawa Exhibition grounds. One hundred and sixteen horses remained in Regina. Of the Force's total of 845 saddle horses that year, 729 were used at nine strategic points from Ottawa to Vancouver, as mounted squads intended to support local authorities during industrial disturbances. By 1922, however, the need for such squads had declined, and so had the number of RCMP horses.

By 1930 mounted squads existed only at Vancouver, Edmonton, Winnipeg, Rockcliffe and Regina. At the training centres of Rockcliffe and Regina the squads were made up of senior recruits who had received riot-drill training.

During the depressed 1930s, these squads had to be used during strikes and demonstrations at various points including Saskatoon, Saskatchewan; Blairmore, Alberta; and Vancouver, B.C. The Regina squad was used in 1935, during the riot that occurred after the Force was ordered to halt the "On-to-Ottawa" trek of the unemployed. Then the need for such squads gradually diminished, until by 1938 only two remained, at Rockcliffe and Regina.

The old and the new at Prince Albert barracks in 1917.

Meanwhile, although the Force's general need of horses diminished, some new needs did arise. For example, one of its responsibilities since taking over federal duties in eastern Canada in 1920 was the policing of several Indian reserves in southern Ontario. For this a few horses were transferred to reserve detachments.

In 1928, when three police horses died of poisoning at the Six Nations Indian Reserve at Ohsweken, near Brantford, the police suspected local Indians. They circulated a poster offering a reward for any information that would lead to the arrest of the culprits. However, a police investigation revealed that the horses had been watered with pails that had held a solution used to spray the police potato patch, and the pails had not been thoroughly cleansed before the horses drank from them.

Since the Force had resumed the provincial policing of Saskatchewan in 1928, it also needed horses for the outlying detachments still using them. Similarly, when it resumed the provincial policing of Alberta and undertook similar policing in Manitoba in 1932, again it needed more horses for a few detachments. Nevertheless, by 1928, more cars than horses were being used for patrol work.

By this time the police had such difficulty in obtaining enough suitable animals even to fill their reduced requirements that they had to accept horses outside their set standard of between 15.3 and 16 hands in height. Occasionally, suitable horses no longer needed on detachments were transferred to mounted squads. But the problem remained. By now there was such a limited demand by the public for

Men and horses of the newly-named Royal Canadian Mounted Police in summer camp on the banks of the Ottawa River, on the site of what was to become "N" Division, the eastern Canada training division at Rockcliffe, Ontario, 1920.

Constable L. H. Nicholson, later a commissioner of the RCMP, ready for a saddle horse patrol at Balcarres, Saskatchewan, in the late winter of 1924-25. By this time the RCMP was again using the Universal saddle.

horses of the police standard that breeders no longer found it profitable to raise them.

During the 1930s the quality of most of the relatively few detachment horses deteriorated so badly that the police team was often the poorest in the district. Occasionally a detachment member made a patrol with a better team borrowed from the local livery stable. On one detachment this system worked well until the RCMP patrol sergeant arrived to find the constable away on patrol with a borrowed team, while the police team hauled the local dray wagon.

Fortunately for the senior author of this book, the police team he used at Meadow Lake, Saskatchewan, during the winter of 1934-35 was of top quality and in fine condition. Then a constable less than a year out of training, he drove by team and cutter (a small, light sleigh) through deep snow, the last miles over a trackless, frozen lake, to interview a trapper living forty-five miles away. As the police cutter neared the trapper's cabin, the trapper locked his two half-wolf sleigh dogs in a shed. They howled incessantly while the interview took place in the cutter, and the longer they howled, the more nervous the police horses became.

As Kelly and his team, Kit and Bess, set out over the snow-covered lake heading for home, the team was obviously relieved. Without any urging they moved at a very fast trot, the howls of the wolf-dogs still ringing through the clear air. Half a mile from the cabin, Kelly looked back and saw the dogs, which the trapper had

RCMP mounted troop on riot duty in the Crows Nest Pass, Alberta, winter of 1934-35. (A. R. Foster)

mistakenly released too soon, racing towards his small sleigh. Soon, yapping and snarling, they reached the back of the cutter, and the horses, having heard them closing in, became frantic.

Kelly was trying to keep his team on the track they had made on the way to the cabin, but their trot had turned into a gallop, and they were more often off the track than on it, which slowed them down. The dogs were able to close in, and one of them snatched off the buffalo robe hanging over the back of the cutter. After pausing briefly to tear at the robe, they again took up the chase. They sped up alongside, trying to jump on the horses' backs, but each time falling back in the snow, allowing the team and cutter to gain a little ground. By this time, however, the terrified horses were no longer galloping, but plunging ahead, which further slowed them down, and again the snarling dogs tried to manoeuvre alongside to renew their attacks on the horses.

Constable Kelly knew then that he must shoot the maddened wolf-dogs, although up to that time he had thought he could avoid doing so. Standing in the lurching cutter with his service revolver cocked, he knew it would be difficult to hit such a target, but he fired at the nearest dog, and it immediately fell motionless in the cutter track. The other dog stopped to savage it and made no further attempt to follow the team. After another mile or so, the well-lathered Kit and Bess quieted down to a walk, and in due course reached the Hudson's Bay post at the head of the lake. Kelly was thankful for having such a splendid team. A lesser one could never have escaped those maddened wolf-dogs, and a patrol which should have been merely a pleasant cutter ride would most likely have ended in tragedy.

As cars became more common, the policemen on detachments with only horses were generally allowed to make patrols with hired cars or with their own private cars, for which they were paid mileage. Thus the detachment horses were used less and less often, and they became too costly to maintain. Gradually they were replaced by police cars.

Even after the police had disposed of their horses on southern Saskatchewan detachments they experienced a temporary need for a few. In 1938-39 an outbreak of cattle smuggling from Canada into the United States required border patrols in areas where the police could not use cars. Two constables using horses from the Regina training depot made preventive patrols in Saskatchewan along the Canadian-American border.

In Alberta, meanwhile, a constable patrolled the border in his area. He used a car where possible and also took a trailer in which he transported a saddle horse for use where he could not travel by car. The last of the police patrol horses in Alberta was sold in the early 1940s.

At the outbreak of the Second World War in 1939, the Canadian government established a Provost Corps with RCMP members, and because of the mechanization of modern warfare, their military training included the use of motorcycles, and no RCMP horses were involved in that war. On the Canadian home front, RCMP training in equitation was curtailed. Eventually it was discontinued, after which a skeleton staff was retained, and the horses were turned out to pasture. After the war equitation returned gradually, with only a small percentage of recruits given this training at first. By 1947, however, equitation training was again in full swing.

In the spring of 1954, general recruit training was extended from two 3-month semesters to two 4-½-month semesters. For some time before this, equitation training had been given haphazardly, sometimes before Part I, sometimes between Parts I and II, and sometimes after the completion of Part II.

With the extention of general recruit training to nine months, equitation training was integrated more closely with the other training, and consisted of one hundred hours of riding and fifty hours of stable duty in each of the two semesters. This system continued until 1966 when recruit equitation training was abandoned.

During the 1950s and the early 1960s, the Treasury Board of the federal government constantly questioned the value of recruit equitation training in

A northern Saskatchewan detachment RCMP team used by the author in the mid-1930s, typically fat and lazy since cars were now generally used for patrol work. (William Kelly)

One of a fine team of RCMP horses, a mare named Bess, used by the author at Meadow Lake, Saskatchewan, 1934. (William Kelly)

Hired team pulling a "caboose", heated sled, on patrol in northern Alberta, 1947. The protrusion is the stove pipe. (A. R. Foster)

relation to the expense involved. They pointed to the fact that the efficiency of the Force had not suffered during the war and suggested that perhaps mounted training should be abolished.

Many RCMP officers disagreed. They believed that young recruits matured through the discipline acquired by learning to care for horses and to ride in cavalry style. The riding master at Regina agreed with those officers. He believed that: "The Mounted Police horse... is the equine detector of courage, or lack of it, in police candidates. Skilled tuition in equitation will replace timidity with boldness and develop a disregard for the inevitable bodily bruises which even the most proficient must experience. Handling of horses promotes mental alertness and rapid acceleration of muscular reflexes."

Other senior members of the RCMP, although acknowledging the value of recruit equitation training, agreed with the Treasury Board and pointed out that thousands of efficient members of other police forces had never taken equitation. Moreover, the RCMP itself contained efficient policemen taken over from provincial forces that had never had such training.

In the summer of 1966, the need to economize drove the federal government to announce that mounted training of RCMP recruits would be discontinued. The

Hired saddle horse being ferried across a lake to continue a police patrol. Fort Vermilion, Alberta, 1947. (A. R. Foster)

A horse being auctioned off in Regina in 1966, after the RCMP discontinued recruit equitation training. (RCMP Museum, Regina)

Force would retain its Musical Ride, however, which would continue to perform at home and abroad as part of Canada's public-relations program, as it had been doing since the early 1920s with some regularity. In future the Musical Ride would be based at "N" (Training) Division at Rockcliffe, near Ottawa. Also, the Force's breeding program, which had been re-established in the early 1940s in Saskatchewan, would be transferred to a new location close to Ottawa.

Mounted Police horses were entering a new era. In the earliest days of the Force's history, they had enabled the NWMP to establish law and order over the vast western prairies. During the following decades, with the NWMP and the RNWMP, they had travelled hundreds of thousands of difficult miles on patrol and escort duty, and they had worked to exhaustion as trailbuilders to the Canadian north. Later, they had helped the RNWMP and the RCMP to keep the peace during strikes that otherwise could have resulted in violence, bloodshed and tragedy. Still later, however, mechanization of the RCMP had led to their decline as useful working animals. In future, the only horses of use to the Force, and hence of use to Canada, would be the sleek, black beauties of the Musical Ride who, as ambassadors of goodwill, would continue to perform at home and abroad, for the pleasure of vast numbers of delighted onlookers.

RCMP Special Constable "Old Yellow Woman" on his own horse in 1953 celebrating twenty-five years' service in the Force assisting the RCMP to police Indian reserves.

Driving the breeding herd to pasture across Battle Creek at the Fort Walsh ranch. (Michael Burn)

4

BREEDING

THE FORCE BREEDS ITS OWN HORSES

The Force first bred some of its own horses in 1878. The police had encountered such difficulty in obtaining suitable saddle horses during their first four years in the North-West Territories that they then established a breeding farm at Pincher Creek, thirty miles west of Fort Macleod.

Some time before 1882 the government provided the farm with a Thoroughbred stallion named Clandeboye, the only Thoroughbred horse in the entire Macleod district. In 1882, however, the police found that operating the farm took too many men away from other duties. The NWMP leased the Pincher Creek farm to the Stewart Ranch Company, already a major supplier of remounts for the Force. Terms of the lease included the provision that the company would take care of the fifty-two police-owned brood mares and the sixty two-year-olds then at the farm, and any other horses the Force might send there for breeding or recuperation.

Although the original lease was for only one year, available records give only a few details of operations at the farm after that. The annual report of 1884 records sixty horses and one stallion at Pincher Creek, but after 1884 the number of horses at Pincher Creek seems no more than would be necessary for regular police duties.

In 1888, Veterinary Surgeon J. Burnett reported with satisfaction that horse-breeders were trying to breed out any tendency of the horse to buck, and that all of the 127 remounts purchased at Calgary, Macleod and Pincher Creek that summer had turned out to be first-class horses. However, a good number of these horses he had recommended for purchase in spite of the fact that they did not come up to the 15-hand standard. Also, many horses stationed throughout the Force died from contagious diseases or were off duty because of other diseases or wounds—841 cases having been treated that year. So the NWMP continued to have difficulty in getting enough suitable horses.

Burnett's report for 1889 specified the kind of horse required: "One standing from 14.3 to 15.2 hands in height, fine clean cut head, long neck, high crest, broad round quarters with plenty of good flat bone, and strong feet." He went on to explain how breeders could easily achieve that kind of horse and then bemoaned the attitude of some ranchers.

By way of illustration, the veterinary surgeon told of his visit to a ranch where three stallions were kept: a Thoroughbred, a coach horse and a Clydesdale. "An extra nice well bred mare" had been bred to the Clydesdale. When Burnett asked why she had not been bred to the Thoroughbred instead, the horse wrangler informed him that "it was not the Thoroughbred's turn."

In 1900, Commissioner Perry raised the standard for NWMP saddle horses to between 15.2 and 16 hands in height in the hope that the breeders would come around, but to no avail. Veterinary Surgeon Burnett now recommended a government stud or breeding farm because otherwise the outlook was bleak. He suggested that two Thoroughbred stallions and fifty selected mares would make a good start. The government ignored the suggestion.

Four years later, Commissioner Perry tried indirectly to persuade the government to establish a breeding farm for RNWMP horses. He suggested that just as experimental farms were advantageous to farmers, so an experimental breeding station in the west would be of equal value to "horse raisers". At the same time, Burnett stressed that such a breeding station would also be of benefit to the police. The government again failed to respond.

In 1910 Perry again reported on the difficulty of securing suitable RNWMP remounts, and now he endorsed the earlier suggestion of Veterinary Surgeon Burnett that the police should be allowed to raise their own horses. Two years later, Perry was still protesting. "It is not possible to secure the class of horse of ten years ago," he stated. "They are not bred in this country....I think it worthy of government consideration that the government take up the breeding of horses for its own permanent corps." He seemed to suggest that if the government would not let the RNWMP breed its own horses, the government should raise them for the army, in which case they would presumably allow the Mounted Police to share in the benefits.

In 1920, the RCMP officer responsible for purchasing police horses reported that the task was more difficult than ever. People in eastern Canada and the United States were buying the first-class horses from western breeders to use as hunters and show horses, while the lower-grade animals were in demand by police forces in the United States.

Almost two more decades passed before the Force at last did get authorization to establish its own breeding program, and then it was not so much because it lacked suitable horses as because its commissioner wanted all black ones.

In 1937, as assistant commissioner, S. T. Wood had headed the RCMP contingent at the coronation of King George VI. When he saw the scarlet-tunicked Life Guards of the Household Cavalry riding black horses and he noticed how the black of the horses emphasized the glowing colour of the tunics, he envisioned the scarlet-coated riders of his own Force riding black horses. The following year, when he became commissioner, he ordered that the RCMP should purchase only black horses. This severely limited the number of Canadian horses from which the Force could draw. It soon became evident that the only way the RCMP could get enough black horses was by breeding them itself.

The year after Commissioner Wood's appointment, the RCMP set up a limited breeding program in the stables at "Depot" Division barracks in Regina, Saskatchewan, most likely with the approval of the Canadian government or at least of the minister in charge of the Force. The police soon realized that one stallion and a few mares could not possibly fulfil the Force's needs; a much bigger program must be undertaken. No doubt the Second World War delayed the acquisition of suitable property. But in 1942, in ranching country in southwestern Saskatchewan, the Force acquired property on which to establish a remount breeding station.

Fort Walsh Remount Station consisted of 720 acres which contained the still barely discernible site of Old Fort Walsh in the Cypress Hills, plus 2,305 acres of adjoining land leased from the province of Saskatchewan. Using the site of Old Fort Walsh seemed especially appropriate considering that from 1875 to 1878 it had been a remote but important NWMP outpost, and from 1878 to 1882, which included the time Sitting Bull and his bands of Sioux Indians were in the Fort Walsh area, it had been the headquarters of the Force.

Commissioner Wood, however, did not approve the site of Old Fort Walsh merely for historic or sentimental reasons. It was an ideal area for breeding horses. In fact, the ranchers in the district had supplied the Force with horses since the

Rear view of the Regina stables, where the modern RCMP horse breeding program began in 1939.

Fort Walsh ranch, the site of the RCMP horse breeding program from 1943 to 1968.

An aerial view of the RCMP breeding station at Pakenham, Ontario, where the Force relocated their breeding program in 1968.

earliest days. Its hills and valleys were covered with large stands of aspen, poplar and white and lodgepole pine, interspersed with wide areas of open range land, scarcely any of which had ever been ploughed. Battle Creek and other fresh-water streams flowed through the valleys and deep gullies. The woods gave cover to such wildlife as elk, antelope and deer, and wild birdlife flourished in the uplands and the nearby woods. Commissioner Wood believed that the year-round outdoor life of the district's horses toughened them, that the hilly terrain developed good muscle and that feeding on the natural grasses provided better nourishment than the horses could get on cultivated land.

By the spring of 1943 the new property was ready to receive the nucleus of RCMP breeding stock from Regina: twenty-three mares, eleven foals and the rented stallion Fred Tracey. Fort Walsh soon became known as "the ranch", and the experienced man hired to operate it as "the wrangler".

Commissioner Wood took such a keen interest in the raising of black police horses that when he retired, in 1951, he was appointed a special constable (without pay) of the RCMP so that he could remain close to the project. Until 1965, when he became terminally ill, he and his family spent most of each spring, summer and autumn at the Fort Walsh ranch.

Meanwhile, in accord with the views of ex-Commissioner Wood, the RCMP raised their horses in range fashion for many years, because he believed that in this way the Force could raise "tough" horses able to withstand the rigours of recruit equitation training and the Musical Ride. During summer and autumn the horses ran loose over many square miles of range land along with the horses of neighbouring ranchers. During the autumn round-up the police identified their horses by the fused "MP" on the right shoulder, the registered brand of the Force since 1887, and drove them back to the police ranch where they wintered on ranch property. By 1950 RCMP horses were no longer branded, but were tattooed on the inside of the upper lip with a regimental number.

The horses fed on the range except for a minimum of supplementary feeding during late winter, and even early spring foaling was done on the open range if the weather was not too severe. Because of these things it was impossible to obtain the best breeding results. Indeed, the appearance of the police horses during those years gave the impression that they were undernourished.

In the mid-1950s the care and feeding of the breeding stock was changed. When a new riding master from the RCMP training depot in Regina saw the horses on his first visit to the ranch he immediately ordered increased and regular supplementary

Regina and Rex (twins) and their dam Laura at Pakenham, 1977.

feeding for all the ranch stock. In addition he ordered the stock be kept under cover during the worst winter weather. This resulted in much healthier animals and better breeding results.

When the three-year-olds were ready to be sent to Regina to begin remount training, they were driven in herd fashion to the railroad siding at Maple Creek, about 35 miles away, and shipped the 275 miles to Regina by train. From a nearby siding they were taken to the barracks and placed in an enclosure. Within a few days they settled down and were taken to stalls in the stables, and for about a week the riding staff handled them carefully and gentled them as much as possible. Then their training as remounts began.

In the summer of 1966 the Canadian government decided that the RCMP must economize by discontinuing recruit equitation training. The Musical Ride, however, would be kept as part of Canada's public relations program, with its base of operations moved from Regina to Rockcliffe barracks on the outskirts of Ottawa, Ontario. To have the breeding program near Rockcliffe, the ranch operations would be transferred to a 345-acre farm the RCMP had purchased in the pastoral Ottawa Valley at Pakenham, about thirty miles northwest of Ottawa.

By 1967 the Force had sold its surplus horses at Regina and Fort Walsh by public auction. Musical Ride horses and those horses retained to train the riders (who no longer automatically had equitation training) were shipped to Rockcliffe barracks. The stallions, mares, foals and other young stock were shipped to

Pakenham after fences and buildings had been erected there. The Pakenham Remount Station was officially opened on December 1, 1968, and soon became known as "the farm". The disruption caused by having to ship the brood mares from Fort Walsh to Pakenham in 1968 resulted in no mating of mares and stallions that year. Hence in 1969 no foals were born, but breeding was resumed.

Pakenham differs greatly from Fort Walsh. Whereas the ranch was hilly, most of the farm at Pakenham is as flat as the flattest prairie; and whereas the range on the ranch had never been cultivated, the pastures at Pakenham have been cultivated for at least 150 years. In addition to providing splendid pasture, the Pakenham hayland permits the cutting of enough hay to feed not only the breeding stock there, but also the Musical Ride and equitation horses at the Rockcliffe stables. Nevertheless, there is one obvious similarity between the Fort Walsh ranch and the Pakenham farm: as the ranch had the fine fresh water Battle Creek, the farm has the equally desirable Waba Creek.

The nearness of the Pakenham remount station to the Rockcliffe stables has many advantages. Remounts in training at Rockcliffe can readily be returned to the farm for periodic rest and conditioning. The riding staff can frequently visit the farm to discuss the breeding program with those employed there. Today, the Pakenham Remount Station is considered a model breeding operation.

The number of horses in the Force varies from time to time. During the summer of 1984, there were 84 Musical Ride and equitation horses at the Rockcliffe stables. At the Pakenham breeding farm there were about 60 mares and young stock, making a total of 144 RCMP horses at that time. Among the horses at the breeding farm were two two-year-old near-Thoroughbred stallions: Amigo, sired by Gauchesco, put down in early 1984, and Apollo, whose sire, Sky Cast's Double, was formerly used by the Force as a stud.

Although the Force's experience in raising its own stallions has so far been unsuccessful, it is trying again with Amigo and Apollo. Success with these two would save the Force the great inconvenience of having to obtain satisfactory sires from private sources. On the other hand, the problem with raising its own stallions is that each one is bound to be related to some degree to some of the mares in the breeding program, whereas a stallion purchased from outside sources and unrelated to the mares can be used for all RCMP mares. The situation demands that the Force must retain more than one sire of its own breeding, but it has the advantage that if the RCMP can use its own high-grade stallions, it will be able to retain the desirable qualities it has already bred into its horses.

MARES AND STALLIONS

When the Force began breeding its own horses in 1939, the height standard was that set by Commissioner Perry in 1900: 15.2 to 16 hands. By the mid-1970s the standard was raised slightly: 15.3 to 16 hands. This range of height is no longer important, however, as the horses raised by the RCMP, with very few exceptions, are 16 hands or more by the age of five or six years. The present standards in other respects are the same as they have been ever since the breeding program began about forty years ago: weight, between 1,200 and 1,300 pounds; Hunter conformation; colour, black; and good temperament.

When the breeding program began at Fort Walsh in 1943, the RCMP did not want to breed pure Thoroughbreds. It needed horses with more stamina—more heavily boned animals better able to carry men weighing from 160 to 200 pounds, and able to withstand the rigours of equitation and Musical Ride work. Hence the Force aimed to obtain the necessary stamina by using grade mares, generally of Standardbred and draught cross, and to obtain the desirable quality of spirit by breeding such mares with Thoroughbred sires.

Right from the beginning of the program the RCMP purchased suitable mares from various locations on the prairies. The majority of them came from farms, and were generally a Standardbred/Percheron cross. Sometimes the Force purchased mares of poor quality, relying on mating them with Thoroughbred stallions to improve the stock. Female offspring from such matings were bred to similar stallions, and in due course a desirable type of horse was usually obtained, for both breeding and saddle purposes. Even when dark brown mares were mated with stallions that looked black but were registered as dark brown, the foals often turned out to be black.

By the mid-1950s, however, the Force was still not producing either the quality or the quantity of the horses it needed. It continued to be extremely difficult to purchase enough suitable black stock for saddle or breeding purposes. In a plan worked out with the assistance of officials of the federal Department of Agriculture and Professor Grant MacEwan, a well-known western horseman, the Force decided to aim at producing more and better horses. It did the obvious thing: it bought more brood mares, at a cost of about $250 each.

In an effort to minimize the possibility of raising foals with too fine a bone structure, in 1956 the Force began to experiment with two purebred bay Clydesdale mares from the Dominion Experimental farm at Indian Head, Saskatchewan.

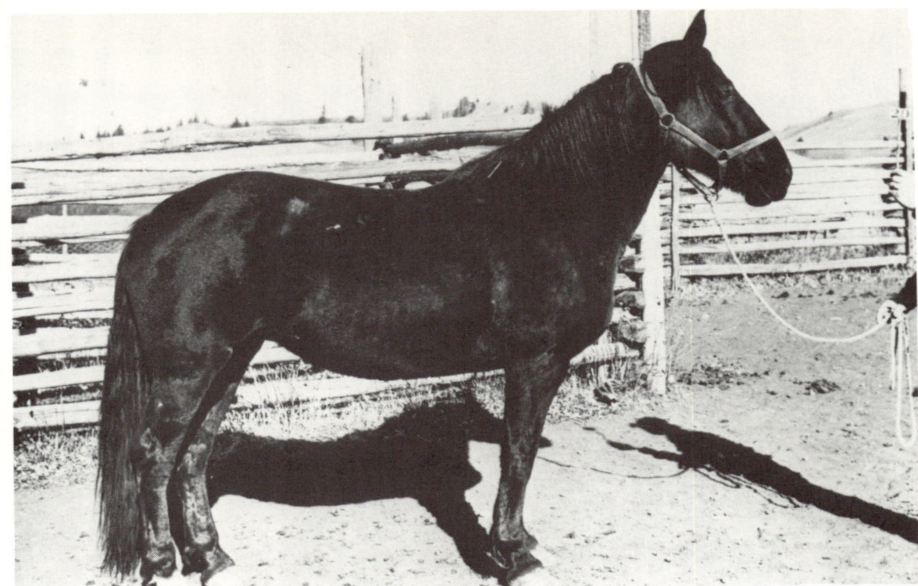

Two early brood mares at Fort Walsh ranch, circa 1950. (RCMP Museum, Regina)

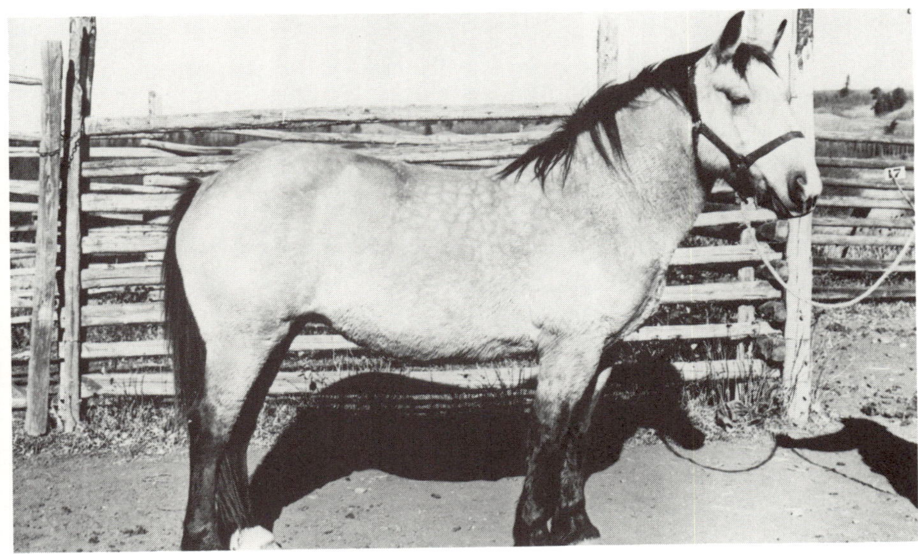

A Clydesdale mare and her foal, circa 1950, part of a breeding experiment at Fort Walsh whereby Clyde mares were bred to Thoroughbred stallions. The experiment was not a success and was subsequently abandoned.

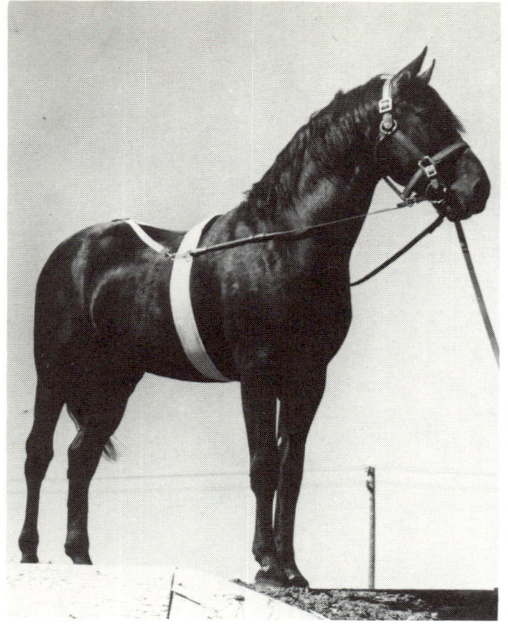

King, one of the early black stallions at Regina and Fort Walsh in 1939. His sire was an American Saddle Horse and his dam a Thoroughbred/Percheon cross. He was used for breeding for seven years and then sold.

These mares were bred to a black Thoroughbred stallion. No one expected that this mating would result in suitable saddle horses. What was hoped for was that any filly foals, who in due course would become brood mares, might produce suitable remounts. This proved generally true but it was a very expensive, uncertain and slow method of getting desirable saddle horses. Eventually the experiment was discontinued, but even today some of the beautiful, sleek black horses of the Musical Ride, three-quarters or more Thoroughbred, have some Clydesdale blood.

Although the breeding program had been stepped up in the mid-1950s, it was not until the mid-1960s that all the horses used in the Musical Ride had been bred by the Force. By the mid-1970s, however, all the RCMP horses, except for the stallions, were of its own breeding.

Some of the brood mares by this time were Musical Ride horses retired to the farm for breeding purposes. Later, young mares were taken from the Musical Ride and used as brood mares because of their good qualities, but not all proved satisfactory and some were returned to the Ride. Other suitable young mares went back to Pakenham after completing remount training, without ever being used as equitation horses.

Mares are chosen for breeding not only on the basis of size, conformation and colour, but also for good temperament. Mares with poor temperament, regardless of how many positive attributes they might have, are not used as brood mares, so that the Force will avoid breeding foals with the same failing. Unfortunately, the

Soldier's Son, a black Thoroughbred stallion used at Fort Walsh from 1947 to 1954.

choice of good temperament is not always possible in the selection of stallions. Sky Cast's Double, for example, used for a number of years in the late 1970s, had a mean disposition which is re-appearing in some of his foals. Consequently the female offspring of this sire are not likely to be chosen as brood mares.

Difficult as it was to find black brood mares for the RCMP breeding program in its early years, it has been even more difficult to find suitable black stallions, although King, the first stallion owned by the Force, at Regina in 1939, was black. King's sire was an American saddle horse and his dam a Thoroughbred/Percheron cross. He proved so unsuccessful as a sire that about fifteen of his foals had to be destroyed, mainly because of deformed fetlocks. Strange as it seems, King was replaced by a chestnut, an American saddle horse named President Roosevelt. He was privately owned and covered only three mares. Of the two foals thrown, one died.

The next stallion, Fred Tracey, was first used at Regina, and then for two seasons at Fort Walsh after the breeding program was transferred there in 1943. He was a black-brown Thoroughbred and was rented from his Ottawa owner at the rate of $35 a foal. His foals inherited his near-black colouring.

From 1945 to 1955 inclusive, the RCMP used ten stallions: two privately owned, one of them on loan to the Force; two on loan from the Canadian Department of Agriculture; one raised by the Force; and five purchased. Of the ten stallions, only two were not Thoroughbreds, one of the two, a black three-quarter Thoroughbred on loan, and the other, a black grade stallion raised by the Force. Four of the eight

The black Thoroughbred stallion Faux Pas, used for breeding with great success by the RCMP from 1956 to 1968. Faux Pas died in 1975 at the age of 27.

Faux Pas winning the Ascot Gold Vase when he was a three year old in 1951. (©Sport & General Press Agency, London)

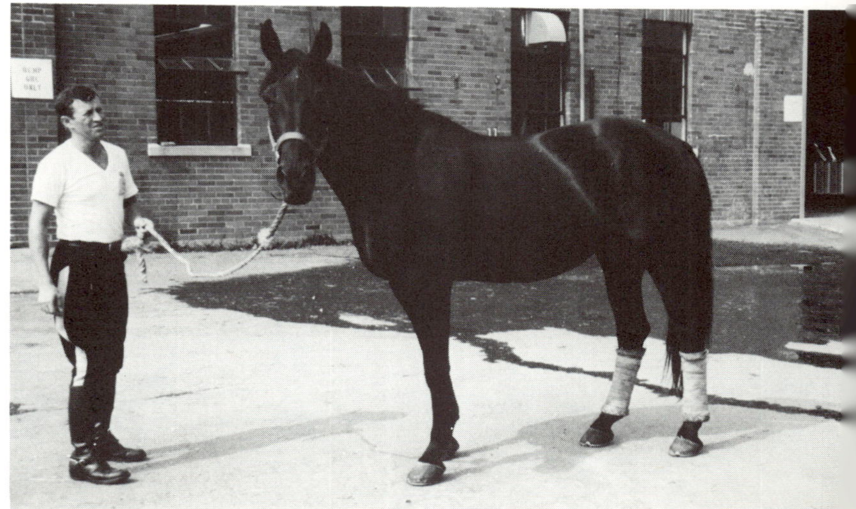

The highly valued Musical Ride mount Clara (a full sister to Burmese, the first horse the RCMP gave Queen Elizabeth) in 1982 at Rockcliffe. Clara was retired briefly from the Ride in 1975 to be bred, and again at age 20 in 1983. (William Kelly)

Thoroughbreds were registered as black, and three of the others appeared to be black but were registered as brown or dark brown because of brown markings. The other Thoroughbred stallion, Raglan, purchased in 1946, was a chestnut. The Force hoped that by breeding the browns and the chestnut to black mares, their foals would be black. Raglan, however, produced few black foals, and was used for only two seasons.

Because of the difficulty in obtaining suitable black stallions, in 1954 the RCMP used Nick, a black grade stallion of its own breeding. He was used for one season only and produced only one foal. His lack of success as a sire, plus the fact that he did not develop physically as well as expected, caused the Force to sell him. In 1974, twenty years after its disappointing experience with Nick, the Force used a second stallion of its own breeding. But Ned, sired by Alton out of a mare named Fairlane, was also used for only one season. He sired only two foals and was then sold.

Meanwhile the RCMP continued to be concerned that its horses, now about three-quarters Thoroughbred, were developing too light a bone structure. Hoping to achieve heavier bone, in 1976 the Force leased Himeryk, a near-black stallion of the Trakehner breed, from his Ontario owner, although they continued to use Thoroughbred stallions. This breed, which originated in East Prussia when English Thoroughbred stallions were bred to native mares, has a slightly heavier frame than the Thoroughbreds. During Himeryk's first season he bred eleven mares. The Force used him until 1980, when he died unexpectedly from a cancerous growth. His foals were black and are proving satisfactory, although the trainers notice that they have a slightly different gait from that of the horses sired by Thoroughbred stallions.

Three stallions used by the RCMP through the years deserve special mention: Faux Pas, Alton and Up-the-Ensign, used by the Force in that order. Faux Pas, born in 1948, was an English Thoroughbred, registered as dark brown, but black to the eye. As a three-year-old he won the Ascot Gold Vase, and later he won some minor distance races as a steeplechaser. The Force purchased him in England in 1955 for the sum of £630, and used him at Fort Walsh from 1956 to 1967. Faux Pas had an even temperament, and through him the Force bred some fine black horses. Queen Elizabeth's favourite horse, Burmese, is a daughter of Faux Pas, and another of Her Majesty's RCMP horses, Centenial, is a grandson through his mother. When the RCMP breeding operation was moved from the Fort Walsh

Alton, a black Thoroughbred stallion used from 1969 to 1974. He died in 1975.

ranch to the breeding farm at Pakenham in 1967, the Force presented Faux Pas to a neighbouring rancher, who kept him until he died at the age of twenty-seven.

Alton was a black Thoroughbred stallion used by the RCMP from 1969 to 1974 inclusive. Alton was born in 1947 in Kentucky and sold in 1952 to the New York State Jockey Club, which used him at the Lookover Stallion Station, in Avon, New York, for eighteen seasons. The Jockey Club donated Alton to the RCMP in 1969, when he was twenty-two years old. During the five years he was with the RCMP, he sired some splendid foals, noted for their fine heads and even temperament.

The RCMP purchased Up-the-Ensign, registered as a dark bay, bred by Major Conn Smythe, of Toronto, from Mr. J. Laughry of Don Mills, Ontario. At that time, in 1974, the Thoroughbred stallion was ten years old, and his racing career had ended as a result of lameness. The Force used Up-the-Ensign successfully until 1981, when he broke a leg while breeding a mare and had to be destroyed. Both Up-the-Ensign and his half-brother, Northern Dancer, the famous Canadian racehorse, were sired by Nearctic, a son of the famous sire Nearco. Major Smythe gave Up-the-Ensign his name at the time the Canadian government was considering replacing the Canadian ensign with the present Maple Leaf flag.

Himeryk, a dark bay Trakehner stallion leased by the Force in 1976 and used for breeding until 1982.

After winning two races as a two year old, Up The Ensign was retired to stud because of injuries. He passed along his elegant head to his progeny.

Anyone who sees the RCMP horses at Rockcliffe, Ontario, or during a Musical Ride performance, sees evidence of how the Force's breeding program has standardized them, not only in colour but also in size and conformation. What cannot be seen is the even temperament which has also been bred into them. Indeed, the RCMP horses have become so standardized that they are now considered a definite type, established by crossing black Thoroughbred stallions with black grade mares. As the present breeding policy continues, the type will be further refined, and the RCMP horses will become as near Thoroughbred as possible without having the name.

FROM FOALS TO REMOUNTS

The breeding season at the Pakenham farm lasts from April to July of each year. Although efforts are made to breed mares as soon as possible after foaling, care is taken to ensure that the next year's foals are not born too early in the year. From the time of breeding until foaling the brood mares are pastured together. During the winter months they occupy stalls indoors and are allowed out for a few hours each day. During the same period they receive a special diet of supplements which promote good health, not only in the mares but also in the foals they produce.

As foaling time approaches the mares are placed in roomy box stalls and carefully watched by an experienced member of the farm staff who is ready to assist if necessary. A qualified veterinarian is always on call.

Healthy foals are on their feet and nursing within twenty to thirty minutes after birth. Weather permitting, they go with their mothers to the pasture the next day. In the main feeding pasture a small area to which the mares have no access is provided for the foals, and when the foals are only a few weeks old they venture beneath the bar that restrains the mares, to nibble from boxes of special feed.

Soon after birth, RCMP foals are named alphabetically according to year; for example, foals born in 1961 all had names beginning with the letter "A", those born in 1962 with the letter "B", and so on. Difficult letters such as "Q" and "X" are omitted. When the alphabet is exhausted, the system is repeated, beginning names again with the letter "A".

The naming and numbering of the foals is the responsibility of the breeding-farm manager, although it has been known for his choice to be changed for some particular reason by a senior member at Rockcliffe. For example, the horse Jock was renamed for a retiring commanding officer, and the horse Shawn was renamed for an instructor's son. It so happened that the initials for those years permitted this to be done. But generally the names selected by the farm manager are the ones that are retained.

At the time a foal is named it is also given a regimental number of a series that continues year after year. This number is tattooed on the inside of the young horse's upper lip sometime during the first year, the male foals being tattooed at the same time as they are gelded.

In the early spring the brood mares and foals return to the stables at night. Later when the weather is warm enough they remain in the pasture full time. Just before and during weaning time in October, the foals are gently halter broken so that they can easily be led and tied up in their stalls when necessary. Also at this time they are gentled around the feet and legs, in preparation for the routine foot care carried out from time to time by the farrier who goes to Pakenham from Rockcliffe.

In the autumn the foals are weaned at about six months of age. As the weather turns cold they are stabled each night but are turned out each day for exercise. As yearlings they are pastured in spring, summer and autumn with the two- and three-year-olds. In winter they spend the days outdoors and the nights indoors. Colts are gelded at one year of age, and all animals receive the fullest possible immunization treatment against tetanus, rabies and various types of encephalomyelitis.

Yearlings at Fort Walsh, circa 1955. (C. W. Anderson)

Two year olds at Pakenham, 1981.

Three year olds at Pakenham, 1981.

The young horses remain at the breeding farm until about April of the year in which they are three years old, when they are taken by horse van to the Rockcliffe stables to begin remount training. During the two years or more spent in training they grow and mature and are then ready for equitation work. Later, some of them become replacements for Musical Ride horses.

Decisions often have to be made as to which young stock to keep or to cull. During the Fort Walsh days a committee met at the ranch in the autumn of each year and made recommendations to the commissioner. Today the close proximity of the breeding farm at Pakenham to the Rockcliffe stables enables the officer in charge of the Equitation Branch and the riding master to pay frequent visits to the farm to discuss the condition of the young stock. In this way the progress of each horse is under continuous review, and any problem is immediately discussed by the farm and equitation staffs.

OFF-COLOUR HORSES

During the early days of its breeding program, the RCMP used chestnut stallions and bay mares as well as black ones. Even when the off-colour animals were mated with the more dominantly coloured blacks, they passed their own colour-coded genes to their offspring, which in turn passed them to their offspring, and so on. As a result, even though black animals are now predominant in the breeding program, the off-colour genes persist, and occasionally a black mare bred to a black stallion gives birth to an off-colour foal.

The explanation lies in the fact that although black genes are dominant to chestnut or bay, the two latter recessive colour genes also survive to a lesser degree and are passed on to offspring in accord with certain laws of nature.

For example, if a pure chestnut stallion is bred to a pure black mare, all the foals will be black in colour. But instead of carrying only black-coded genes, they will carry genes of black and chestnut in equal proportions. If the black stallions and the black mares of that second generation are mated, their foals on average will be in the proportion of three blacks to one chestnut. Of the three blacks of this third generation, one will have only black genes and thus will be pure black. The other two will have black and chestnut genes in equal proportions, and although the black colour is dominant, so that their general appearance is black, these two blacks might have a brown shading, which can be seen in some present day RCMP horses.

Curious mares at Pakenham.

Dry mares jealously watch another mare and her foal being led out to pasture at Pakenham.

A mare enjoys the lush pasturage at Pakenham while her foal sleeps.

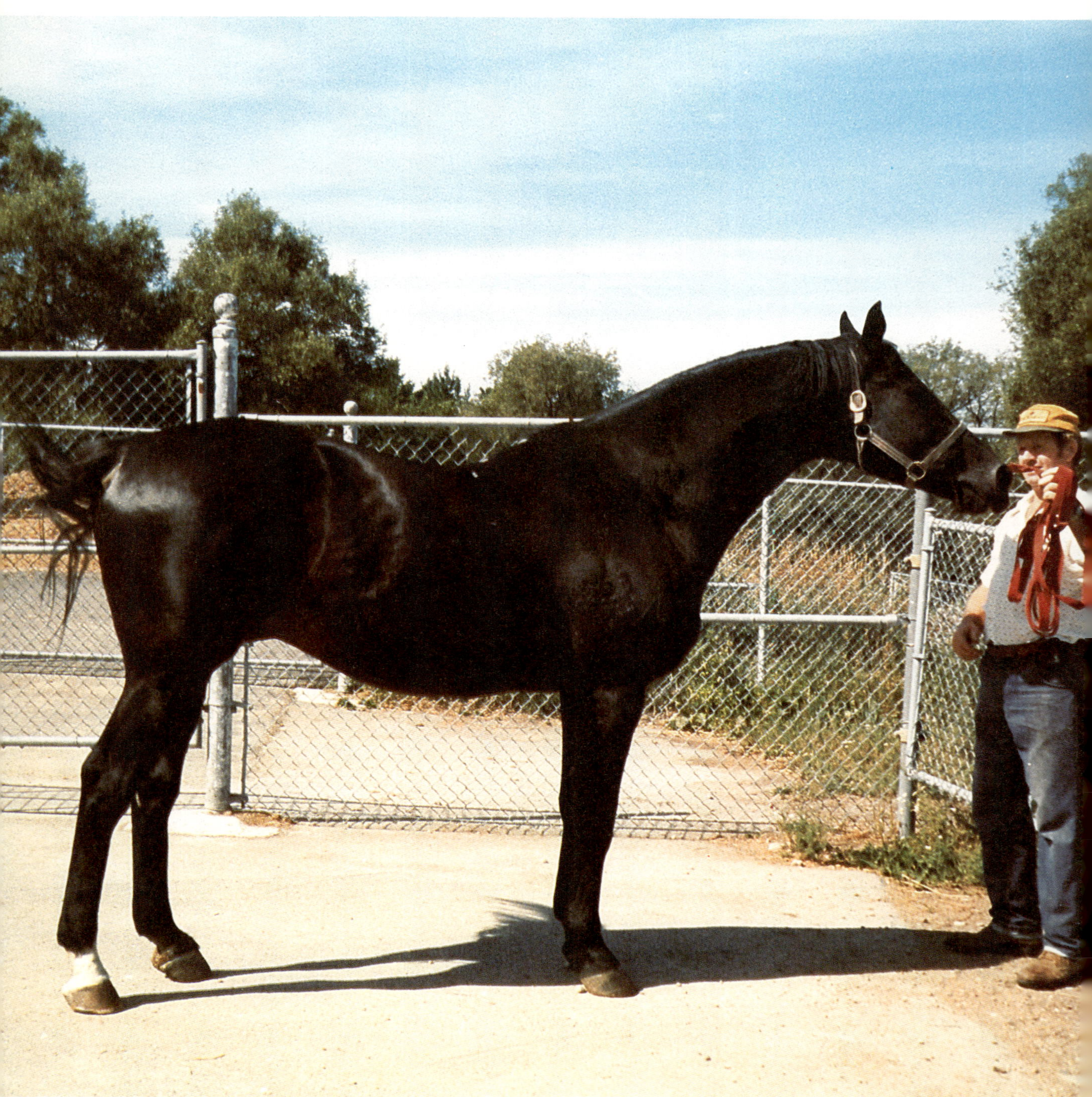

Gauchesco, a black stallion purchased by the RCMP in 1981 and used for breeding until put down in 1984 at age 21.

OPPOSITE: *The classic profile of a well-bred modern RCMP horse.*

Dark bay stallion Up The Ensign, half-brother to the great Canadian race horse Northern Dancer, used from 1974 to 1982, at which point he broke a leg and had to be destroyed.

The RCMP-bred chestnut gelding Larry and his American owner, Olympic rider Karen Stives, competing in two phases of a Three-Day Event. Larry became an international calibre event horse. (Mary Phelps)

The farm manager at Pakenham leading a brood mare and her off-colour foal to pasture.

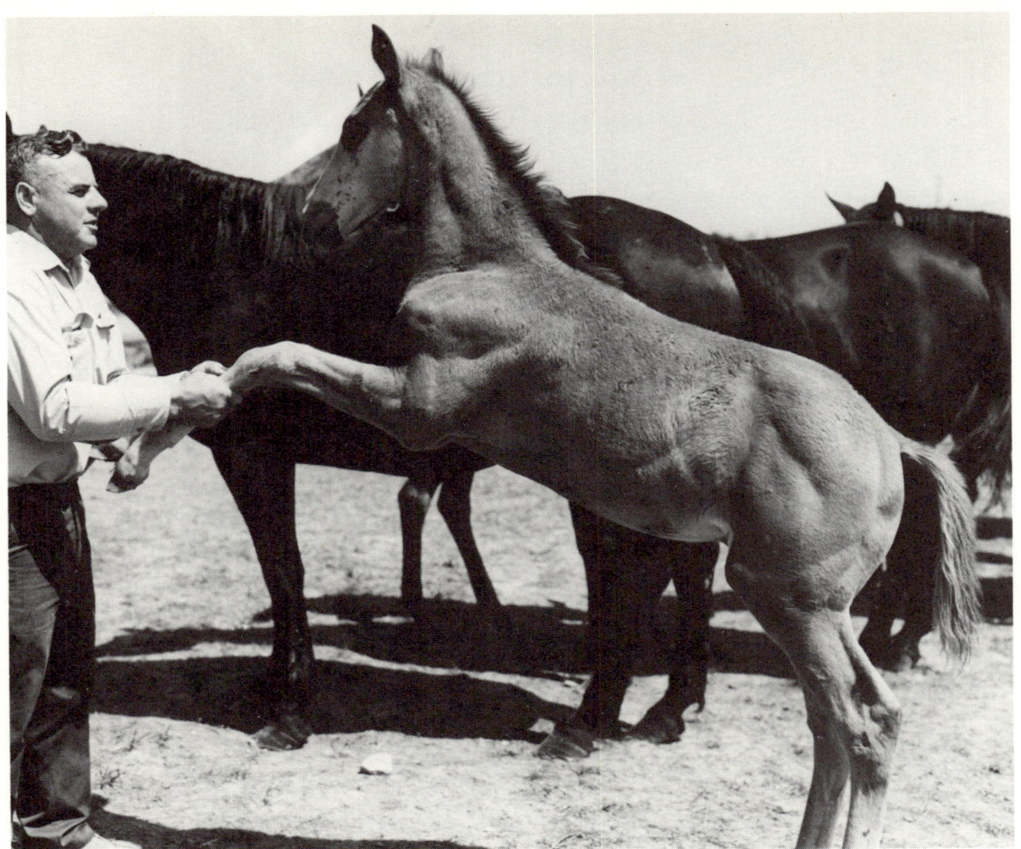

All foals—of whatever colour—are "handled" from an early age at Pakenham.

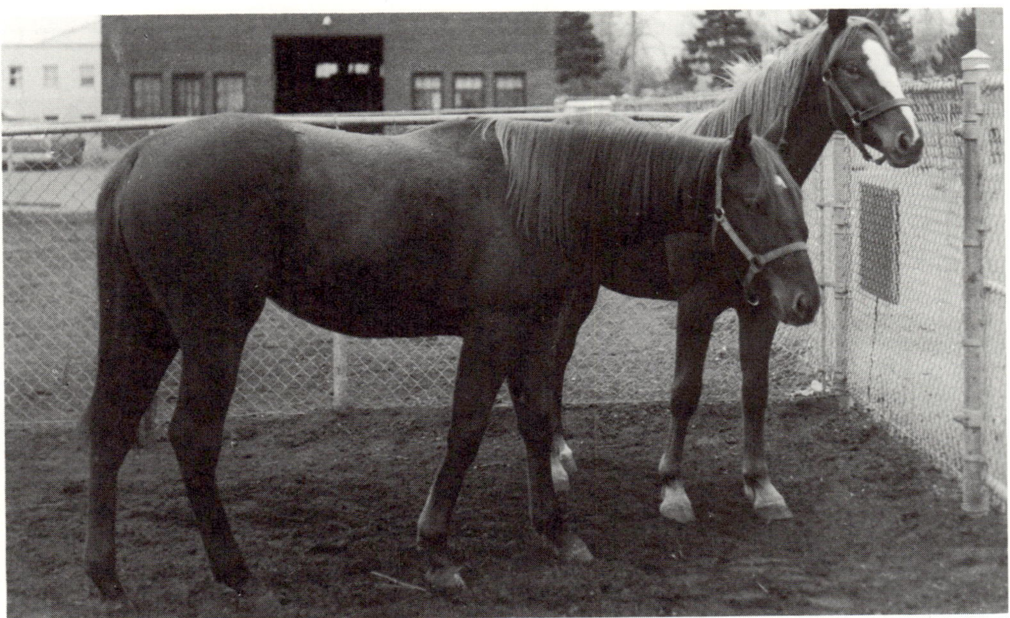

Two apprehensive RCMP-bred chestnut yearlings about to be sold.

Moreover, even after many generations of breeding out undesirable genes, the recessive chestnut or bay genes sometimes come to the fore. Thus black breeding stock at Pakenham occasionally produces an off-colour foal. Evidently, careful genetic engineering must prevail if the RCMP breeding program is eventually to produce only pure black horses.

The Force does not retain its off-colour horses. At about one year of age they are turned over to Crown Assets Corporation to be sold by sealed bids. There is always a great demand for such yearlings, especially by persons active in the equestrian world.

Larry, a chestnut born in 1972, was sold as a yearling to an Ottawa man for $1,212. As the horse developed, his owner received many offers from persons who wanted to train the horse for show jumping and three-day eventing. At last, when the man was offered more than $30,000, he sold Larry to Karen Stives, a noted American horsewoman. She gave her horse the official name of Silent Partner for competition purposes, but kept the name Larry for general use.

Ms. Stives then trained the chestnut for Three Day Event competition, which calls on the full range of a horse's ability and its rider's skills. The first day of these competitions is taken up with dressage. The second day features a speed and endurance section which includes a steeplechase course, two circuits of roads and a course of cross-country obstacles. The third day highlights a show jumping event.

Since 1979 Larry has been very active in Three Day Event competitions in the United States and, on one occasion, in the Netherlands. In the United States by the end of 1983 he had placed first twelve times and had placed second five times. In the Netherlands he placed sixth, a commendable showing against many of the world's best Three Day Event horses and a credit to the RCMP breeding program.

RETIRED HORSES

Most horses no longer of use to the Force are cast and sold, but the best-loved ones have been retired and allowed to live out their days on pension.

The most renowned of these was "Old Buck". As a three-year-old buckskin bronco, he was purchased in 1873 by Acting Commissioner W. Osborne Smith for use by the NWMP on its March West in 1874. 'Buck' became the mount of fifteen-year-old Trumpeter Bagley and served the Force for many years. When he was no longer useful, probably between eighteen and twenty years old, he was allowed to roam freely over southern Alberta between Fort Macleod and Lethbridge. He regularly visited Mounted Police detachments for the special welcome he rightly expected. In 1907, after he had been with the Force for thirty-four years, "Old Buck", about thirty-eight years old, was put down.

A few other horses retired by the Force in the early days after long service were also kept "on pension". They had gained the respect of their riders during many years of innumerable long saddle and wagon patrols. As one officer remarked in pleading for them to be retired with dignity, they were well worth their daily "handful of oats".

Horse Reg. No. 1842 served with the early Force for twenty-two years. For part of that time he was loaned to Earl Grey, Canada's governor general in the early 1900s. After the horse was retired, he whinnied with pleasure whenever he saw a uniformed member of the Mounted Police. Eventually, Reg. No. 1842 was returned to Depot Division, Regina, where he died.

Another horse with long service was Corona, born in 1924 and purchased by the RCMP in 1927 when police patrol horses were being replaced by automobiles and motorcycles. Corona's service was spent in the training depots at Regina and Rockcliffe, where he was used in the training of recruits and on Musical Rides. In 1937 he was a member of the mounted troop that went to London to appear in the Coronation parade of King George VI. After his regular term of service ended, Corona was kept around the Rockcliffe stables more or less as a pet, and in 1956, at thirty-two years of age, he was finally put down for humane reasons.

Members of the Force have generally objected to favourite horses being sold for such "undignified" occupations as delivery work, or being sold to persons who might not treat them with the consideration they deserved. In the 1920s when it came time for Laddie to be disposed of, the men in the training division "chipped in" and purchased him so that he could be put out to pasture with dignity.

Another horse, not as lucky as Laddie, was cast and sold to a local delivery man in a nearby town. On his first day on the job, as the driver made his first delivery, the horse kicked up his heels and galloped to the police barracks. When he arrived there, having shed the wagon and most of his harness, he ran into his old stall. The police surgeon stitched up his badly gashed shoulder, after which one of his former riders bought him from the disgruntled delivery man for five dollars, then arranged for him to be kept in a nearby pasture.

5

TRAINING AND TACK

THE TRAINING OF REMOUNTS

> Because this is the first time of a great many new experiences to which these young animals will be exposed—it is of the utmost importance that every reasonable care is taken to introduce each of these new experiences in a quiet and uneventful manner which is conducive to a growing and continued confidence on the part of the young horse.
>
> While it is recognized that every horse is an individual animal subject to a variety of traits, it is nevertheless a creature of habit in which experiences of the previous day[s] determine its acceptance of training. *RCMP Equitation Branch Policy Manual: Remount Training*

The present attitude of the RCMP toward the breaking-in and training of remounts is a far cry from that of the Force in its early years. In those days the task of breaking broncos was shared among hired cowboys, often Métis, and the police, who presumably used the same methods as the skilled and experienced cowboys.

The following description of the breaking of NWMP horses is based on an account given by a member of the Force who served at Regina in 1891, and who watched a herd of thirty broncos being broken to the saddle.

After the horses were driven into a small corral, a cowboy lassooed a chosen bronco around the neck or feet. Feeling the rope securely fastened, the horse stood still, his body all aquiver, his ears flickering at great speed, his eyes staring wildly at the man holding the rope. The cowboy advanced slowly, and the horse, aware that the man was approaching, stepped back. A long and tedious process finally resulted in the cowboy's getting close enough to touch the horse and tie the rope around his neck. Then the cowboy led the horse round and round, lessening the animal's fright as much as possible. At last he led it into an empty larger corral.

A remount wearing a cavesson with rings for attaching a lunge line.

When the horse had quietened down, the next step was to put a saddle on it. First the cowboy threw a blanket over the horse's head, but only after the horse had put up a fight, then he strapped it into place. To curtail the horse's movement the cowboy roped a front foot, pulled it off the ground, and fastened it under the bronco's body. With the horse thus deprived of sight and movement, the cowboy was able to place a blanket and saddle on its back. The cowboy then fastened the saddle girth, but with great difficulty as the horse expanded its own girth. At last, one hole at a time, the saddle girth was securely fastened. Then the cowboy removed the blanket from the horse's head and after another fight he managed to put on a bridle and bit.

The cowboy sprang onto the horse's back, and a second cowboy untied the horse's foot and lowered it to the ground. Now the main fight between horse and cowboy began. As the horse found itself in this unusual situation, it first tried to shake the rider off its back. Failing to do this, it attempted to roll. But the rider, expecting the move, raked the horse's sides with his sharp spurs and the horse remained on its feet. Standing still, it tossed and shook its head, trying to remove the bridle. Then the animal lowered its head between its forelegs for a moment or two, its eyes shining like fire, its body quivering with fright and nervous excitement.

Suddenly stretching its forelegs to the front and arching its back, the horse leaped wildly forward into the air with an indescribable scream of rage. The cowboy expected the move and remained firmly in the saddle while for the next ten minutes or so the horse continued screaming and bucking. By now the cowboy was trying to get the horse to leave the corral through the gate held open by the second cowboy. When the horse saw the open gate it gave a mad kick and a snort, then lowered its head between its legs and made a dash across the open prairie, stopping occasionally to indulge in another spell of wild bucking. After two hours of such antics the horse, bleeding at the mouth and sides, gave up the fight. The cowboy rode it back into the corral and unsaddled the exhausted animal. The first and most important step in "breaking" a remount was over. After several similar but less violent lessons the horse became sufficiently compliant for recruits to ride it.

When the RCMP ranch at Fort Walsh bred the Force's remounts, the training of those remounts began when the three-year-olds arrived at the Regina stables. For about a week the young horses were kept in the stables and gentled while men handled and groomed them. Then they were taken into the riding school, one at a time, each with an older horse alongside. Each three-year-old was trained to stand still while a dummy resembling a man was moved back and forth near it, so that the horse would not be alarmed when a man walked toward it. After several sessions

Purchased remounts at the Regina barracks in 1939.

A winter exercise ride at Regina in the 1930s.

with the dummy the horse was saddled and bridled, seldom an easy task, and led about the riding school alongside an older horse. Then a man held the remount's head while another man mounted it, after which the remount and its rider were led around the riding school, either by a man on foot or by a man mounted on an older horse. Later each remount was trained to stand still while a rider mounted and dismounted, and finally it was ridden under the control only of its rider. The young horses were then trained to walk and trot as their riders indicated, and much later they learned to canter.

By the walking and trotting stage, the remounts were sufficiently trained to be used by the more experienced recruits in the regular equitation classes for recruits. Now the remounts were put among the trained horses, and they learned mounted drill movements such as forming half sections and sections, and turning into line, under the guidance of their experienced recruit riders, assisted by seeing the movements of the more experienced horses also taking part in the drill.

Although the remounts learned quickly, so that in about three months they mastered their basic training, lessons and reviews continued for about six months in all. Only after that were they pronounced fully trained, although during the last few months they had progressed far enough to be used to help teach inexperienced recruit riders.

Since 1966, when the RCMP retained horses only for the Musical Ride, and after which the breeding operation moved to Pakenham, Ontario, and the base of the Musical Ride to "N" Division at Rockcliffe, the training of remounts has altered radically. Present training covers a period of twenty-five months, divided into ten segments. Eight of these are actual training periods of two to three months each, and the other two are one-month periods of review and conditioning during the fifteenth and twenty-third months.

The system of extended training has proved advantageous in several ways. It allows the horses to become more mature before they have to bear the weight of their Mounted Police riders, who are usually much heavier than civilian riders. It also allows the horses to develop gradually, with no forcing. Thus they are better able than horses trained under the old system to withstand the rigours of the Musical Ride and the stressful travel involved. This means that horses can now remain longer in the Ride, which is more economical. A further advantage of the longer training period ensues for the Musical Ride horses and their riders. It allows time for such advanced work as dressage, a much more demanding discipline than is normally required of ordinary saddle horses. Dressage develops precision in a horse's movements and increases the animal's ability to respond quickly and correctly to its rider's aids.

Each year, as the training of three-year-olds begins at Rockcliffe riding school, they are apportioned among the instructors, usually in groups of four or five, depending on the year's crop. Every instructor must comply with a set program. He must also keep a diary showing how long each horse spends on each exercise, the horse's reaction to training, and his own comments on the animal's progress and its temperament. Information from an instructor's diary might eventually help the RCMP to decide whether to keep or cull a certain horse.

During the young remounts' first three months of training, the Rockcliffe instructors take great care that the habits they form are good ones. They are used to having men about them, but they have had very little handling. From the beginning the instructors gain the horses' confidence by giving them tidbits of sugar and oats, just as later during training they will give such tidbits to reward compliance.

The NWMP breaking remounts at Fort Macleod in 1883. (Glenbow Archives, Calgary)

For the first week or two the instructors teach the young horses to lead, and then they lead them around the stables, the paddocks, the riding school, the jumping area and so on, to let them become familiar with their surroundings. During this same period each horse gets used to wearing a soft or "water" bit constantly, even when eating, so that its mouth will gradually harden in preparation for a metal bit.

At the beginning of the third week the instructor takes his horses, one by one, to the riding school. There he introduces each one to the lunge line and the surcingle. The instructor attaches the thirty-foot lunge line to a special halter, or cavesson, which the young horse is wearing. A second instructor holds the cavesson to control the horse from its head, while the first instructor holds on to the free end of the long line. Then the two of them encourage the horse to walk in a large circle. Later there is no need for the instructor at its head. For several reasons, lungeing remains part of the training for the first six months.

The surcingle is a wide band that goes around the widest part of the horse's body. The kind used at first has elastic inserts, so that the horse can breathe without feeling restricted and having cause to panic. Soon the surcingle is used to hold a saddle blanket on the horse's back.

Later the horse wear side reins, also with elastic or rubber inserts, fastened to the cavesson and to the surcingle. These reins hold the horse's head in place and so help harden the mouth, yet still allow the horse to flex its neck and head. When the horse is used to holding its head up, reins without elastic inserts are used.

After a while the horse carries a stripped saddle (without stirrups), one with elastic inserts in the girth until the horse gets used to wearing a girth. The animal now wears the stripped saddle during lungeing and during a new exercise, long lining. In the latter exercise, long lines are fastened one on each side of the bridle, and the instructor walks behind, "driving" the horse. The instructor uses pressure on the reins and at the same time voice commands to encourage the horse to go forward, to turn, to back up or to stop. When the horse responds satisfactorily to rein pressure alone, voice commands are discontinued.

Also during the first three months of training, the young remounts are trained with poles. At first only one of the eight-foot poles is placed on the ground in the lunge circle so that the horse on the lunge line, travelling in either direction, has to step over the pole. During the second three-month period the horse, still on the lunge line, learns to negotiate one, two or three poles at both the walk and the trot.

Between the fourth and the sixth month the horse learns to accept the weight of a rider who drapes his body over the saddle, after which the horse is led around by

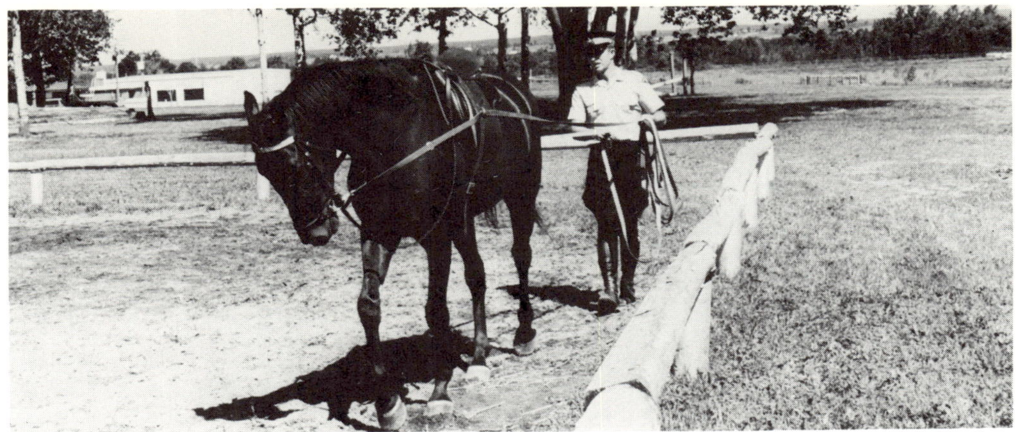

Teaching a remount flexion by long reining.

An advanced remount and rider entering a gymnastic line.

Taking the jump in a gymnastic line.

A well-schooled remount performing a two track or half pass, a dressage movement.

the head. Later the rider sits in the saddle, and the horse is led around the riding school or goes in circles on the lunge line. Still later the horse carries its rider at a walk or at a trot, for only a few minutes at a time, free of the lunge line and with no one at its head. By the sixth month the horse is used to carrying the weight on its back, and the riding periods are gradually extended to thirty minutes.

Once the horses can be trusted to carry riders safely and to obey them, the instructors occasionally give them a change from the monotony of the riding school. In good weather, especially in the summer, some training is carried on outside. Also, as often as possible the instructors or the members of the Musical Ride take them for pleasant rides (hacking) in the countryside. This not only dispels the tedium of indoor training, but it also allows the horses to acquire stamina and to develop their lung capacity.

From the seventh month onward the training becomes more sophisticated. The horse learns things beyond the basic training of an ordinary saddle horse: single transitions at the walk, trot and halt; turns on the forehand; how to lengthen its stride at the walk or the trot. By the end of the ninth month it can negotiate, at a

A remount in training for crowd control, 1938. Such training is no longer given.

walk or a trot, four poles. During the tenth and eleventh months the animal receives several exercises of dressage training, and by the end of the first year's training it has learned to canter.

During the second year, even more sophisticated movements are achieved. By the end of the fourteenth month the horse has been trained in half pirouettes, half halts and double transitions. By the end of the nineteenth month, the animal has learned the strong and collected trot and how to canter full out, but not yet to gallop. The animal goes on to stepping or jumping over obstacles up to eighteen inches high.

In the last two months of training the horse learns to wear a double bridle, so that its rider can use double reins and thus have better control over his mount. Now the horse learns the collected canter and the flying change. It also completes a course of jumping in which it negotiates a series of eight jumps, two and a half feet high with a three-foot spread.

At last the horse is thoroughly trained, fit for equitation in the Force, and equally fit for the Musical Ride, since it can now easily learn the cavalry movements which form the basis of the Ride. By now, if the horse were to be offered for sale on the open market, it would bring in thousands of dollars. With the exception of the few horses that are trained privately and especially for dressage competition, the horses of the RCMP are very likely the best-trained saddle horses in Canada.

EQUITATION TRAINING OF RECRUITS

From the Force's inception in 1873, the NWMP and the RNWMP gave recruits some equitation training. In the early years, when horses were the only means of transportation, such training was essential, although the more work demanded of the men, the less time was available for training. Indeed, many members acquired most of their riding skills on long mounted patrols, in the earliest years using the military Universal saddles, and later with the more comfortable western-style saddles.

In 1932 a more formal period of general recruit training, both academic and physical, was established. During the second half of a six-month course recruits received about 120 hours of equitation training, although they became acquainted with the horses from the day their training began.

In fact, the recruit was never allowed to forget that he belonged to a mounted unit, and the theme of his life was "horses, horses, horses". Wearing drab brown fatigues, he spent forty-five minutes at each of the three daily stable parades—6:30 A.M., noon and evening—cleaning out the stables and feeding and grooming horses.

Each Saturday, at 11:00 A.M. precisely, the commanding officer inspected the barrack rooms, accompanied by his staff. He and his two officers wore trim blue uniforms; the two NCOs wore scarlet tunics, blue breeches and high boots; and all wore spurs. Each recruit, dressed in immaculate regular dress of brown serge, blue breeches, high boots and spurs, stood stiffly at attention by his wrinkle-free bed. On the wall at the side of the bed hung a bridle whose leather and metal the recruit had polished to perfection the previous evening.

From the barracks the CO and his staff strode to the stables, where the scarlet-tunicked riding master awaited them. There they found everything put in order by the recruits earlier—clean stalls, sleekly groomed horses, and saddles as highly polished as the bridles in the barrack rooms. After inspection on Saturday and again on Sunday, one of the training squads took over the cleaning of the stables and the feeding of the horses. On these days there was no further grooming

RNWMP recruit equitation class being instructed in the raising of a sick horse, Regina, 1917.

of horses, and the recruits hurried through their chores in anticipation of a few rare hours of freedom.

In addition to their regular work with the horses, recruits were detailed in turn to the daily duty of stable orderly, which they classified as a "bitch duty". This duty, from 6:00 A.M. to 6:00 P.M., with time out for meals only when the mealtime stable parades took over, required that a single stable orderly keep a stable spotless. After the stable parade had cleaned out the stable and tidied up in general, the orderly had to complete the job and make sure that no stray hay, straw or other material found its way to the space behind the horses.

The favourite sport of stable orderlies was trying to prevent fresh manure from falling in the stall or to the floor behind the horses. As soon as a horse raised its tail, the orderly would make a mad dash with a shovel held out to catch the droppings. The worst thing possible, from an orderly's point of view, was when two or three horses in different parts of the stable raised their tails at the same time. And the worst possible time was immediately before the riding master and the inspector veterinary surgeon arrived to inspect, as they invariably did at some time during the day.

Recruits were also detailed in turn as night guards, and then they had to check the stables several times during the night. On one occasion the nightguard, standing in the doorway of the dark stable, heard footsteps approaching and receding as if someone were walking back and forth inside the stable. Waiting until the sound seemed nearest, he suddenly switched on the light. It shone on a constable who had recently come out of the north with a nervous breakdown. He was carrying a quarter-bushel measure of oats with which he was filling a horse's deep manger.

To the guard's surprise, the horse was an unruly animal appropriately named Broncho. The ill-tempered angular creature would not usually let anyone into his stall without trying to kick the intruder mercilessly, and he was even fed and cleaned from adjoining stalls to avoid injury to the recruits. The only person Broncho tolerated was the constable found feeding him in the dark in the middle of the night. The same constable in daylight could walk into Broncho's stall, slap him on the rump, then saddle him and ride him with no trouble. Anyone else would have been bucked off immediately. Broncho didn't last long as an RCMP horse, and no one was sure why he tolerated the mentally disturbed policeman. Perhaps it was because Broncho sensed the fear in the other constables, whereas the exceptional constable was not afraid.

Recruits were always eager to start equitation training, and most felt it was unfair that during the three months of Part I training they did all the work of caring for the horses without the pleasure of riding them. But with the beginning of Part II training they took equitation. In squads of thirty-two men each they received two hours' equitation a day, five days a week, until they graduated. By the time equitation began, the men knew that they would not be allowed red serge jackets until they had completed their training. They also learned that they would not be allowed to ride with spurs until their instructors were convinced that they would not injure or alarm the horses, usually well into the course.

The most eager recruits were those from the prairies who had ridden western style most of their lives. They found, however, that getting rid of habits learned in that style of riding gave them as much trouble as the non-riders had in learning to ride cavalry style. To begin with, the experienced riders were nearly always the target of the instructors' scathing remarks, to the amusement and gratification of the non-riders, who at first had been jealous of the experienced ones' skill.

A five year old remount by the Trakhener stallion Himeryk after a washdown. (William Kelly)

A remount on the lunge line with full tack including rubber donut side reins, which are not engaged to full effect.

OPPOSITE: *A remount being vacuumed with an electric body brush.*

A remount being acquainted with the weight of a rider. The saddle has been stripped of its stirrups, and the rider is not wearing spurs at this early stage in the young horse's training.

A remount on the lunge line navigating a single cavaletti at the trot.

Riding instructor Staff Sergeant Dunn and Perry in a collected canter.

Staff Sergeant John Dunn on Perry in an extended trot, 1984.

Taking the chicken-coop jump at Rockcliffe.

The western riders, however, knew from experience what the non-riders had been told again and again but still sometimes overlooked, which was that a horse has a habit of extending its girth when a saddle is thrown on it. After first tightening the leather girth, each recruit should re-tighten it a few minutes later. Those who failed to do this found their saddles slipping. Some fell off, at the worst catching a foot in a stirrup and being dragged around the riding school. Fortunately, scarcely anyone was ever seriously hurt.

The men learned to jump without stirrups and with arms folded, and with the reins tied around the horses' necks to avoid pulling on the animals' mouths. Some riders fell off as the horses rose to take the jump. Occasionally one who made it to the far side found to his surprise that he had bounced in front of the saddle and was leaning forward, clasping the horse's neck with both arms as he slid down it to the tanbark of the riding-school floor.

Graduates of the equitation course accumulated many stories, not only about themselves and their comrades but also about notable characters among the horses. The latter, especially those who had often repeated the course, became very knowledgeable about what was expected of them. In fact, in the early stages of recruit training they understood the instructors' commands better than the riders did. As a result, the horses often complied with the commands while the riders were still trying to figure out what they were supposed to do. One recruit wrote home, and many others had the same idea, that he often wondered if he was riding the horse or the horse was riding him.

The instructors meanwhile were always quick to point out that recruits were easy to obtain but good horses were obtained only with great difficulty. One corporal instructor, a graduate of a British cavalry training school, seemed indifferent to the difficulties experienced by his men and was forever shouting in his strong English accent, "Take care of that little hawse!"

One day the same instructor, sitting smartly erect on his own horse, watched with annoyance as an inept recruit's mount carried him around the riding school at top speed, travelling inside the circle of other riders.

"Stop that little hawse!" the corporal yelled again and again.

The recruit was so engrossed in his own problem that he forgot that a trainee should always be respectful to his superiors. As he sped past the instructor once more he yelled back, "This is no time for fooling, corporal!" It was some time before the recruit's comrades could carry on as usual, straight-faced.

Practicing for trick riding at Regina.

Recruits taking a grid of jumps at Regina, circa 1935.

Some horses are still well remembered for their less than endearing traits. Bena, for example, had a remarkable ability to throw any rider unexpectedly, even a trained one. Rogue, appropriately named, was able to assess the prowess of his rider. The less the prowess, the more trouble Rogue caused. He often disrupted a training session with his misbehaviour, while the instructor put all the blame on the rider. But the instructors knew more about the situation than they admitted, and many a know-it-all recruit was assigned to Rogue, who in his way contributed to the desired discipline.

Lucky, who served in the Force for twenty-one years, from 1941 to 1962, frustrated many recruits. He would move out of formation unexpectedly and stand like a rock, waiting until a horse which had annoyed him came full circle back to him. Then he lashed out with his hind feet to the ribs of the offending horse, and only then would he move back into his place in the ride formation. Recruits who hurt Lucky's mouth in trying to force him back into line before he was ready, usually found themselves down on the tanbark.

Recruits not only developed their own repertoires of horse stories, but they heard others from other Mounted Police. For instance, it was widely circulated that Laddie could buck on command, but his more amiable trick was to laugh on command by stretching his neck and raising his upper lip. Some horses could "shake hands", or lie down on command, or cake-walk by exaggeratedly raising their front feet as if dancing. Imp could tell you his age by stamping his foot. He also liked to hold the bag of his rider's grooming kit in his mouth while he was groomed. Bobbie was known to be a well-mannered horse—until he heard the bagpipes: then he would try to put as much distance as possible between him and them. Several of the Musical Ride horses were known for their talent of going through the movements of the Ride without riders on their backs, much to the chagrin of those riders who had been bucked off during a performance.

One horse at Depot Division, Regina, was often turned out with other horses in a pasture adjoining a golf course. The pasture's barbed wire fence was obviously meant to prevent horses from reaching the lush grass on the fairway of the course. But the one horse used to squeeze himself under the lowest strand of the wire and enjoy the golf course grass—until he would spot someone coming to return him to the pasture. He would then hurriedly squeeze himself back under the wire to his own side of the fence, only to repeat his escapade at the first opportunity, without ever being scratched by the barbs.

Summer equitation camp, Hidden Valley, Saskatchewan, circa 1957.

The last RCMP recruit equitation troop based at Rockcliffe, Ontario, summer, 1966. Most of these horses had been born and raised at the Fort Walsh, Saskatchewan, RCMP ranch.

A member of the Jamaican police sent to "N" Division at Rockcliffe for mounted training.

By the end of the course all recruits became fairly proficient riders, trained to handle a carbine when mounted, and trained to some degree in riot drill, which involved the use of a trunchéon about three feet long, in tactics generally used by mounted police when dealing with unruly crowds. It was a proud day when they donned their recently issued scarlet serges and took part in the passing out parade before the commanding officer and guests, often watched admiringly by recruits who were still doing stable chores and had yet to win their spurs.

SADDLES

Throughout the more than a century of Mounted Police existence, the Force has had only four basic types of saddles in general use: three models of the Universal Pattern saddle, the Wood Arch, the Flat Iron, and the Angle Iron Arch; the California; the Colonial; and the Stübben. It has experimented with several other types, however, including the McClellan and the Whitman, and it is possible, though not certain, that during the March West, a few of the Universal Pattern Drivers' Saddle, a modification of the Wood Arch, were used by the men riding the horses that pulled the gun carriages.

The number of horses available for the original 150 members of the NWMP at Lower Fort Garry during that first winter of 1873–74 was at first only thirty-three, and although more were purchased, the total fell far short of one horse per man. That total is not available, but it is known that during that first winter only fifty saddles were in use. They were the Universal Pattern Wood Arch saddles borrowed from the Canadian militia which was stationed at Winnipeg twenty miles to the south, and of which the commanding officer was Lieutenant Colonel W. Osborne Smith, who was also the Acting Commissioner of the NWMP until Commissioner French arrived. One feature of the Wood Arch saddle was a high cantle (the curved arch at the back of the saddle), which gave support and protection to the rider. This saddle had been very popular with the British cavalry in the Crimean War, and perhaps for this reason it was incorrectly referred to by the militia and the Mounted Police as the "Cavalry Saddle".

When Commissioner French arrived at Lower Fort Garry in mid-December 1873, he found the borrowed saddles were unsatisfactory. Early in January he reported his displeasure to the Canadian government: "50 sets of old pattern military saddlery with the high wooden cantles have been issued....It all *must* eventually be returned to the Militia department being entirely too heavy and clumsy for our work....Strong light saddles will be required with wallets, valises, etc., etc." (A wallet was a container strapped on the pommel on the front of the saddle, and a valise was a leather or cloth container fitted to be strapped behind the cantle or elsewhere.)

Later in 1874, when French was in Toronto recruiting, buying more horses, and preparing for the March West, he purchased from England three hundred saddles, of a modified form of those used at Lower Fort Garry. French's choice was the Universal Pattern Flat Iron Arch saddle, which the British had been experimenting with since 1872 and which had eliminated the high wooden cantle. French also ordered three Royal Artillery Officers' Saddles, one for himself and two for other officers.

The twenty-three officers in the March West had to purchase their own uniforms and equipment, but there is no record of what saddlery they purchased other than the three Royal Artillery Officers' saddles. Neither is there any record of whether officers were allowed to use the saddlery obtained for NCOs and men of the various original ranks of constables, although it is likely that in the earliest days they were allowed to do so. Later, most of the officers purchased their own equipment, including saddlery.

It seems unlikely that breast plates and cruppers were used on the March West. After two years, however, the horses at some police posts were wearing these articles, which probably indicates either that their use was optional or that they were used as they became available.

The Universal Flat Iron Arch saddles that travelled with Commissioner French and his contingent from Toronto to Dufferin were more than enough to equip the horses of the 275 officers and men who set out from Dufferin on the March West. Certainly a few weeks after they left, most of the horses were wearing them. The Force's first historian, J. P. Turner, suggests, however, that about half of the Wood Arch saddles borrowed from the militia at Winnipeg were never returned, and that probably some of them were used on the march. French and two of his officers used their privately purchased Royal Artillery Officers' saddles.

The Universal Pattern Iron Arch saddles soon gave evidence of defects. The arches almost always spread, especially in the hot weather that plagued the men and horses during the march, causing the pack and the seat to rest too heavily on the horse's back. The saddles were fitted with too many buckles and straps for attaching equipment to them, and the steel stirrups and buckles rusted quickly and were difficult to keep clean. The saddle had a tendency to roll from side to side, and the packing in the panels loosened and gave the horses sore backs. The position of the girth caused many galls, and some of the police found that the lack of the high-spoon cantle was a disadvantage when carrying a valise. Soon after the Great March West began, the men constantly complained about their Iron Arch saddles.

As the North-West Mounted Police settled in the west and travelled south to the United States, they noticed that American horsemen invariably used western "stock" (California) saddles. This American "cowboy" saddle had originated in Mexico, where the saddles imported by the Spanish conquistadores in the sixteenth century were copied and modified. The high pommel and cantle and the straight-leg seat were features which had been developed in Europe for the benefit of mounted men who wore armour and fought in the battles and tournaments of the Middle Ages. In the stock saddle these features had been adapted by Mexican and American cowboys, and the police immediately realized the advantage of using such comfortable saddles for patrol work. Almost at once a few commissioned officers purchased western saddles for their own use, and as early as February 1875, Inspector J. M. Walsh suggested that it would be a good idea to issue a few California saddles to each Division. Commissioner French agreed, but the Canadian government took no action on his recommendation.

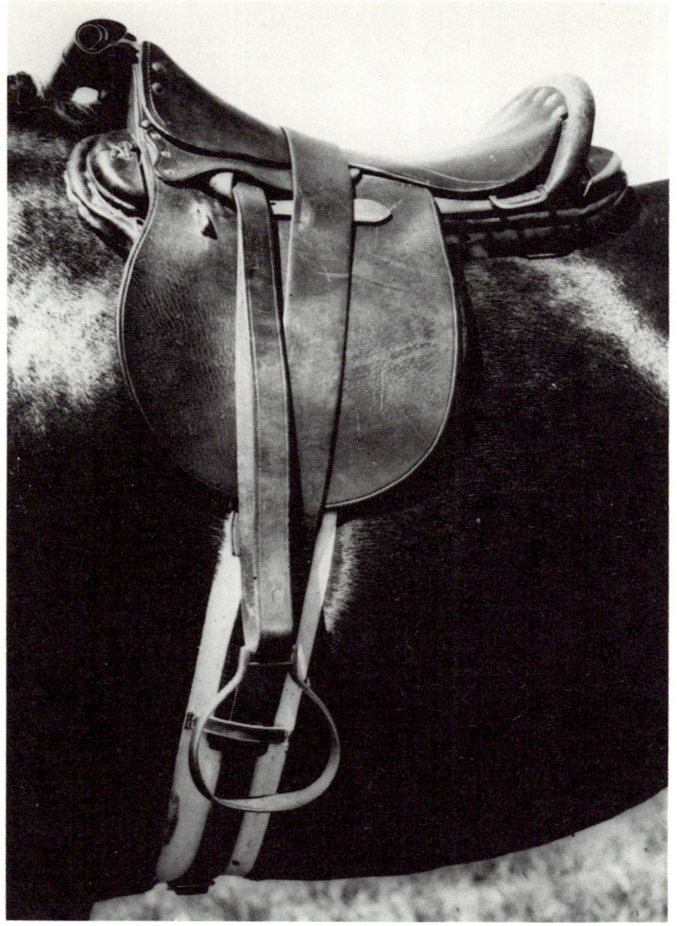

Universal Pattern Wood Arch saddle, used by the NWMP on the March West in 1874.

When Major-General E. Selby Smyth, accompanied by a police escort, made a long patrol in 1875 to inspect the posts of the new organization, he saw the advantages of the California saddle. He recommended to the Canadian government that the NWMP should be equipped with western-type California saddles, which were well-designed, light, without buckles, and low in price. In classifying the California as "light", however, in comparison with the "heavy" Iron Arch, Selby Smyth made the same error as would others after him. He assessed the weight of the Iron Arch saddle fully outfitted with all its attached equipment in full marching order, for a total of sixty-five pounds, while the approximately thirty-five-pound weight he ascribed to the California saddle was of the "stripped" saddle, with no equipment included. Actually, the stripped weight of the Universal Pattern Iron Arch saddle was only about seventeen pounds. The weight of the California saddle was its greatest disadvantage.

The California saddle became the official saddle of the NWMP in 1884 and was used until 1922, when it was replaced by the Universal Flat Iron Arch saddle.

The Canadian government ignored the major-general's recommendations, perhaps partly because of Veterinary Surgeon Poett's report at the end of that year. Poett commented that a good feature of the Universal was its very high pommel, which allowed a free current of air to pass beneath the saddle. He remarked that if this saddle was in good state of repair and properly put on, the horses would very seldom have sore backs. A disadvantage of the California, he pointed out, was that it was apt to produce the "dreaded disease" of fistula of the withers.

Whatever the merits of the Universal Pattern Iron Arch saddle, it was obviously unsuitable for breaking broncos. By 1876 the NWMP had thirty California saddles in use, most of them at Fort Walsh where, by this time, breaking broncos was a daily activity, as it had always been at Fort Macleod. Compared with the Iron Arch saddle, the more comfortable California provided a better seat and more stability, which allowed the rider to have better control of his horse. It also allowed the

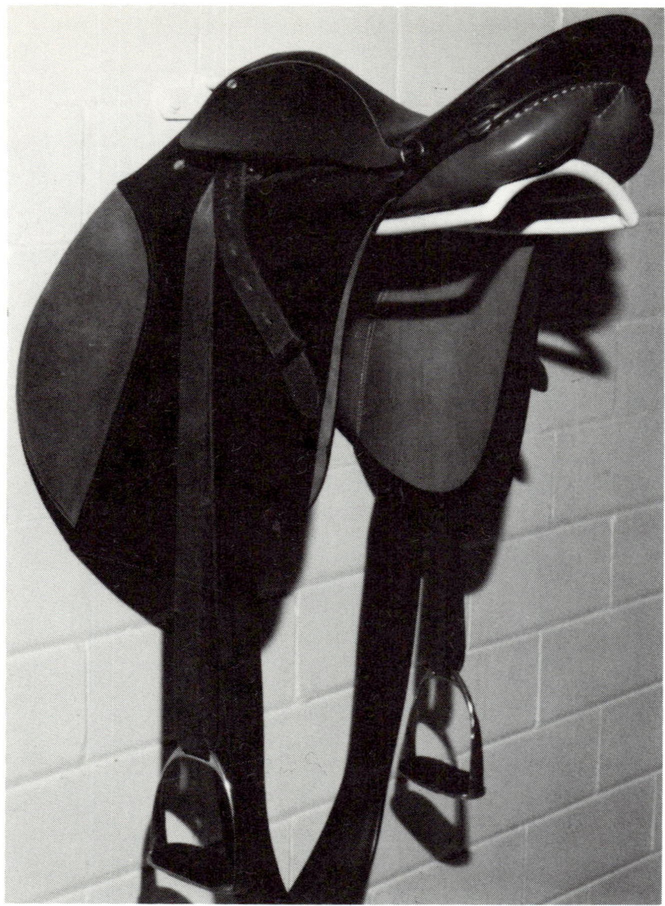

The Stübben "Tristan Extra" saddle, used by the RCMP Musical Ride from 1971.

weight of the rider to be more evenly distributed, which helped to prevent the horses from developing sore backs. Although it was acknowledged to be heavy, its benefits far outweighed those of the Iron Arch.

Moreover, many of the men needed the help of those comfortable, protective saddles. After Commissioner J. F. Macleod succeeded Commissioner French in 1876, he acknowledged their poor riding ability by recommending that the men should be transported in wagons rather than on horses. He wrote caustically, "I need not go further into details of the system I have proposed but will only add that to make our men effective to fight on horseback against such enemies as we might meet in the N. West; they will have to be engaged as children and made to ride every day till they grow up."

The unsatisfactory performance of the Universal Pattern Iron Arch saddle led to its modification in 1878, and for about six years the Mounted Police used the new model. The arches of the 1878 Universal Pattern Angle Iron Arch saddle were made with angle iron for more strength, and the girth was moved farther forward. This saddle, like its predecessor, however, had many defects, including a low cantle, which again had the disadvantage of not allowing the seat and the pack to be kept off the horse's back. Hence this type in turn proved unsatisfactory.

As the NWMP continued to search for a better saddle, it acquired two western stock-type McClellan saddles from the U.S. War Department in Washington, D.C., one covered in leather, and the other in buckskin. Both models were very popular with the U.S. cavalry. Their construction was simple, they could withstand weather, and they were said to be lighter than and superior to any other military saddle of that time. An outstanding feature of the McClellan saddle was that the stirrups were set forward of centre, to distribute the weight of the rider and his pack more evenly over the horse's back. Also, the pommel and the cantle were of wood reinforced with steel, and the saddle, when complete, was open throughout to allow air to circulate over the horse's back. But the NWMP never succeeded in persuading the government to provide the necessary funds to equip it with the superior and suitable McClellan saddles.

Over the next few years Mounted Police officers and men constantly voiced conflicting opinions in private and in public about the saddlery of the Force. Superintendent Sam Steele favoured the California saddle, which he had used since 1875. Veterinary Poett still didn't like it. He now blamed the California saddles used at Fort Walsh for the increase in fistula of the withers at that post, probably, he said, because there was less air circulating under the saddles. Superintendent James Walsh favoured the Whitman saddle. He had used one for several years and had found it at least the equal of the California, with the advantage of being lighter in weight and cheaper. However, nine Whitman saddles purchased for the Marquis of Lorne's escort in 1881 lasted only two years. Commissioner Irvine, who had succeeded Macleod in 1880, recommended a saddle which he wanted to have built to his own design, and which he declared would have the best features of both military and stock saddles, but nothing came of his recommendation.

In 1883 the Canadian government at last reached a decision and established the California as the Force's basic saddle. One hundred were purchased from a dealer in San Francisco, California, at $23.50 each. Soon another 250 were purchased at $24.50. As the Universal saddle seemed more suitable for drill on the barracks square, however, it continued to be used by some recruits in training. The California saddle was warmly welcomed by many of the Mounted Police. Although most of the NWMP horses were generally well broken, they were often used for patrol work soon after they had passed the bucking stage. At the same time, many of the men who should have been able to, could not ride very well. The California saddle allowed even an inexperienced rider to stay on his horse and control it better than if he had been using a Universal Pattern saddle.

Over the next few years, two senior officers, Superintendents A. H. Griesbach and A. B. Perry, complained bitterly about the weight of the California saddle when fully equipped for patrol work. They strongly suggested that it be replaced by a lighter-weight military-type saddle. Their criticism probably lost some significance, however, because by that time many patrols were being made by team and wagon, and thus the patrol horses accompanying them could travel with relatively light packs.

Griesbach, the first of the original men to sign on at Lower Fort Garry in 1873, and always in sympathy with the horses, complained further, that the use of the California saddle, with its horn, high cantle and stiff-legged seat, gave the rider too much of an advantage over the horse, and he also regretted that the stock saddle failed to encourage good horsemanship. Rumour had it that if a bucking bronco threw a recruit, Superintendent Griesbach would berate the recuit for falling off. Moreover, if anyone supported the use of the heavy California saddle by remarking that cowboys' horses did not suffer from its use, Griesbach retorted that cowboys had several horses at their disposal, and they were not forced to use the same horses day after day, as the police were.

NWMP horses during that period had to endure more than the burden of heavy saddles. The quality of the felt in the numnahs, or felt saddle pads, was so poor that the horses developed sore backs, and riders often had to use blankets under the numnahs. In 1884 Commissioner Irvine requested new numnahs, "leather bound where the cinches cross, and particularly where the ring of the cinch rests," but the government did not grant his request. When the numnahs began to last only four months, Irvine recommended, again with no result, that they be made from the same material as was used by the Imperial Cavalry "until a suitable article is made in this Dominion". Three years later it was Commissioner L. W. Herchmer who was complaining, but by then the Force was using saddle blankets, so the problem of sore backs had diminished.

Although the California-type saddle was used by the Mounted Police for about thirty-five years, after only a few years politicians pressured the government to make the Force purchase its saddles in Canada, and Canadian manufacturers began producing a saddle modelled after the California. In 1887, after much testing in the field, Veterinary Surgeon J. F. Burnett recommended the purchase of California-type saddles manufactured by Hutchings in Winnipeg. During the decade after the Force began using the Hutchings saddle, it was modified a number of times in accord with suggestions from the men who patrolled by saddle horse thousands of miles a year. The NWMP also experimented with five other saddles, but they failed to find one more suitable than the California.

When Commissioner A. B. Perry took office in 1900 he again criticized the California saddle. Then, from the NWMP officers serving in the Boer War, he received favourable reports on the use of the saddle in South Africa. After that Perry merely recommended modifications to lighten the California saddle, and it continued in use for almost two decades.

By 1919 the RNWMP had mechanized to the extent of three cars, six trucks and fifteen motorcycles, and patrol work by saddle horse was diminishing. As roads were improved, more cars were used for police work and there was even less need for horse patrols. When patrol horses were necessary in sparsely settled areas, they were often used as teams drawing democrats (light wagons or sleighs), and there was less need of saddles.

Another factor also contributed to the decline of the California saddle. From 1919, Mounted Police duties included dealing with industrial disputes, referred to within the Force as "strike duties", for which the Universal Pattern saddle was more suitable than the California. The Force had also since then undertaken more ceremonial duties, including the Musical Ride, and again the Universal saddle was more suitable. So in 1920 the RCMP began using the Universal Pattern Angle Iron Arch saddle with which the NWMP had been equipped in 1878, and it was in use again for many years.

In 1948, the Musical Ride at Regina was using the Colonial saddle, English Officers' Pattern, which was better padded than the Universal Angle Iron Arch saddle, and more comfortable for both men and horses. After a few years, at the request of the RCMP, the manufacturer modified the saddle slightly by removing the two leather-covered wooden burs which projected a few inches beyond the front arch of the saddle. Not only the Ride used this Colonial saddle, but gradually it was also used by recruits in training in Regina. In the mid-1950s, probably at the whim of a senior riding instructor, the Universal saddle was brought back into use again for a year or two. By 1958, however, the Colonial saddle was again in favour in Regina. It remained in use there until 1966, when recruit equitation training was abolished.

The Musical Ride, which was transferred from Regina to Rockcliffe, Ontario, that same year, continued to use the Colonial saddle until 1971. Before the Musical Ride arrived at Rockcliffe, the riders at the training depot there had been using the Universal saddle, although it had gone out of use at Regina, but gradually they, too, came to use the Colonial saddle.

Since 1971 the Musical Ride has used the Tristan Extra model of the German-made Stübben saddle. The regular Tristan model was modified to meet RCMP requirements by the addition of a knee roll and "D" rings, and by the lengthening of the saddle flaps to accommodate the riders' high Strathcona boots. The Stübben is a great improvement over any saddle previously used by the Force for ceremonial purposes and is very popular with the riders, so it will probably remain in use for many years.

THE SHABRACK

The name "shabrack", or "shabracque", which designates the saddle cloth used by mounted military units, is derived from the Turkish "shaprack". Some authorities insist that the term "shabrack" should be used only when a unit's battle honours are inscribed on it. There are no battle honours on the RCMP shabrack, but the term seems to have come into common use in 1920, when the organization became the Royal Canadian Mounted Police.

For many years the shabracks have been of dark blue cloth edged with yellow piping. The single wide piping used by NCOs and constables has remained standard for those ranks over the years.

The NWMP began using the fused "MP" on the rear corners of its saddle cloths soon after 1887, when it registered that symbol as its brand. The fused "MP" was at first used for all ranks and has, like the single wide piping, continued to be used for NCOs and constables.

The piping and the insignia on officers' shabracks have been changed over the years according to the wishes of officers in charge of various mounted units. For example, in 1937 the shabracks of the officers of the Coronation Contingent of King George VI carried a fused "MP" surmounted by a crown. In 1948 officers at one post replaced the fused "MP" with the letters "RCMP" and retained the crown. In 1953 the officers of Queen Elizabeth II's Coronation Contingent, both trained at Regina, used only the bare fused "MP". From the early 1960s for about two decades, the insignia on officers' shabracks were generally the letters "RCMP" surmounted by a crown.

The piping edging the officers' shabracks similarly lacked standardization, at least from the 1920s, apparently because of the various decisions of officers in charge of the mounted units at Regina and Rockcliffe. Sometimes the piping was single wide at one of those locations, and at the same time double narrow at the other place. But from the early 1960s for about two decades, all officers used double narrow.

In 1982 Commissioner Robert Simmonds issued a policy standardizing shabracks, probably the first such directive. Officers' shabracks are now of dark blue material with double narrow yellow piping, with each rear corner bearing the same crest of the Force as the one approved for regimental blazers. Those of the NCOs' and constables' remain as before, of the same dark blue material with a single wide yellow piping all around and the fused "MP" on each rear corner.

BRIDLES

The early NWMP used various kinds of bridles, often called collars or headstalls. Those which Divisions "A", "B" and "C" obtained from the militia at Lower Fort Garry in 1873, and then used when training their thirty-eight locally purchased horses, were undoubtedly the regulation army type of that time. Some bridles were fitted with Pelham (English cavalry) bits and double reins. This made them unsuitable for police patrol work, as each horse on patrol carried a halter rope and a tether rope, so that a second rein was surplus equipment. It is impossible to classify the bits used during the first few years, as the kind of bit was usually a personal choice, in spite of the efforts of the various commissioners to standardize the Force's equipment. The Pelham bit, however, remained in general use for about ten years.

Divisions "D", "E" and "F" used bridles which Commissioner French had purchased from McLaren's of Montreal, Quebec. No description of them exists, although records show that the commissioner wanted bridles of simple design: "A plain headstall with bit and halter attached is all that is likely to be required."

After Major-General E. Selby Smyth's inspection of the Force in 1875, he reported to the government that the Pelham bits were weak and not standing up to use, and he recommended standardizing the headstalls. Earlier that year Commissioner French had requisitioned two hundred Standard Cavalry Pattern bridles, apparently in an effort to standardize such equipment through progressive replacement of worn-out bridles.

The commissioner received only fifty-eight bridles, not of Standard Cavalry Pattern, but of a type designed by Colonel Hugh Richardson of the Department of Justice in Ottawa. The police saddlers made another fifty bridles of the same pattern. However, French preferred the cavalry bridles and made a further request for them. The following year he received a shipment of 150 bridles from the firm of Borbridge in Ottawa. The bridles were similar to the Richardson ones, but they were merely described officially as "halters with two reins for each bit and bit straps". During the next few years the Mounted Police horses wore bridles of various types, some supplied by Ottawa, some made by the police, and some of the "mend and make do" variety.

Until 1884 the Pelham bit remained the most widely used. Curb, snaffle and Portsmouth bits were also used, perhaps according to the personal preference of the police, and certainly in many cases according to the nature of the horse. Meanwhile, the Whitman bit gradually came into use. As early as 1880, Commissioner A.G. Irvine had recommended it in his annual report.

> I have already informed the Department that I considered the 'Whitman' bit more suitable for the force than the English cavalry [Pelham] bit. The latter is too heavy for prairie work. The 'Whitman' bit is a pleasant one for a horse, does not irritate or chafe the mouth, answers also as a strong curb bit suspended by a swivel snap which hooks to any bridle or halter; is a powerful bit, giving the rider perfect control of his horse.
>
> I recommend the English cavalry head collar, which with proper care would last for years, a five ring halter to be exclusively used in the stables, and the English cavalry head collar for outdoor service.

As Commissioner Irvine also pointed out, "With the 'Whitman' bit, bit heads [over-the-head leather straps] would not be required." That was because the Whitman bit was fastened to the bridle with a snap instead of being used with the over-the-head leather straps as other bits were. Thus the Whitman bit could easily be removed by unsnapping, leaving the bridle immediately usable as a halter. After 1884, when the California saddle became the official saddle of the NWMP, the Whitman bit began to replace the Pelham bit for general use.

Bridles continued to be a source of complaints until 1886, when Commissioner L. W. Herchmer recommended that the Force should be allowed to make its own small leather articles, including bridles, halters, belts and holsters—something the saddler major had been recommending since 1883. The government finally agreed. Within three years, while police saddlers worked under the supervision of

The double bridle, which includes a Weymouth bit and a bridoon (snaffle) bit and also a curb chain, currently used by the RCMP Musical Ride.

The Ride mascot guarding the tack room at Rockcliffe.

Saddler Major Horner, the Force became self-sufficient in supplying its own bridles, halters and other pieces of saddlery and kit. Saddler Major Horner and his men seem to have done their work well, for there were no further complaints from the men about bridles.

Since those early days there have been many changes in the bridles of the Force. Today a single bridle is used for training and exercise purposes, while on ceremonial occasions the attractive Weymouth double bridle is used. This bridle combines a curb bit and a snaffle bit or bridoon bit, each with its own set of reins. Attached to the ring on the double bridle is a white headrope which hangs around the horse's neck. There is no longer any practical use for the headrope. In earlier days, however, when the bit was removed, the bridle became the halter, and the headrope became the halter shank.

The present ceremonial bridles have white brow bands, secured on each side by brass rosettes bearing the badge of the Force. What appears to be a martingale has always been called a breastplate by the Mounted Police, and the breast portion of the breastplate displays a large badge of the Force. The breastplate, although serving only as decoration today, had a practical value when horses were used for patrol work. From two points on it, one on each side near the withers, two small leather straps were attached (as they still are) to the front of the saddle to prevent the saddle from slipping back. The breastplate used by the RCMP differs from a martingale in that the latter is attached at one end to the reins, or the noseband, or even directly to the bit.

ARTISANS

The artisans of the Force have always been of vital importance in keeping its horses and equipment in good condition. When the North-West Mounted Police was established in 1873, the organizational structure provided for the three non-commissioned officer ranks of saddler major, wheeler major and farrier major. Other "mechanics", as they were sometimes called, worked under their supervision: farriers (shoeing smiths), blacksmiths, wheelwrights, gunsmiths, harness-makers, saddlers, carpenters and others.

The three NCO ranks received twenty cents per day in addition to their regular pay of one dollar. The pay scale also allowed extra pay for twenty "mechanics" of fifteen cents per day in addition to their regular seventy-five cents. These more highly paid "mechanics" were to be distributed as: one saddler, one blacksmith and one carpenter for each of the six Divisions, plus two extras to act as spares where necessary.

Commissioner French had many of these artisans with him when in the late spring of 1874 he took the Force's second contingent from eastern to western Canada in preparation for the March West later that year. From the time they de-trained at Fargo, North Dakota, the artisans certainly earned their extra pay.

Before the contingent could march north to Fort Dufferin, Manitoba, the saddlers, harness-makers, wheelwrights and carpenters had to fit together the pieces of saddles, bridles, harness and wagons which had been shipped by train to Fargo in pieces, most of them distributed haphazardly, and even in different boxcars. Then, almost as soon as the cavalcade of horses and wagons set out on the trail from Fargo, the saddlers had to repair the new saddlery and harness that was proving less substantial than it should have been. Before long the wheelers were busy repairing broken wagon wheels, and the carpenters fixing wagons that threatened to come apart.

During the March West the artisans proved invaluable. They shod horses and oxen at portable forges. They repaired wagons, ox-carts, mowing machines and hay rakes. They improvised missing parts for worn and damaged saddlery and harness. In fact, the unique skills of the artisans enabled the great March West to continue; without them it is doubtful the NWMP could have reached its destination.

Later, when the NWMP set up detachments in various parts of the prairies, these same artisans helped not only in keeping horses and equipment in good condition, but also with the buildings and their furnishings.

As the years passed, the ranks of saddler major, wheeler major and farrier major were discontinued. Those artisans still employed were given regular police ranks. In more recent years such necessary artisans as farriers and saddlers are engaged as civilian employees.

Today, RCMP horses are kept only at the stables at Rockcliffe, Ontario, where the Musical Ride is based and where equitation training is given to members who volunteer for it, and at the nearby breeding farm at Pakenham. Two permanently employed farriers attend to the horses at both places, and one of them accompanies the Musical Ride on its travels. The RCMP also permanently employs a saddler, who works at Rockcliffe in a shop near the stables. These three RCMP artisans are as vital to the Force as were the old-time artisans of earlier years. The saddler keeps saddlery and leather equipment in good repair and also, with the exception of the basic saddles, makes all the leather equipment. This includes halters, single and double bridles, surcingles, girths, breastplates, headropes, and lines used in the training of young horses. He also makes the lances used in the Musical Ride. In preparation for the European tour of the Ride in 1974, the present saddler, assisted by his recently retired father who as the Force's saddler had begun the project, made 1,960 pieces of leather equipment, each piece cut separately and stitched by hand. The saddler estimates that he and his father spent at least 720 hours on this work alone.

No one appreciated the specially made equipment more than the riders. All standardized in size and colour, it enhanced the appearance of the already magnificent group of horsemen. Above all, the riders knew that it would withstand the wear and tear of an arduous European tour much better than similar equipment purchased from a commercial source.

6

THE MUSICAL RIDE

THE "RIDE" THROUGH THE YEARS

The Musical Ride figures are based on cavalry drill which, in its present form, began to take shape during the eighteenth century, when Frederick the Great of Prussia revolutionized cavalry tactics and trained his cavalry to a standard which became the envy and ideal of other European nations, which then imitated the Prussian tactics. Since the basic cavalry formations were line and column, cavalry drill movements were concerned with transitions from one to the other, and with changes of pace and direction. The attack, or charge, which became the culmination of those movements, depended on its momentum, direction, timing, and the shock produced by a solid line of galloping horses and riders clashing with the enemy.

During the nineteenth century, peacetime duties of cavalry regiments often involved them in public ceremonies. It seemed natural to combine choreographed cavalry movements with the music of regimental bands, partly for entertainment, but also because the performance requires the utmost in timing, co-ordination and control of horses. Musical Ride training and performing also relieves the tedium of the daily drill periods and routine duties. The first British Musical Ride is believed to have been performed in 1882 by the 1st Regiment of Life Guards at the Royal Tournament at Islington, London.

Although when the NWMP made its Great March West across the vast Canadian prairies in 1874 its weapons, in case of need, were revolvers and carbines, its scarlet-tunicked riders carried lances to impress the Indians. The lance has remained as part of the Force's mounted equipment for use in ceremonies, mounted sports and Musical Rides. The men and horses of the original NWMP were soon scattered in small groups over tens of thousands of miles of unsettled prairie, but the

The Ride performing at the New York World's Fair, 1939.

importance of drill, both mounted and dismounted, was never forgotten. Wherever a sufficient number of men and horses were stationed, cavalry and foot drill were the order of the day, and the men made them part of their entertainment by using their skills as horsemen.

The first recorded display of riding by the NWMP took place at Fort Macleod in 1876, under the direction of Sergeant-Major Robert Belcher. Belcher and others who directed mounted training in those early days had been members of British cavalry regiments and had had experience in performing such displays. Only after the men at the main posts had formed their own bands, however, did riding displays take the form of Musical Rides as we know them today.

In 1886 the NWMP completed the building of a riding school at headquarters at Regina, thus allowing mounted training all year around. A Musical Ride was then formed by riding master Inspector W. G. Mathews, formerly riding master with the Third Hussars in England, in cooperation with Sergeant-Major George Kempster, who had served with the Life Guards in London during the first two years the Guards had performed the Musical Ride there. A third British army veteran, NWMP Reg. No. 1365, Jacob Farmer, had had considerable experience with military bands, so Commissioner Herchmer placed him in charge of the headquarters bands, both mounted and unmounted.

During the first three months of 1887, the NWMP Musical Ride, composed of men who had returned from summer detachments to Regina for the winter months, gave five performances. The bandsmen, in an effort to preserve life, limb and instruments, were usually unmounted. Regina "society", led by Lieutenant Governor E. Dewdney and Mrs. Dewdney, enthusiastically patronized the performances. This resulted in the satirical Toronto weekly, *The Grip*, characterizing the Ride as "Lady Dewdney's Own" and a great extravagance, whereas the riders should have been attending to their police duties.

Of the various groups of mounted policemen who had organized many volunteer bands since the earliest was formed at Swan River, North-West Territories, in 1876, many had often tried to develop mounted bands from already established unmounted ones, but only a few mounted bands survived even briefly. Undoubtedly the greatest problem arose from the fact that the horses, many of them broncos, couldn't be persuaded to walk with dignity while men on their backs made strange and frightening noises.

The earliest mounted band of recorded police history developed out of an unmounted band formed in 1886 by the police at Fort Macleod. At Fort Calgary a

An eleven-piece mounted NWMP band at Calgary in the early years. (RCMP Museum, Regina)

Training for the Ride in the early 1920s in Vancouver. (R. L. Trolove)

The "March Past" at St. Louis, Missouri, 1949. (C. W. Anderson)

few years later another mounted band emerged, although this one sometimes performed unmounted on as the occasion dictated.

From 1887 onward, unmounted bands gave much pleasure at NWMP headquarters in Regina, entertaining at concerts and playing at dances, formal and informal. In 1905 the bandsmen, some of them excellent musicians, tried to provide additional pleasure by forming a mounted band of the recently designated Royal North-West Mounted Police. Unfortunately many of the horses there, as elsewhere, were western broncos. During rehearsals they often stampeded as soon as the music started, although on a few occasions they allowed the band to perform.

Sometime later there came an important occasion at which Commissioner Perry expected to astound visiting officials with the Force's mounted band. As soon as the band began to play, the horses threw their riders and galloped off, eventually disappearing over the western horizon. The officer commanding headquarters ordered a telegram sent to the Moose Jaw detachment, about forty miles to the west, asking the detachment men to be on the lookout for some police horses last seen galloping in that direction. The runaway horses were caught later and returned to barracks, but there is no record of any subsequent performance by that Regina mounted band or any other mounted band of the RNWMP or the RCMP.

Meanwhile, the NWMP Musical Ride had soon acquired a reputation in both Canada and the United States. In 1887 a painting by the well-known American artist Frederic Remington, entitled "The Charge of the NWMP Musical Ride", appeared in *Harper's Weekly*, a notable American publication. The painting was highly romanticized. Remington's policemen were extremely dashing, and his horses had never been seen on the western prairies, and probably nowhere else, except perhaps among Arab sheiks and their followers.

For several years the Musical Ride was performed sporadically, but it became very popular nonetheless, especially on the prairies, which sadly lacked ceremonials and entertainment. The highlight of 1904 probably came for many prairie people when the Ride performed at annual agricultural fairs at Regina and Fort Qu'Appelle in the North-West Territories, and at Winnipeg and Brandon in Manitoba. After 1910, however, the number of performances dwindled, and from 1914 to 1918, during the First World War, other more pressing duties prevented any performances of the Ride.

Performances were resumed in 1920, when the Royal North-West Mounted Police became the Royal Canadian Mounted Police, and 160 horses were transferred with their riders to Ottawa, the nation's capital. While permanent barracks and stables were being built at Rockcliffe, a few miles from the centre of Ottawa, men and horses were accommodated at Lansdowne Park, the Ottawa Exhibition grounds. Training for the Ride began soon after the police arrived in mid-March. The next summer the Ride performed in Ottawa, marched 75 miles to Brockville to perform, and then marched back to Ottawa. No doubt the horses played a useful public relations role, especially as many eastern Canadians knew little or nothing about the Force, and presumed that the Mounted Police were in Ottawa mainly to guard public buildings.

From 1920 until the outbreak of the Second World War in 1939, two different

The Musical Ride at the Royal Winter Fair, Toronto, Ontario, 1949.

Musical Rides occasionally performed in various parts of Canada and the United States, one based at Rockcliffe, the other at Regina. Other Rides were occasionally trained, for local performance only, at other places where enough horses were stationed, in Vancouver, for example.

In 1924 in the absence of a complete Musical Ride, a ten-man mounted squad appeared at the Wembley Exhibition in London, England. In 1930 the Ride went to England for the first time, to perform at Olympia, also in London. In 1932 a trick riding team went to London.

In 1934 the Ride paid its first visit to New York City. The publicity and acclaim it received irked one constable who had been left behind at Rockcliffe. After the Musical Ride returned, he placed a notice on the bulletin board: "We have read about you in the newspapers, we have seen you in the newsreels, we have heard you over the air. Now you are back for God's sake don't talk about it."

Musical Ride horses being loaded on a plane at Ottawa, en route to Ireland, 1977.

Two years later the Ride again visited New York. Two members in uniform, sightseeing on Broadway, stopped in front of a theatre where large posters advertised a film about "The Royal Canadian Mounted". They began talking to the doorman, who was wearing a hybrid uniform of the Force, and soon a large crowd gathered to watch. A policeman friend of the doorman came to clear the sidewalk.

"Beat it, you guys!" he shouted at the two genuine policemen. "Get back to your own theatres!"

The Second World War prevented performances of Musical Rides during 1939-45, just as the First World War had prevented them earlier. During the Second World War, however, the Force did maintain its horse strength. This was also the point at which the breeding program was established at Fort Walsh, Saskatchewan.

After the war, mounted training of recruits was gradually resumed, and in 1948

The RCMP *Musical Ride on tour, using stabling accommodation in a hockey rink in Sydney, Nova Scotia, 1973.*

the Musical Ride was formed at Regina, with horses from the Regina and Rockcliffe stables. Although it was known as the first Ride with all-black horses, several of them would have been more accurately described as brownish-black. As if trying to make up for lost time, the 1948 Ride performed within a few months at the Royal Agricultural Fair in Toronto, and in the United States at Portland, Oregon; Harrisburg, Pennsylvania; and New York City.

Between 1949 and 1961 (although not every year), Musical Rides from Regina and Rockcliffe performed in Canada and the United States. In 1951 a Musical Ride troop provided an escort for Princess Elizabeth and Prince Philip when they visited Canada. Two years later, when Princess Elizabeth became Queen Elizabeth II, a Musical Ride troop acted as the RCMP contingent in her coronation procession. While the troop was in Britain it performed the Musical Ride in England and Scotland.

In 1961 the RCMP decided that the Musical Ride would be performed annually. Up to this time, in spite of numerous requests, it had been impossible to plan performances far in advance, as there had always been doubts about whether or not the Ride would be organized. The new policy would allow planning to proceed smoothly, even for years ahead.

From 1961 onward, a Musical Ride has been formed each year. In 1963 there were more performances than in any previous year: 120 performances in eighteen centres, before an estimated 608,000 people. In 1964 the Ride went to three Maritime provinces for the first time (excluding Newfoundland), and to six large American cities. The following year it made a more extensive tour of the United States, performing in Ohio, Michigan, Colorado, Wisconsin, Minnesota, Kentucky, Tennessee, Texas and Louisiana. On January 1, 1966, eighteen Musical Ride horses and their riders attended the Tournament of Roses parade in Pasadena, California, as an escort to British Columbia's float.

The year 1966 was a landmark one for the Musical Ride. For some years past, rumours had persisted that the RCMP would get rid of its horses. During 1966, however, the Canadian government decided to do away only with recruit equitation and to keep the Musical Ride as a public relations attraction. The Ride, henceforth, would be based in Rockcliffe, and equitation training would be given only to those riders who had not received such training as recruits in earlier years.

During 1966 the Ride performed at seven major exhibitions in western Canada. Then, with the RCMP band in attendance, it helped British Columbia celebrate its centennial year by visiting, for the first time, twelve small cities in that province. Later it appeared at the Ottawa Winter Fair. The Ride ended its busiest year to date by going to New York City, where it took part in Macy's Thanksgiving Day parade. The main purpose of this appearance was to further the advance publicity campaign for Canada's centennial the following year. By this time an estimated 1,373,000 persons had seen the Ride perform.

Canada's centennial year, 1967, was even busier for the Ride than the previous one. It performed in all Canadian provinces (except British Columbia, where it had performed in 1966), and it spent a week at Expo '67 in Montreal. The seventy-two performances during centennial year included several at Rockcliffe, its new home, and several in Newfoundland, where it had never before performed.

Since 1967 the RCMP Musical Ride, now firmly established, has continued to perform regularly in Canada and the United States and occasionally elsewhere. It travelled by air for the first time in 1968 when it flew from Washington, D.C., to

The Musical Ride at the Royal Agricultural Show in England (Windsor Castle is in the background), 1977.

Inside the stables at Rockcliffe, Ontario.

Bermuda, thus demonstrating the practicability of using planes to transport the Ride. In 1969 it flew across the Atlantic Ocean for the first time, to perform at Windsor and in other British cities, and in 1970 it flew across the Pacific Ocean for the first time, to perform at Expo '70 in Japan. The following year it flew to San Francisco, California. In 1974 the Ride again flew across the Atlantic, en route to Europe, where it gave performances in Belgium, Denmark, Holland, Switzerland and France. Transport between these countries was by horse van. This tour ended with a Channel crossing by boat to Britain, and after performing there, the Ride returned home to Canada by air.

The Ride did not leave the North American continent again until 1977 when it flew to Ireland to perform in several Irish cities. It then travelled to England by sea, and took part in Queen Elizabeth's Silver Jubilee procession from Buckingham Palace to St. Paul's Cathedral. Before flying home to Canada, it performed in cities in England, Wales and Scotland. From 1977 to 1984, the Musical Ride has performed only in Canada and the United States, although it continually receives requests from other countries.

Performances must be planned at least a year, and sometimes longer, in advance. Arrangements must be made for transporting the horses and their riders, for feeding and stabling the horses, and for housing the riders. Sometimes horses must be stabled in hockey rinks and in parking lots. On occasion, in parks or fields near the places where they perform, they use large tents for stables. Plans must cover periods up to six months when the Ride is on extended tours and travelling thousands of miles by land, sea and air in several foreign countries, such as when it performed in Britain and five continental European countries in 1974.

Performances of the Ride in foreign countries often have to wait several years until the RCMP receives enough requests to make a tour worthwhile for men and animals to travel to distant places. One consideration is that the costs incurred must be acceptable to those who have requested the Ride, since those sponsors pay all expenses.

Such extensive travel is harder on the horses than performing, and the policy adopted after 1966, of training three-year-olds for at least two years before they are used on the Ride, has proved invaluable. The animals can better withstand the rigours of travel once they have reached full adulthood, and consequently can remain longer with the Ride. The average age of Ride horses in 1982 was eleven, but two horses that year were eighteen years old, and one or two others were almost as old. Unless horses are injured, they usually remain with the Ride until they are too old for it, although some mares are retired earlier, to be used as brood mares.

Performances almost invariably elicit favourable comments. Some onlookers acclaim the horses' beauty and grace, some praise the overall colourful scene, while others admire the combination of the rhythmic music and the intricate equine movements. The Right Honourable Antony Head, Britain's Secretary of State at the time, and an expert on Musical Rides, wrote the following letter to Commissioner L. H. Nicholson after watching a performance at the Earl's Court Arena in London after the coronation of Queen Elizabeth II in 1953.

> I went yesterday to the Military Tournament and was particularly struck by the smoothness and precision with which your musical ride was carried out. I have twice had to train musical rides [as an officer of the Household Cavalry] myself and have seen many others. I would like to assure you that I have never before seen a ride so well executed. The dressing and timing were quite excellent and I do congratulate you on the movements of the ride, many of which were most original and most effective. I thought it was a performance more than worthy of the Canadian Mounted Police.

Even today, after an additional thirty years of RCMP breeding and training of its horses and of Musical Ride experience, such a response would be high praise indeed.

THE PERFORMANCE: MOVEMENTS AND MUSIC

The Musical Ride takes thirty-six horses on its travels. Thirty-two take part in the performance, one horse is used by the inspector in charge of the Ride, and the other three act as spares to replace sick or injured horses or those in need of a rest.

Thirty-three gleaming black horses prance into the arena, with the officer leading eight rows of four abreast, to the music of "The Maple Leaf Forever". Excited crowds immediately applaud, and the horses seem to respond to their excitement. The scarlet tunics of the riders glow, polished leather gleams, spurs glisten and the red and white pennons of the lances flutter, all adding to the brilliance of the scene.

The inspector in charge leads the Ride before the guest of honour, who stands in a conspicuous place in the grandstand to take the salute. The riders turn their heads and eyes to the right, the officer raises his sword, and the guest of honour acknowledges the salute. The Ride marches in column to the centre of the arena and halts, facing the guest of honour. The inspector rides forward, salutes the guest of honour, and in a loud voice asks his permission to begin the performance. When permission is given he signals the Musical Ride and then rides to the end of the arena. From this vantage point he watches the performance, which begins as soon as the music starts.

Generally a brass band is in attendance, sometimes the RCMP's own but more often a local one. In the latter circumstance, a member of the RCMP band is usually present to conduct, because of his familiarity with the music and the way in which it should be played. When the Ride occasionally performs in a small community with no band, music is supplied by the tapes, amplifiers, and loud speakers which are used by the Ride in training sessions.

The whole performance of the Musical Ride is based on the cavalry training of men and horses, and the manner in which they move in sections (fours), half-sections (twos), and singly, at either the trot or the canter. Only part of the performance, however, relates directly to cavalry drill movements. The entry of the Ride, in sections, into the performing arena, and the manner in which the horses then wheel, right or left, are based on cavalry drill. The last movement of the performance, "The Charge", is taken directly from a cavalry movement in battle, and the "March Past" at the end is a cavalry drill movement.

The figures of the Musical Ride are not drill movements, but have been choreographed so as to take advantage of the cavalry training of men and horses. The figures are formed by horses simulating such things as a wagon wheel, a gate, a star, a maze and a dome. In doing so they form intricate patterns, in sections, half-sections, and singly, often with considerable "threading of the needle" (horses crossing one another's paths), to arrive at figures which are easily recognized. As one figure is completed, the horses keep moving, now to the tune of carry-over music, and get into position to begin creating the next figure. The timing and co-ordination, and the control of the horses by their riders, are very important, although this is not always realized because of the apparent ease with which the figures are performed.

Between the two halves of the performance (the first half at the trot to music in 4/4 time, and the second half at the canter to music in 6/8 time), the horses rest while the riders perform a stationary mounted lance drill which simulates the use of the lance by old-time cavalry. Each rider moves his lance around his horse's body, especially the head, but his well-trained horse does not flinch.

As the second half of the performance nears its end, the horses form up in two ranks at one end of the arena. They stamp and fret, knowing what is to follow. A trumpet call rings out, exciting, strident and chilling—The Charge. That call is followed by a long drum roll, during which the riders in the front rank remove their lances from the lance buckets and arc them down to The Engage position. At a signal given by the rider on the lead horse at the extreme right of the front row, all the horses dash forward at a fast gallop, urged on by the wild cries of their riders. The Charge ends at the far end of the arena, and the riders in the front rank return their lances to their buckets. Another trumpet call—The Rally—rings out. The horses canter back to where they started The Charge and form up in the original eight rows, four abreast.

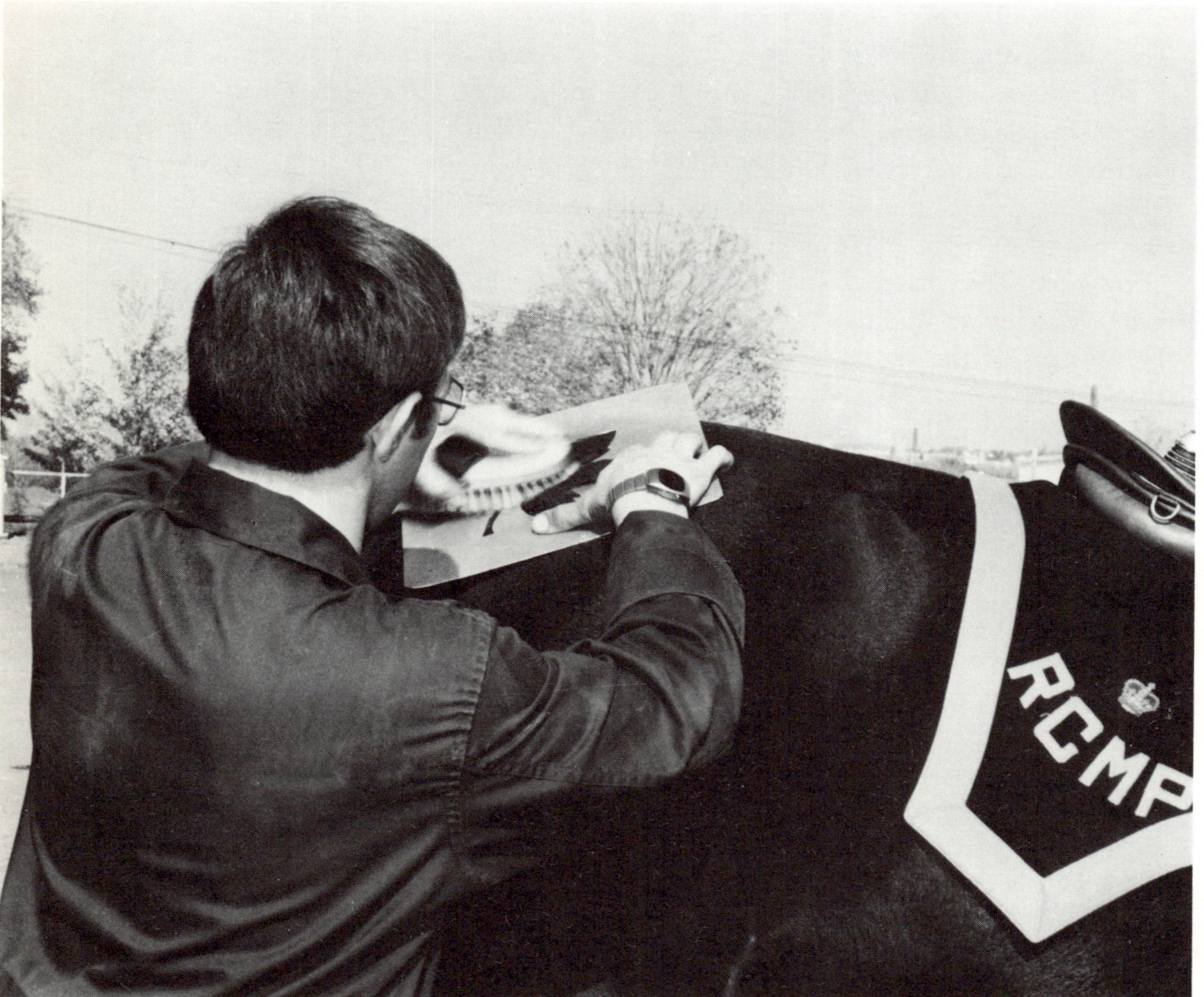

Before each performance of the Ride, a maple leaf is stencilled on both sides of every horse's rump. The dampened hair is brushed against its natural direction.

OPPOSITE: A dress rehearsal at Rockcliffe.

MP

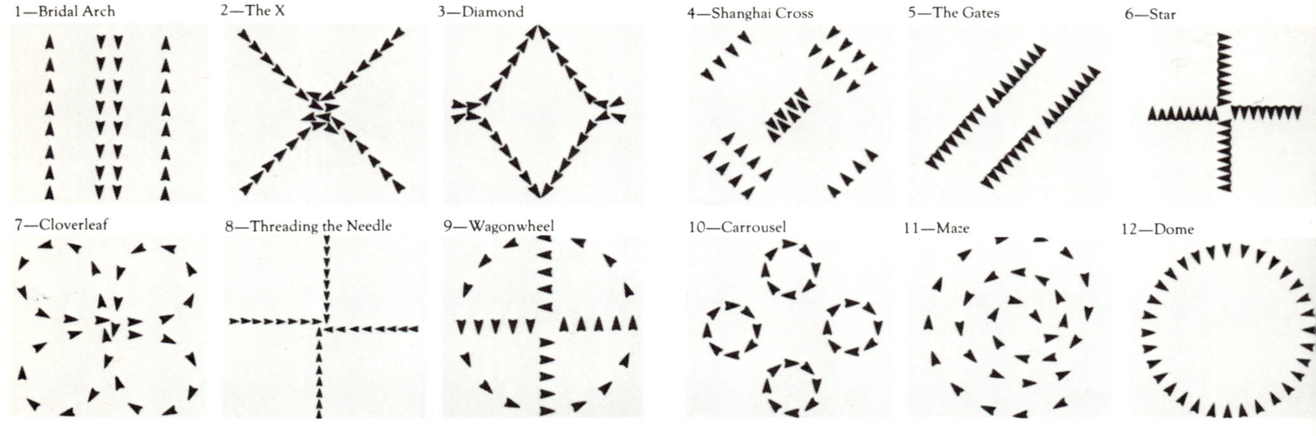

Some of the Musical Ride figures.

Musical Ride in training at Rockcliffe, Ontario, 1959.

The inspector then resumes his place at the head of the column, and as the band begins to play the RCMP "Regimental March", the Ride moves off in The March Past. Now the riders again pass the grandstand and salute the honoured guest. The horses prance out of the arena to the music, and the crowd applauds until the last one is out of sight.

Usually performances go smoothly, but riders sometimes lose their hats or inadvertently tilt them, or even, occasionally, fall off their horses.

Several riders fell during their performance at the World's Grain Show in Regina in 1933. An American flyer who had recently broken a continental speed record had been engaged to fly over the grounds during the afternoon. Although he happened to arrive during a Musical Ride performance, he swooped low over the grandstand and "buzzed" over the horses. The horses broke ranks and several threw their riders. The horses quickly re-formed, and all but one of the thrown riders managed to re-mount. One horse, however, refused to allow his rider to catch him, and at last the rider, tired of trying, stood to one side as the Ride continued without him. The riderless horse performed perfectly. When the horses lined up for the Charge the rider managed to re-mount, to the sustained applause of the delighted crowd, who were probably not so much applauding the rider as the horse.

Music played during performances of the Musical Ride varies from year to year and within a given year. In the accompanying list of examples, the tunes under the trot heading, while always played for trot figures, are not always played for the same trot figures each time. It is the trot rhythm (4/4 time), not the tune, that is important. The same principle applies to the canter (6/8 time) portion of the performance. Nevertheless, certain tunes in both trot and canter sections are invariably played for specific figures; for example, the tune "Buttons and Bows" is always played for the "Bridal Arch" figure, and the tune "Wagon Wheels" for the "Wagonwheel" figure. Some music is used for all performances, year after year: "The Maple Leaf Forever", the trumpet calls for "The Charge" and "The Rally", and the Royal Canadian Mounted Police "Regimental March".

Lance drill, like the canter movements and figures, is performed to music in 6/8 time. The thrust of the lance is made on the count of one, with a rest on counts two and three, then the parry, a defensive movement in actual combat, is made on count four, with a rest on counts five and six. The next thrust uses the same timing, and so on to the end of the drill.

Popular Melodies of Musical Accompaniment
for the Musical Ride

The March On (4/4 time)	"The Maple Leaf Forever"
Trot (4/4 time)	"Vive La Canadienne"
	"Ca-na-da"
	"Raindrops Keep Falling on My Head"
	"Buttons and Bows"
	"Alouette"
	"Canadian Sunset"
	"Wagon Wheels"
	"The Keel Row"
	"The Surrey with the Fringe on Top"
	"Country Gardens"
Lance Drill (6/8 time)	"The Last Gleam"
	"Blow the Man Down"
	"All Day on the Prairie"
Canter (6/8 time)	"Hey Look Me Over"
	"Irish Regimental Marches"
	"The Campbells Are Coming"
	"Bonnie Dundee"
	"A Hundred Pipers"
	"Repaz Band"
Charge	"Trumpet Call—The Charge"
Rally	"Trumpet Call—The Rally"
March Past (4/4 time)	"The Royal Canadian Mounted Police Regimental March"

Commissioner R. H. Simmonds inspects the Ride before its first public performance in 1981.

The "March On".

The "Wagonwheel".

The "Bridal Arch".

The "Dome", which is pictured on the back of the Canadian fifty-dollar bill.

The "Cloverleaf".

The exciting final movement—the "Charge".

A head-on view of the "Charge".

THE RIDERS

Before the abolition of recruit equitation training in 1966, riders were usually chosen from the squads graduating in the spring of the year. They were expected to perform throughout the season, usually summer and autumn.

The only exception to this practice occurred in 1953, when the Queen Elizabeth II Coronation contingent was the first such contingent to perform the Musical Ride. These riders, as were the members of the coronation contingents of 1911 and 1937, were chosen from the working members throughout the Force. The members of the Coronation-Musical Ride contingent of 1953 were mostly young men from all the Divisions, with at least five years' service. All of them had had equitation training, and some had previous Musical Ride experience. After taking part in the coronation procession, they performed the Musical Ride for two full weeks at the Royal Tournament at Earl's Court Arena in London, and then went to Scotland to perform at the Royal Scottish Agricultural Show at Alloa. Upon returning home, the riders, as usual, returned to regular police duties.

Since 1966, all members of the Musical Ride have been volunteers. They have completed their police training, which does not include equitation, and have been working as regular members of the Force in various parts of Canada.

Each year thirty-six volunteers, usually in three groups of twelve, receive a three-month preliminary course in equitation. Then eighteen members are chosen to begin three months of actual Musical Ride training during the late autumn and winter, so that they will be ready to perform the following spring. At the end of this training period each member is assigned to the horse which he will ride in the Musical Ride and which will remain with him during his Musical Ride service.

Members serve for two years only, and the eighteen newly trained members replace the eighteen men on the Ride who have completed their two years. Thus, at the beginning of each performance year, there are eighteen members with one year's experience and eighteen newly trained riders.

Although the riders have never held permanent positions, some of the riding instructors have had more or less permanent careers as such. All instructors have received RCMP basic training and have done police work in various parts of Canada before becoming instructors. Few of them, if any, joined the Force to become riding instructors, and in due course some of them request permission to return to the practical police work for which they were trained. These requests might come about because the routine of instructing no longer appeals to them, or because

there is a limit to promotional opportunity within the small staff of instructors at the Rockcliffe stables. When they do leave, they are replaced by younger men who have taken equitation training and who have shown an aptitude for the work of instruction.

Until 1981 all the riders were men, although women had been serving as regular members of the Force since 1974. There had always been some doubt about the ability of women to withstand the daily routine of the Ride, which includes the lifting of heavy kit boxes, and there was also some doubt as to whether women could satisfactorily wield the heavy lances during Musical Ride lance drill. In 1980, however, women were allowed to volunteer for the Ride. Six volunteers were accepted for the preliminary equitation course, and two of them were chosen to take the specialized training. They performed satisfactorily with the 1981 Musical Ride, and each year since then two women members have participated in the Ride.

THE LANCE

The lance, which has become an important part of the Musical Ride equipment, was first taken west by the North-West Mounted Police in 1874. Advisors to the Canadian government believed that scarlet-coated riders carrying lances would impress the Indians they would encounter on their westward march, and later during prairie patrols.

The lance, with a shaft of male bamboo, is approximately nine feet in length, including the 12½-inch chrome-plated steel tip at the lance point and the 6¾-inch chrome-plated steel butt at the other end. It is from 1 inch to 1¼ inches in diameter and weighs about 3 pounds 14 ounces; the point of balance is at the top of the leather hand grip. The Force's saddler at Rockcliffe makes the lances, puts on the 18-inch dark brown leather grip about 24 inches from the steel butt, and adds a white leather sling above the grip. The carpenter puts on the steel butt and tip, and finally a red and white crimped pennon is attached to the top of the lance below the point.

The pennon supplied to the NWMP on its March West was of a British regulation pattern in red and white. The authoritative *Journal of the Society for Army Historical Research* (Vol. XXV, p. 95) states: "When the four Light Dragoon regiments were converted into Lancers in 1816 they were given the uniform borrowed from that of the Polish Lancers of Napoleon's Guard, and it is noteworthy that the lance pennons of the British Army have always been of the Polish national colours, red and white."

Half-section wheeling in a Ride movement.

MP

The British custom of crimping the pennon came from their own 16th Lancers. That regiment was so heavily engaged in the Battle of Aliwal in 1845, in northwest India during the First Sikh War, that the next day their pennons were so matted with blood that they looked stiff and starched. Later the 16th Lancers crimped their pennons in memory of that battle, and other British lancers adopted the custom, which continued even after lances were used only for ceremonial purposes.

The assignment of colours is a royal prerogative, and with the approval of King George V, a Canadian proclamation dated November 21, 1921, assigned red and white to Canada as its national colours. Consequently the Mounted Policeman, as he rides his horse on ceremonial occasions, could hold no more appropriate colours aloft on his lance.

During the Musical Ride the men perform their stationary lance drill to music about half-way through the performance. Lance drill, which allows the horses to rest before the second half of the performance begins, was never part of recruit equitation training, and only the riders in the Musical Ride have ever been required to learn it. When the lance is carried upright its butt rests in a leather "bucket" attached to the right stirrup, but it is removed when certain figures in the Ride are performed. When it is carried parallel to the ground during "The Charge", it is said to be in The Engage position.

One of the two female members of the 1981 Musical Ride in full dress carrying her lance at rest in the lance bucket attached to her stirrup.

Queen Elizabeth II arriving on Parliament Hill in Ottawa to open Parliament.

7

Special Occasions

Ceremonial Occasions in Canada's Capital

Since 1952, when Governor General Vincent Massey initiated the practice, the RCMP has provided a mounted escort for governors general en route to Parliament Hill for the opening of Parliament. The RCMP also provides a "Sovereign's Escort" for Queen Elizabeth when, being in Canada, she goes to open Parliament or to visit or address the House.

A full escort for such occasions is made up from members of the Musical Ride: usually thirty-two mounted men and two mounted officers, plus two postillion riders and two other men who ride on the raised seat at the rear of the landau. The guidon, the regimental flag, or Colour, is usually paraded, and this entails an additional three mounted men, one carrying the guidon and two acting as escorts.

The original guidon of the RCMP was presented to the Force in 1935 by Lord Bessborough, then governor general of Canada and representative of King George VI. The presentation recognized the role of the Force in every Canadian military venture from the time of the North-West Rebellion in 1885, mention of which is inscribed on the guidon.

Traditional use of such a guidon goes back to the days when knights in battle carried standards and guidons. The use of standards was reserved for such senior military units as the Household Cavalry Regiments in Britain, while guidons were allotted to lesser units such as the Lancers and Dragoons. When classified according to its Colour, the RCMP is considered in the latter category, although it follows the British system by tradition rather than by obligation.

The main difference in appearance between standards and guidons is that standards are uniformly square or oblong, while guidons come to a double point or swallow tail. The RCMP guidon, of scarlet cloth fringed with gold, displays the badge of the Force surrounded by battle honours and crests. In 1973, the centennial year of the Force, Queen Elizabeth II presented the RCMP with the present guidon, which contains the most recent honours for military service during the Second World War.

The landau is a special type of four-wheeled carriage with a top of which the front and back halves can be raised and lowered separately as befits the occasion or the weather. Four specially trained RCMP horses draw the landau, two behind two, with the near (left) horses ridden by two scarlet-tunicked riders, postillion fashion. Two other members of the Force ride on the high seat behind the body of the landau, ready to assist passengers to enter or alight.

The landau was built in the 1890s in Melbourne, Australia, of hand-wrought iron and hand-carved wood, for the Earl of Hopetoun, then Australian governor general. When the earl returned to England he took the landau with him.

In 1904 when Earl Grey became governor general of Canada, he bought the carriage from the Earl of Hopetoun for $4,000. Later, when Earl Grey's term as governor general ended, he gave the landau to Canada for use by his successors. They continued to use it until Viscount Willingdon became governor general in 1926, after which a car was used for ceremonial purposes.

On the appointment of Vincent Massey as governor general in 1952, the landau was taken out of storage, and since then it has been used again for ceremonial purposes. In 1971, sixty-seven years after the landau was brought to Canada, it was completely restored for the first time.

The RCMP horses that draw the landau wear what is officially called postillion harness. When it became necessary in 1977 to replace the fifty-year-old harness, the only manufacturer the Force could find was in England. The 1977 harness was made by hand from the hides of nine heifers and two calves.

Although the harness, like the landau, is stored by the RCMP, it is the property of the governor general and hence carries royal crests. Stylized maple leaves and all the royal crests from the previous collar harness have been incorporated into the newly designed breastplates. The new harness was used for the first time on October 18, 1977, when Queen Elizabeth II rode in the landau, escorted by the RCMP, to open the third session of the thirtieth Parliament of Canada.

As the RCMP Musical Ride is based at Rockcliffe, near Ottawa, men and horses of the Ride are often called upon to perform various ceremonial duties. Some of these duties, like the escorting of governors general and heads of state, are

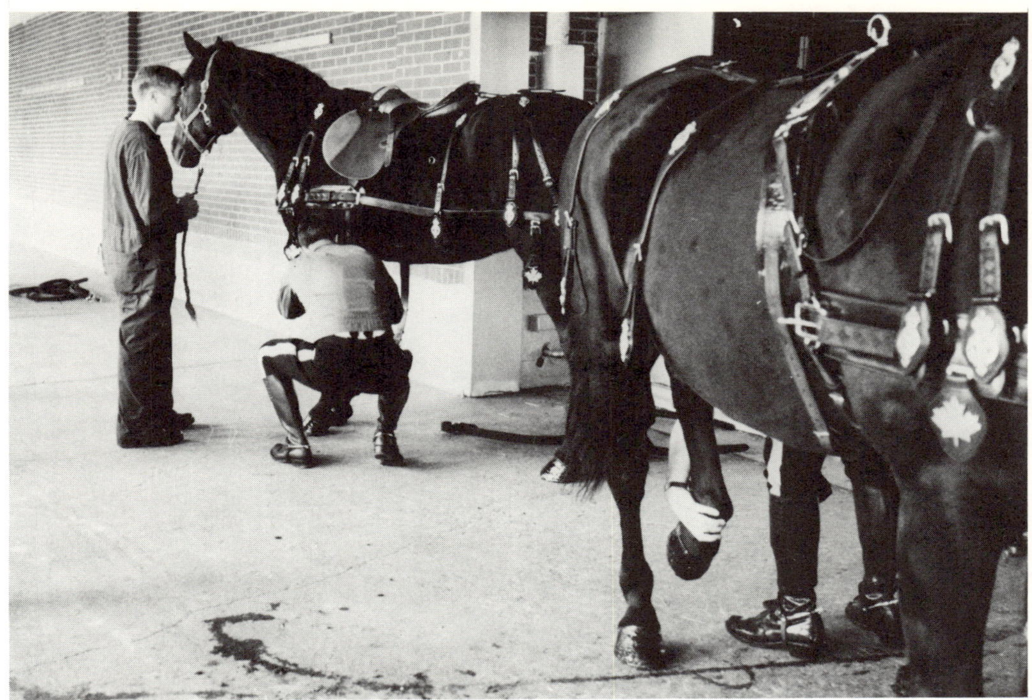

Getting the landau horses ready at Rockcliffe stables.

conducted with the utmost formality and decorum. Others, like the annual Ottawa Children's Christmas parade in which only a few horses and riders take part, are considerably more informal and less elaborate.

It is customary for the RCMP to provide mounted escorts for ambassadors newly arrived in Canada. Each new ambassador is escorted from the Lester B. Pearson Building (which houses the Department of External Affairs) to Government House, where he presents his credentials to the governor general. Later the mounted escort accompanies him back to the Lester B. Pearson Building. The ambassador rides in the landau drawn, as usual, by four horses with two postillion riders, while the rest of the escort on such occasions consists of a mounted officer and four mounted men.

In 1980 a mounted honour party carrying the Colour of the Force took part in a sombre ceremony when the body of the late John Diefenbaker, former Prime Minister of Canada, was taken from the Parliament Buildings to a local church. Also in 1980, the RCMP provided a full mounted escort for President José Lopez Portillo of Mexico when he went to Parliament Hill to address Members of Parliament in the House of Commons. In 1981 a similar escort was provided for President Ronald Reagan of the United States when he went to address Members of Parliament.

Governor-General Vincent Massey preferred this older style of livery for the RCMP carriage riders.

The Musical Ride horses took part in many extra duties in 1981 when Canada played host to the heads of state of various nations who attended an economic conference at Montebello, Quebec. As each head of state arrived at Montebello, about fifty miles east of Ottawa, he or she was met by an honour guard of four mounted members of the Force. A similar guard of honour was on duty on Parliament Hill as each head of state arrived there for the concluding meeting of the conference.

It is now traditional for the RCMP to provide men on beautiful black horses to take part in welcoming important visitors to Canada's capital. Thousands of other visitors ask to see a "mountie" and his horse, thanks to the world-wide publicity that has made the RCMP the most romanticized police force in the world. Indeed, many people from other countries perceive the Mounted Police and their horses as the unique symbol of Canada. Perhaps that explains why a scarlet-tunicked member of the RCMP and his horse, on duty on Parliament Hill during the summer months, are one of the most photographed subjects in Ottawa. In a country that pays scant attention to pageantry, the glamorous RCMP and their sleek black horses will always be popular.

OPPOSITE: *Children's Day at Rockcliffe.*

JUBILEES AND CORONATIONS

The first mounted troop of the Force ever to leave Canada was a contingent of NWMP members which sailed to England in 1897. Its mission was to attend Queen Victoria's Diamond Jubilee which, being the sixtieth anniversary of Queen Victoria's ascension to the British throne, elicited great rejoicing, jubilation and pageantry. Hence the gathering of military and other units in London in 1897, including units from the colonies, as they were then called, to take part in the Diamond Jubilee procession. In June 1897, Superintendent A. B. Perry, Inspector R. Belcher, thirty NCOs and constables, and twenty-seven horses formed a contingent which, after training, left the prairie city of Regina for London. All the horses except one had been raised, up to the age of four years, on western ranches.

A trans-Atlantic crossing during the last part of the nineteenth century took from ten days to two weeks, and much longer during stormy weather such as the NWMP and their horses encountered. The horses suffered terribly in their cramped quarters in the hold of the ship, small by today's standards, ruthlessly and interminably tossed by the huge waves. Three horses died at sea.

Fortunately, the horses of that contingent of 1897 were not required to make the return journey to Canada. One of them was the horse ridden the previous year by Sergeant W. B. Wilde when he was shot and killed while attempting to arrest the Indian, Charcoal. Sergeant Wilde had been a member of the Life Guards before he emigrated from England to Canada, and his horse was presented to that regiment by the Canadian prime minister, Sir Wilfrid Laurier, who had gone to London for the Jubilee celebrations. The other twenty-three horses were presented to the British government.

In 1902, a horseless contingent of twenty-four members of the NWMP went by sea to England for the coronation of King Edward VII, who had succeeded his mother, Queen Victoria. The coronation was postponed, however, because of the king's illness, and the NWMP returned home. Later that year, when the coronation did take place, two other NWMP members went to represent the Force. They were Sergeant-Major Knight and Sergeant Richardson, VC, who had won his Victoria Cross in the Boer War, recently ended. During the coronation procession, the two men rode in the colonial escort on borrowed horses. Probably the unfortunate experience of shipping horses across the Atlantic five years earlier had influenced the Canadian government's decision not to send any horses to King Edward VII's coronation. If it had taken place as originally planned, most likely the whole NWMP contingent would have ridden in the procession on borrowed horses.

The RNWMP contingent to the coronation of George V in 1911.

The RCMP contingent to the coronation of George VI on parade at the Regina barracks, 1937.

Corona, born in 1924 and destroyed in 1956 at thirty-two years of age, was the last surviving equine member of the 1937 coronation contingent, and a veteran of many Musical Rides. (T. V. Little photo, Ottawa)

To be a member of a contingent representing the Force overseas is always an honour, and it must have been a great disappointment to the men of the 1902 group who did not, after all their intensive preparations, share in the excitement and the celebrations. Preparations for such special contingents include choosing the best horses and saddlery, and new uniforms and special training for the men, who also have been chosen with care, as representatives of the various Divisions of the Force. Especially in the early days, the Force made great efforts to ensure that its contingents were as smart and as well trained as possible, in order to compete favourably with military contingents from Britain and from other parts of the Empire (now the Commonwealth). As "colonials", they knew that they would be critically scrutinized, especially by the home-based British. Fortunately for the "colonial units" of NWMP members over the years, they were invariably and publicly praised for their smartness in processions.

Two RCMP horses of the contingent to Queen Elizabeth's coronation grazing after being unloaded at the London docks, 1953. Robert Simmonds, the constable holding the horses, later became commissioner. (P. A. Reuter)

In 1911, a mounted troop of seven officers, seventy-five NCOs and men, and eighty horses of the RNWMP crossed the Atlantic by ship to attend the coronation of King George V, but this time the horses travelled with less discomfort. The members of the troop had been selected from the whole Force, in numbers that varied with the strength of the various Divisions. A few men had been selected from the Yukon, but they had died in the ill-fated MacPherson-Dawson patrol (by dogteam) earlier that same year, without knowing that they had been chosen for the honour of joining the coronation troop.

The horses also travelled well in 1937, when the RCMP sent a contingent of two officers, thirty-five NCOs and men, and thirty-five horses, again by sea, to share in the coronation celebration of King George VI. After the coronation, the men and horses were invited to the Royal Mews at Buckingham Palace, for a private review by King George, Queen Elizabeth, and the young princesses, Elizabeth and Mar-

The RCMP 1953 coronation contingent marching from the London docks through the city en route to their tent stables in Hyde Park. (P. A. Reuter)

garet. It was rumoured that Princess Elizabeth had made a special request, by way of her mother, for this review of the men and horses of the RCMP, so that she and her sister could have a close view of the scarlet-tunicked men and their famous horses.

Sixteen years later, in 1953, when Princess Elizabeth was crowned Queen Elizabeth II, another RCMP coronation contingent travelled to London. Of its forty-six men and forty-six horses, four men and four horses would act as escorts for the Canadian prime minister, the Right Honourable Mr. Louis St. Laurent. Four of the other horses would be ridden by senior army officers, who had practiced riding at the Rockcliffe barracks for three months before the contingent left Canada. Thirty-six other horses and their riders would march in the coronation procession, and the remaining horses and men would act as spares.

Under the command of Assistant Commissioner D. McGibbon, the coronation

The 1953 contingent training in Hyde Park. (Spice Photos)

OVERLEAF: *The coronation parade, 1953. (Keystone London News Agency)*

contingent of 1953 made the last sea voyage of a mounted group of RCMP en route to London or the continent of Europe. Henceforth such visits would be made by air. Compared with the disastrous sea voyage of the Diamond Jubilee contingent in 1897, the sea voyage of the 1953 Coronation contingent was luxurious. During a smooth crossing, the horses travelled in a CPR freighter with ten men to attend them, while the rest of the party travelled in the comfort of an ocean liner. As they had left Canada on April 25, more than five weeks before coronation day, the men had plenty of time in London, not merely for training and for cleaning their equipment, but even for sightseeing, and the horses had time for a rest.

The senior author of this book, then Inspector W. H. Kelly, was stationed in London at that time as the liaison officer between the RCMP and European police and security agencies; hence he was on hand to make arrangements for the billeting of the men and the stabling of the horses. On one occasion when he visited the

HEROES

tent-stables in Hyde Park, he found two RCMP corporals laughing hilariously. They could only explain by pointing wordlessly to two men nearby, looking at the horses. When at last they could speak, they made sarcastic remarks about the appearance of the two visitors, who were dressed exactly alike, in dark trousers, short black jackets vulgarly known as "bum freezers", and gleaming black patent leather shoes. They also wore extremely small black bowler hats ridiculously high on their heads, and they carried walking sticks. Kelly, who had been based in London for eighteen months, at first perceived them only as ordinary "men about town", but then he recognized them as two very senior officers of the Canadian Joint Staff located at Ennismore Gardens, not far from Hyde Park. The corporals became incensed that these Canadians had become so over-Anglicized. As Kelly left, he heard them muttering heartfelt prayers that the two army officers would soon be ordered back to Canada, to be promptly re-Canadianized.

The 1953 coronation contingent differed from earlier such units in being, at the same time, the Musical Ride. The horses, too, differed from earlier coronation and jubilee contingents in being all blacks. Although the Musical Ride horses in the autumn of 1948 had been accepted as blacks, actually some of them were very dark bays and others had brown patches. During the following five years, true blacks had been added as they were bred and trained, so that by 1953 the coronation Musical Ride contingent was truly an all black horse Musical Ride group. It must have been a great satisfaction to ex-Commissioner S. T. Wood, by that time a special constable at the breeding ranch in the Cypress Hills of Saskatchewan, to know that a RCMP unit with all black horses would, on coronation day, June 2, parade along the very London streets where, years earlier, he had seen the Household Cavalry with their scarlet tunics and black horses and had conceived the idea of using black horses for the Force.

Coronation day dawned cold and wet. Soon after the mounted escort for the Right Honorable Mr. Louis St. Laurent left the Hyde Park tent-stables, the coronation troop also moved out, to take its place in the procession, and then to stand there in intermittent rain for more than two hours, with the men dismounted, waiting for the conclusion of the coronation ceremony taking place in Westminster Abbey. When the ceremony ended, Queen Elizabeth II and her entourage emerged from the great Abbey. The Queen and H.R.H. the Duke of Edinburgh entered the "golden" State Coach, and the long procession began to move.

In spite of the rain, heavy by this time, pomp and ceremony prevailed. The units of the red-coated Foot Guards, in tall bearskin hats, marching like jointed toy

Selected RCMP members and horses of the 1953 contingent in a BBC television studio.

soldiers; the horsemen of the Household Cavalry in beplumed helmets clattering along; and the more than a dozen bands of 2,000 bandsmen; constituted only a small part of the whole procession that wound its circuitous way along five miles of elaborately decorated, rain-washed London streets.

The cold, wet weather seemed not to diminish the cheers of the three million people standing on sidewalks, watching from windows, or sitting in stands built along the route. Nevertheless, by the end of the parade, the swords of the RCMP officers and the carbines of the men showed signs of rust, the brims of their soggy stetsons drooped, and streams of rain flowed from their horses and saddlery. The RCMP contingent, which was, of course, only one small segment of Canada's official representation, elicited rousing cheers all along the route, especially when it passed Canada House in Trafalgar Square. Indeed, one London newspaper remarked that, after Her Majesty and Sir Winston Churchill, the RCMP and the Queen of Tonga, who had declined to ride in a closed carriage in spite of the downpour, shared the greatest acclaim of the crowds.

A private inspection at the request of Her Majesty Queen Elizabeth II at the Royal Mews at Buckingham Palace, after her coronation in 1953. (P. A. Reuter)

Four members of Canada's armed forces on RCMP horses they used in London for the 1953 coronation procession. These men trained at Rockcliffe for their appearance in the procession.

On June 10, the RCMP and their horses moved from the tent-stables in Hyde Park to the Earl's Court Arena in the west end of London. There, for ten days, the Musical Ride performed twice a day at the Royal Tournament, a military tournament held annually since 1880. The Musical Ride faced stiff competition from the performances of such British units as the King's Troop of the Royal Artillery, the

Household Cavalry and the King's Squad Royal Marines, but the crowd's applause indicated that the Musical Ride was one of the most popular displays. From London the Ride entrained for Alloa, the host city that year for the Royal Highland and Agricultural Show, thirty miles from Edinburgh, Scotland. The Ride performed at Alloa twice daily for a week.

After the Ride returned to London, Queen Elizabeth invited the RCMP coronation contingent to visit the Royal Mews at Buckingham Palace. There, on the afternoon of July 7, Her Majesty, H.R.H. the Duke of Edinburgh, Prince Charles and Princess Anne privately reviewed a contingent of RCMP men and horses, just as Princess Elizabeth, her sister and her parents had done in 1937 after the coronation of her father, King George VI. Queen Elizabeth and the Duke of Edinburgh spoke to each man, while the children looked on. The Queen asked the men about their work, about their homes in Canada, and especially about the horses they rode, and she made favourable comments to the commanding officer about the part the troop had played in her coronation procession.

Twenty-five years later, in 1977, eighty years after Queen Victoria's Diamond Jubilee, another Musical Ride troop went to help celebrate Queen Elizabeth's Silver Jubilee. This time horses and riders flew across the Atlantic as far as Ireland, en route to London, where they were scheduled to take part in the Jubilee procession from Buckingham Palace to St. Paul's Cathedral. In Ireland the Musical Ride performed in several cities before travelling by ship across the stormy Irish Sea to England, where they were also scheduled to ride in the Lord Mayor of London's procession a few days before the Jubilee procession.

Severe storms over the Irish Sea delayed their arrival in England, and they missed the Lord Mayor's procession. The only RCMP member who did take part in it was the man who had flown to London to ensure that arrangements for his fellow riders were in order. In the absence of the Ride horses, and no doubt much to his chagrin, he took part in the Lord Mayor's procession by riding in a carriage.

Fortunately, the rest of the RCMP contingent arrived in London in plenty of time to take part in Queen Elizabeth II's Jubilee procession. Also in that procession were two former RCMP horses presented some years earlier to Her Majesty. Centenial, ridden by the Prince of Wales, and Burmese, ridden by the Crown Equerry, Sir John Miller, followed immediately behind the "golden" State Coach which carried the Queen and the Duke of Edinburgh. After the Jubilee celebrations, and before returning to Canada by air, the RCMP contingent remained in the British Isles to perform the Musical Ride in various English, Scottish and Welsh cities.

The RCMP escort en route to Government House.

Three members of an RCMP royal escort. The centre member carries the Force's guidon, which is always part of a royal escort.

Governor-General Madame Sauvé and her husband with full RCMP *escort leaving Parliament Hill after she was sworn in on May 14, 1984. (The Citizen, Ottawa)*

U.S. president, Ronald Reagan, thanks his RCMP *escort on their arrival at Government House, March 1981.*

Tent pegging by an RCMP rider in NWMP uniform, 1973.

Practicing synchronized display jumping.

SPORTS AND EXHIBITIONS

Public displays of horsemanship have long been traditional for mounted organizations, both military and police. Although the Musical Ride has always been the most popular of the Force's exhibitions of riding, over the years men and horses have also given, and still give, other demonstrations of their skills, particularly on sports days.

The Force has originated such days wherever there were enough men and horses stationed to make the effort worthwhile, some of the earliest being held at Fort Walsh in the early 1880s, with Indians as both spectators and participants. The police consistently had the advantage in the unmounted game of football, although on one occasion an Indian, shouldered and sent flying by a constable, made an effort to diminish that advantage by trying to catch and scalp the constable, who fortunately outraced his pursuer to the safety of the fort. In the sport of bareback wrestling, however (the object of which was to wrestle the opponent from his horse), the Indians always won.

During the earliest years of the Force's history, sports days were held at the forts which housed the original Divisions "A", "B", "C", "D", "E" and "F", and in later years at western cities where a sufficient number of men and horses were stationed in barracks, such as at Regina, Calgary and Edmonton. As settlers flocked to the prairies, the Mounted Police barracks became the centres of social activity, including not only sports days, but also garden parties in summer, and dances during the autumn and winter. In those days, however, when horses provided the main form of transportation, the general public was very knowledgeable about horses and riding. This, coupled with the fact that entertainment was less readily available than in later years, meant that the police displays of horsemanship were especially popular. Some, but not all, sports days included the Musical Ride. Sometimes, too, the police held gymkhanas in which the families of members of the Force participated.

Usually, however, only the Mounted Police took part, in events that needed special skills. Tent pegging, for example, required the rider to gallop with an outstretched lance, and use the lance to pierce a four-inch-wide piece of wood that had been pounded into the ground like a tent peg, after which he carried off the "peg" on his lance, held high aloft. The "Ring and Peg" event also had galloping horsemen, lances pointed forward, shoulder high, each rider trying to push his lance point through a small ring suspended at the rider's eye level from a high post.

A group of trick riders at an RCMP gymkhana held at the Regina barracks in the late 1920s.

In addition to the usual straightforward jumping contests, others required the rider not only to urge his horse over obstacles, but at the same time to shoot at balloons tied to the obstacles, or to pierce such balloons with a sword.

Other popular events for individual competition included wrestling on horseback, musical chairs, and obstacle races over courses littered with barrels. The wheelbarrow race required a rider to dash from a starting point to a second point, where there was a wheelbarrow containing a passenger, usually a pretty girl. He then got off his horse and wheeled the barrow to a third point, taking his horse with him. There he remounted and galloped back to his starting point. Team events also found favour, especially the "Balaclava Mêlée", which set riders, protected by helmets and masks, attacking each other with long truncheons. The "Post and Ball" game, in which two opposing mounted teams tried to push a ball about four feet in diameter across the opponents' goal line, was mild in comparison.

Sergeant C. Walker, a graduate of an English cavalry school, served with the RCMP as a riding instructor for many years.

The most nerve wracking of all displays at Mounted Police sports days was the "Victoria Cross" event, aptly named after the Victoria Cross medal, which is awarded for conspicuous valour in battle, invariably involving the saving of life at the risk of the recipient's own. Entrants in the "Victoria Cross" event lined up at one end of a short track, at the other end of which was a dummy tied to a post. The dummy represented a wounded comrade, and the object of the contest was to rescue that comrade, and to carry him, on horseback, to the "safety" of the starting point. Making the rescue more difficult, men flanked the dummy, armed with revolvers, rifles and shotguns from which they shot blank ammunition at the approaching horses and riders.

It was difficult at the best of times as riders tried to coax their frightened horses forward. Snorting animals wheeled and reared. Riders fell, and only the lucky ones caught their horses and remounted to face more gunfire. The snorting and

Spearing the balloon with a sword while taking a fence.

Shooting the balloon while taking a fence.

trampling of the horses, the explosions from the guns and the utter confusion of the riderless horses and dismounted men created chaos. Only the most phlegmatic of horses could be persuaded to help rescue the "wounded man".

A "Victoria Cross" event at a Calgary field day in the early 1900s ended in even more than the usual chaos. Some of the police had hauled an ancient seven-pounder field gun from the barracks square to the gymkhana grounds and placed it near the dummy, to be fired with black powder and a light wad to add to the noise at the height of the battle. The constable delegated to fire the field gun also, on his own initiative, stuffed a piece of turf into the barrel for a more realistic effect. As the frightened horses snorted and screamed, the boom of the cannon resounded amid the barrage of the defending force. The chunk of turf slammed into the rump of a terrified horse, which bucked off its rider and bolted. Weaving his way among the distraught horses and their confused riders, the dismounted constable lashed out at every man he encountered, and even the spectators were forced to back away. There is no record of who, if anyone, won that "Victoria Cross" contest, or if the Calgary incident was the reason that the event has since been deleted from the Force's exhibitions of horsemanship.

Since the mid-1920s, after the RNWMP became the RCMP and moved its headquarters to Ottawa, spectacular sports days have been held at Rockcliffe, Ontario, where, near Ottawa, the new "N" Division was established to receive the men and horses transferred from western to eastern Canada. In 1949, the year after the Musical Ride was re-formed, having been disbanded early in the Second World War, "N" Division held an equestrian sports day with about three thousand guests in attendance. The program closely resembled those of earlier days: Individual Jumping; Individual Tentpegging (Lance); Individual Tentpegging (Sword); Half-Section Jumping; Section Tentpegging (Sword); Post and Ball Race; Musical Chairs; Wheelbarrow Race; Bareback Wrestling; Balaclava Mêlée.

During 1973, in celebration of the Force's centenary, a large RCMP exhibition travelled all over Canada giving various displays, including those of police dogs, choir singing, physical training, and music by the RCMP band. Since the Musical Ride was often performing in other parts of Canada during that centennial year, equitation horses travelled with the exhibition and, with their riders in old-time uniforms, they gave many displays of riding proficiency. Like all exhibitions of the Force, the centenary displays were well received, although most likely no RCMP group will ever be more popular than the famous Musical Ride.

Practicing for a trick riding display.

The "Balaclava Mêlée".

THE FORCE AND HOLLYWOOD

Although artists and authors have used the Force and its horses as popular subjects ever since artist Henri Julien accompanied the NWMP on its March West in 1874, Hollywood has given it the most publicity.

Some films, even those made in consultation with the Mounted Police, have distorted the true image of the police and their horses by overly romanticizing and glamorizing them in the interests of the box office. This has often irked members of the Force. In fact, Commissioner James MacBrien proposed during the 1930s that the word "mounted" be dropped from the Force's title in order to portray it more realistically, as a modern, efficient law-enforcement body. But the general appeal of the "Mounted" Police was too strong with the Canadian public, and nothing came of MacBrien's proposal.

Although the film companies pay lip service to the Force's objections to their treatment of stories by hiring ex-members as consultants, or by having the Force supply serving members, free of charge, the image portrayed of the Force is still unrealistic. In the hope that Hollywood might portray the Mounted Police more realistically, sometimes troops of horses and riders have been loaned to film companies. This has never improved the plots, but it has saved the companies a lot of money in their not having to hire dozens of cowboys and horses, and then train them to act like the men and horses of the Force, and in not having to provide their own uniforms and equipment. Whenever the Force has co-operated with them, the film companies have tried to convince the public, through extensive publicity, that their films also have been made with its complete approval. The Force, however, has never approved of Hollywood's depiction of its activities.

The earliest film in which the Force allowed its men and horses to take part was a five-hundred-foot semi-documentary, *The Riders of the Plains*, made by the Edison Moving Picture Company in 1910, and partly filmed at the RNWMP barracks at Regina. It was not until *Rose Marie*, released in 1936, was filmed by Metro-Goldwyn-Mayer, partly in British Columbia, that the Force again loaned men and horses to a film company.

The highly romanticized *Rose Marie* was based on the operetta *Rose Marie*, which ran for several years in the 1920s on the stages of New York and London. It is set in the "North West", with Nelson Eddy playing a singing sergeant in the RCMP, and Jeanette McDonald as Rose Marie, a French-Canadian opera star. She goes from Montreal to the North West looking for her brother, who has escaped from jail,

Members of the Force and their horses in Hollywood in the mid-1930s. (RCMP Museum, Regina)

and is wounded and in hiding. There she meets the sergeant, who falls in love with her. The story is interrupted from time to time with such popular solos, duets and choruses as "Rose Marie", "Indian Love Call" and "The Mounties", and after many complications all ends happily. *Rose Marie* gave the RCMP more publicity than any other film about the Force, although, like the others, it was an unrealistic portrayal of life as a Mounted Policeman. Even the RCMP could not object to that delightful film, however, except that the Force became known as a "Rose Marie" police force, and eventually its members came to detest the term.

Force members on location in Saskatchewan for the shooting of Alien Thunder *in 1972.*

The RCMP provided sixty men and sixty horses for *The Canadians*, released by 20th Century-Fox in 1961. This film presented a shocking mish-mash of Canadian history. In connection with the Cypress Hills massacre of 1873, it featured Sitting Bull, the American Sioux Indian chief who defeated General Custer at the battle of the Little Bighorn in 1876 and who didn't arrive on the southern prairies of the Canadian North-West Territories until 1877. The RCMP deputy commissioner who served as technical advisor to 20th Century-Fox could do nothing to prevent the film director's distortion of Canadian history. The RCMP felt even worse since Commissioner C. W. Harvison, in the light of earlier films, had objected to supplying the men and horses. The film company, however, had persuaded the Canadian government to bring pressure on the Force, no doubt because they would employ a number of Canadians on location at the site of old Fort Walsh, and because the company had promised to spend about $500,000 in Canada in making the film.

Minx (the dam of Burmese, the first horse the RCMP *gave to Elizabeth* II*) on location during the shooting of* Alien Thunder. *The Force member holding her wears* NWMP *period dress.*

About a decade later, *Alien Thunder*, based on the Riel Rebellion of 1885, was filmed by Onyx Films near Batoche, in Saskatchewan. The RCMP supplied a troop of men and horses with 1885 uniforms and saddlery for the film, which was released in 1973, the Force's centennial year. *Alien Thunder* received the usual Hollywood treatment, but could be enjoyed if, as one historian of the Force, R. C. Featherstonhaugh, had written to an assistant commissioner about an earlier film, the viewer left his "historic glasses" at home.

Films on the Force have generally followed two themes, "Love versus duty" and "The mountie always gets his man", and many people came to believe, wrongly and to the annoyance of the Mounted Police, that the latter is their motto. Nevertheless, the more than 250 Hollywood-made films of varying lengths about the Force, some with horses and some without, have been so widely distributed, in so many countries, that they have established the RCMP as the world's best-known, most glamorous and most romantic police force.

MP

8

THE HORSES THE RCMP GAVE THE QUEEN

BURMESE

No Mounted Police horse ever became a public personality while still with the Force, but one did after it left. That horse was Burmese, whose progress from prairie to palace reads like a fairy tale. As a filly-foal born at the Fort Walsh breeding ranch in Saskatchewan in 1962, she was so undersized that it seemed certain the RCMP would have to discard her. Yet she grew to meet RCMP standards and eventually became Queen Elizabeth II's favourite horse, living at Windsor Castle.

Burmese's sire and dam were a strange pair. Her sire, Faux Pas, was a registered dark brown Thoroughbred race horse, though black in appearance, who in 1951, as a three-year-old, had won the Ascot Gold Vase. After the RCMP purchased him in England in 1955 at the age of seven, he was taken immediately to Fort Walsh, where the breeding career of the even-tempered stallion lasted from 1956 to 1967, during which time most of his foals were black.

Burmese's dam, Minx, was a non-descript short-legged black mare of uncertain background, bought in 1959 by the RCMP from a farmer in Manitoba for her breeding qualities which, like Faux Pas', included a highly desirable even temperament. Minx's first foal in the RCMP was born in 1961, and her second, in 1962, was Burmese. Minx remained in the Force until the mid-1970s, and was the dam of about ten black foals, all of which served in the RCMP either as equitation or Musical Ride horses.

Burmese was a beautiful foal, and in many ways she seemed a perfect example of the kind of horse the RCMP aimed to breed: pure black, with perfect conformation, and gentle but spirited. Unfortunately, she was remarkably undersized. But instead

Burmese, the lead horse of the Musical Ride, 1968.

of culling this otherwise perfect foal at six months of age, the RCMP kept her for another year. At eighteen months she was still undersized but otherwise still perfect, so again the Force kept her instead of culling her.

When she was two years old the RCMP sent her from the Fort Walsh ranch to the Regina stables. They hoped that a year of regular food, exercise and grooming, plus indoor living, would enable her to catch up with the other horses of her age, who would not go to Regina until they were three years old.

Burmese grew as the police had hoped and in 1965, at age three, she became a recruit equitation horse. Everyone was pleased when the beautiful and likeable filly showed promise of becoming a Musical Ride horse. In the summer of 1966, however, the Canadian government announced that the RCMP would discontinue recruit equitation training, which meant that Burmese, like the other equitation horses, would be sold. The Force, however, was permitted to keep the Musical Ride. The riding instructors replaced three of the older Ride horses with the three best equitation horses, which of course included their favourite, Burmese.

A few months later while touring with the Ride, Burmese and the other horses were running loose in a field. The sleek black mare ran into barbed wire and gashed her chest. Again the RCMP were afraid that she was lost to them, but a local veterinarian tended her wounds with remarkable skill. When the police asked for his bill, he said they owed him nothing: he had long admired the RCMP and was pleased to be of service to them.

Fortunately for Burmese, the Musical Ride tour in western Canada was coming to an end, and she returned to Regina with the other horses. After good rest and care during the remainder of the autumn and the following winter, by the spring of 1967 she had recovered completely, with no visible scar, and she resumed her role in the Musical Ride. That year, Canada's centennial, the black mare performed so well that she became the leading file, that is, the right hand horse in the leading section, ridden by the most experienced rider of the group. From this leading position, the leading file's rider controls the Ride by giving signals with a nod of the head to the other riders when a change in movement is required. Hence the leading file must be alertly responsive to its rider's aids and keen to perform. Burmese had both those qualities, and it seemed that she would remain with the Musical Ride for the rest of her working life.

Then, in the autumn of 1968, the beautiful black mare was again favoured by good fortune. Staff Sergeant Ralph Cave, the riding master at Rockcliffe, suggested that the RCMP should present one of its horses to Her Majesty, Queen Elizabeth II,

Burmese with a member of the London Metropolitan Police, Mounted Division, during her reorientation training for Her Majesty's Birthday Parade, 1975. (Commissioner of Police, New Scotland Yard)

the Honorary Commissioner of the Force. The Queen agreed to accept one, and the RCMP chose its best horse, Burmese.

Her original training in the mid-1960s, however, fell far short of the training given to RCMP horses even a few years later. She had been "broken" and was in an equitation squad, being ridden by recruits, only a few months after she began her training as a three-year-old. Thus she received most of her basic training "on the job", and her further training, as a Musical Ride horse, was hurried and skimpy. She had never had the intensive training that would fit her to be a recreational saddle horse for Queen Elizabeth. The RCMP chose Corporal Frede Rasmussen, a riding instructor engaged earlier because of his excellent qualifications, to mold Burmese into such a horse.

The black mare's new training involved much of the basic training now given a young horse on the lunge line, to make sure that she was sufficiently supple laterally, and that her balance in that exercise was satisfactory. Later she was trained over spaced poles and over similarly spaced low jumps, so that she would lengthen her stride and further improve her balance. After she had learned these lessons and many others, Corporal Rasmussen let her put them into practice in the large open spaces surrounding the Rockcliffe barracks and acquainted her with all the aids known to a fully trained rider such as Queen Elizabeth. He included jumps of all kinds in her training program, and guided her over undulating ground, signalling by the judicious use of his hands and legs that she was to speed up or slow down. Also, he made sure that she acquired stamina by taking her for long, hard rides, and at last he reported to his superiors that Burmese had become a top-class recreational saddle horse.

In April 1969, Burmese accompanied the Musical Ride when it was flown to Britain. On the morning of April 28, RCMP Commissioner M. F. A Lindsay, George McIlraith, the Minister in charge of the Force, and other Canadian dignitaries assembled on the lawn at Windsor Castle. Nearby were Staff Sergeant Cave on Burmese, and an escort of four mounted Musical Ride members. Soon the Queen arrived, and in a brief ceremony Commissioner Lindsay presented Burmese to her.

The Queen was delighted with the beautiful mare, and later asked if Burmese might perform with the Musical Ride scheduled to appear at the Royal Windsor Agricultural Show in a few days. Although Burmese had not taken part in the Ride for many months she performed well at the show, but not as the leading file. Her rider, at Her Majesty's request, carried the Queen's own pennon on his lance, so that she could easily follow Burmese.

Her Majesty Queen Elizabeth II on Burmese in Her Majesty's Birthday Parade en route to the Trooping of the Colour ceremony. (British Information Services)

The Queen discusses Burmese with Staff Sergeant Ralph Cave after the presentation. (Windsor (Slough-Eton) Express)

Burmese and escort at Windsor Castle for the official presentation, April 1969. (Windsor (Slough-Eton) Express)

Burmese, aged twenty-one in 1983, at her Windsor Castle stable. (Pat Crawley)

In July 1973 Queen Elizabeth was presented with these five horses from which to choose her second RCMP-bred mount. She chose Jerry, the gelding in the centre, and renamed him Centenial.

A few days later, in Windsor Great Park, Queen Elizabeth rode her newly acquired Canadian horse, which by this time was stabled permanently in the royal stables at Windsor Castle. The Queen was so pleased with Burmese that she planned, if possible, to ride her six weeks hence, in the Sovereign's Birthday Parade, which would include the Trooping of the Colour, both of them parts of traditional British pageantry, the latter ceremony known to have been performed as early as 1755, during the reign of King George III. If Queen Elizabeth's plan materialized, Burmese would be the first personally owned horse that Her Majesty would ride in her Birthday Parade. Her earlier mounts, from 1954 to 1968, had been supplied by the Mounted Branch of the London Metropolitan Police, as had the horses her father, King George VI, had ridden in such parades during his reign.

The mounted branch of the London Metropolitan Police then took charge of Burmese and tested her to learn if she would make a suitable royal mount for ceremonials. A policeman rode her along noisy, traffic-clogged London streets, took her to various Guards ceremonies and even to noisy soccer games, and subjected her to highly amplified music. The Metropolitan Mounted Police also tested her patience. A policeman rode her along quiet side streets and made her stand there, and in children's playgrounds, for long periods, as she would have to do during the Trooping of the Colour ceremony.

After several weeks of testing, the police reported to the Crown Equerry that Burmese was a perfectly reliable horse, and that the Queen could ride her with complete confidence. Burmese's Canadian experience with the Musical Ride had prepared her well for the British testing. One more test remained, however. The Queen rode side-saddle in ceremonial parades, and Burmese had never carried anyone side-saddle. Now the black mare took training with side-saddle in the riding school at Buckingham Palace Mews, supervised by a skilled horsewoman who acted as Her Majesty's understudy. After a few training periods, the horsewoman reported that Burmese was as reliable carrying a rider side-saddle as carrying one astride, and so the Queen rode her in further practice sessions.

On June 14, 1969, the day of the Sovereign's Birthday Parade, Burmese was taken from the police stables in Whitehall, where she had been living, to the Royal Mews at Buckingham Palace. The Mews, incidentally, a name derived from the French "mue" and the Latin "murare", meaning "to change", was so called because the early English kings kept their falcons in such "mews" during the birds' periods of mewing or moulting. Although Henry VIII replaced the falcons there with horses, the name "mews" has remained in use. At the Royal Mews, Burmese's police saddlery was removed, and after she had received an extra grooming, she was fitted with the accoutrements of the Scots Guards whose Colour was to be "trooped" that day. The saddle she carried had recently been presented to the Queen by the Worshipful Company of Saddlers, and its value was estimated at £300. From the Mews, the mare was led to the Palace courtyard from which the Queen would ride her to meet the procession, already formed outside the palace gates.

Burmese, only six weeks away from her RCMP Rockcliffe stables across the Atlantic Ocean, then carried Queen Elizabeth II down the Mall to the Horse Guards Parade grounds. The black mare took no notice of the thousands of cheering people, of the blaring of massed bands or of the jingling accoutrements of the Sovereign's Mounted Escort, the Life Guards and the Blues and Royals of the Household Cavalry, following close behind.

The beautiful black mare proved to be an ideal ceremonial horse for the Queen. Unlike some of her less-docile predecessors, she remained unperturbed by what was going on around her as the Queen took the first salute and then rode from one rank of guards to another during the inspections. The patient creature remained motionless during the Trooping of the Colour, in which a specially selected group of the Scots Guards, the honoured regiment of the day, trooped their own special flag, or Colour, past long rows of Scots and other Foot Guards. Burmese still remained motionless, like a jet statue, as Queen Elizabeth saluted from time to time while rows of Foot Guards marched past, followed by the Household Cavalry, all regiments supported by bands, on foot or mounted. Meanwhile, Staff Sergeant Cave, who had first suggested that the RCMP should present one of its horses to the Queen, was seated in the stands at the Horse Guards Parade Grounds, watching the whole proceedings intently and with pride, at the special invitation of Her Majesty.

When at last the ceremony ended, Burmese carried the Queen sedately, as befitted her royal rider, as Her Majesty led the Guards back to Buckingham Palace. There Burmese was rewarded with a royal pat and a few murmured words of thanks.

Each year since 1969 Burmese has been the Queen's mount in her Birthday Parade. For twelve years the parade went smoothly, but in 1981 an incident occurred which could have caused serious injury to the Queen, particularly if she had been riding a horse with a temperament less placid than that of Burmese. As the Queen was entering the parade grounds from the Mall, a man in the crowd fired five blank revolver shots at close range. It was natural for Burmese to be startled, and she bounded forward a few steps. The Queen remained seated and was in full control of the situation within a few seconds.

A member of the Queen's household explained later that while the shots might have had some slight effect on the horse, it was the closing in of the Sovereign's Escort that caused Burmese to bound forward to get out of the way. Later, the press, the British public watching on television, and members of the royal family praised the horse's behaviour during the incident which would have caused many horses to panic.

In 1984 Burmese was twenty-two years old, and obviously consideration will have to be given to replacing her in due course. Nevertheless it seems likely that with the care she is receiving she will remain the Queen's mount for several years to come. When a visiting Canadian asked the horsewoman who now handles Burmese for Queen Elizabeth what makes the mare so special as the Queen's mount, the answer was that she is more than just a well-trained saddle horse of good appearance and suitable temperament. "The difference between riding Burmese and an ordinary horse," the horsewoman said, "is the difference between riding in a Rolls Royce and a mini-car." Much credit is also given by palace officials to the training Burmese received at the hands of the RCMP riding instructor, Corporal (later Staff Sergeant) Rasmussen.

For a few years following Burmese's presentation to Queen Elizabeth, the mare was kept at the Windsor Castle stables. A few weeks before Her Majesty's Birthday Parade she was taken to London to allow the Mounted Division of the Metropolitan Police to re-acquaint her with London street noises and others she would have to endure during the parade.

During her years with the Royal Canadian Mounted Police, Burmese was never used for practical police work, and later, when she became the Queen's horse, it seemed she never would be. In recent years, however, she has spent more time with the London Metropolitan Police, and they exercise her and keep her familiar with city sights and sounds by using her as a patrol horse on regular duty. Her rider is equipped with a police radio, and, like police who patrol in cars, he has a link with the crime records computer. The mounted patrols in which Burmese has been used have resulted in more than 250 arrests. She still spends some time at Windsor Castle, however, when the Queen requires her as a recreational horse.

Burmese also takes part in ceremonies in addition to the Sovereign's Birthday Parade, and this adds to the fairytale-like qualities of her success story. For example, in 1977 she took part in Queen Elizabeth II's Silver Jubilee procession, though not as the Queen's mount. Her Majesty and the Duke of Edinburgh rode in the "golden" State Coach, drawn by eight white horses. Burmese, ridden by the Crown Equerry, Sir John Miller, and Centenial, the Queen's second RCMP gift horse, ridden by Prince Charles, occupied places of honour as they followed immediately behind the State Coach, followed in turn by mounted members of the British nobility and senior army officers, and the Household Cavalry.

All those who have handled Burmese, from her early days on the remote ranch in the Cypress Hills in southwestern Saskatchewan to the present, have been lavish in their praise of her beauty, grace, temperament and intelligence. A letter from Sergeant Robin Porter, of the Mounted Branch of the London Metropolitan Police, to the senior author of this book in April 1984, constitutes a fitting tribute to the remarkable mare:

> I have been most fortunate having been asked to look after Burmese some six years ago. A superb mare. I only wish she were ten years younger. She has never given me a moment's problem and I do not suppose I shall ever have such a well mannered, well schooled honest mount again. I have been associated with the preparation of Royal horses for most of my service and Burmese has certainly made my job easier.

Sergeant Porter's comments constitute a compliment not only to Burmese, but also to the breeding and training of RCMP horses.

CENTENIAL

When the RCMP celebrated its centennial in 1973 it presented a second horse to its honorary Commissioner, Queen Elizabeth II. Perhaps this was partly because Burmese was eleven years old by then and would eventually have to be replaced as the Queen's mount in her annual Birthday Parade.

Whereas Burmese had been chosen for the Queen by the RCMP, she herself chose Centenial when she visited Canada to take part in the celebrations of the Force's hundredth birthday. Before she made her choice, however, Commissioner W. L. Higgitt presented her with a token horse during the celebrations at Regina in July, on the understanding that she could choose her own horse when she visited Ottawa about a week later.

On August 2 when Her Majesty visited the Rockcliffe barracks she was offered the choice of one of five three-year-olds. She chose Jerry, a black gelding, whose name was changed to Centennial, the spelling of which was changed to "Centenial" after the horse arrived at Windsor Castle four years later. In her choice of

The Queen taking a close look at Jerry.

Centenial the Queen might have been influenced by the fact that he is a descendant of the great race horse Man O' War. Centenial's sire, Alton, was, through his dam, a great grandson of Man O' War, thus making Centenial a great-great-grandson of that famous horse. Centenial is also related to Burmese. His mother, Watch, had been sired by the stallion Faux Pas who was also the sire of Burmese, thus making Centenial, through his mother, a nephew of Burmese.

When the Queen chose Centenial, she had ridden Burmese for four years and was especially pleased with the way the mare had been trained. She asked if Centenial could remain with the RCMP and be trained in the same way. Sergeant Frede Rasmussen, who as Corporal Rasmussen had trained Burmese, was still in the Force, so Centenial was turned over to him.

When Queen Elizabeth chose her second RCMP horse as a gift from the Force, he had no mane or forelock, like Burmese in 1969. But as Centenial was not

The official presentation of Centenial to Queen Elizabeth at Windsor Castle in 1977.

delivered to her until 1977, by that time his mane and forelock had been allowed to grow according to the Queen's wishes, just as Burmese's had been once she became the Queen's horse, although the horses in the Force during that time continued to have theirs roached (completely clipped). During at least the first eight decades of the Force's existence its horses had manes and forelocks of varying lengths. Then for about two decades before 1978 they were kept severely roached. In 1978 Commissioner Robert Simmonds ordered that manes and forelocks be allowed to grow, so now the horses have "pulled manes", about four inches long near the ears and withers and gradually lengthening to about eight inches half-way between. The forelocks are kept about five inches in length, thus the hair stays above eye level.

After Centenial was presented to Queen Elizabeth, he was turned over to the Mounted Division of the London Metropolitan Police for crowd orientation training. His Canadian trainer, Sergeant Frede Rasmussen, is on the left.

Burmese and Centenial being honoured at the Horse of the Year Show at Olympia, London, in 1977, after they figured prominently in the Silver Jubilee procession that year. (HRH Prince Charles rode Centenial and Sir John Miller, the Crown Equerry, rode Burmese directly behind Queen Elizabeth's golden coach in the Jubilee procession. (Leslie Lane)

Over the three and a half years after the Queen chose Centenial, he was not only trained to be the best possible saddle horse, but was also used in the RCMP Musical Ride, as Burmese had been used before him. When the Ride went to England in 1977 to appear in the Queen's Silver Jubilee procession and to perform the Musical Ride in Britain, Centenial accompanied it to London. He was presented to the Queen by Commissioner Maurice Nadon, with Sergeant Rasmussen in attendance. By this time Centenial had grown to seventeen hands and the Queen found it difficult to believe that he was the same horse she had chosen almost four years earlier. The Queen suggested, with a smile, that perhaps she would need a ladder to help her get on his back.

A few weeks later, Centenial and Burmese occupied an honoured position in the Queen's Silver Jubilee procession. Still later that year, both horses were honoured at the Horse of the Year Show at Olympia in London. On that occasion they were ridden by members of the Mounted Branch of the London Metropolitan Police dressed in the Queen's livery.

When Staff Sergeant Frede Rasmussen retired from the RCMP in 1978, Queen Elizabeth sent him a personal letter saying how much she appreciated his training of Burmese and Centenial and wishing him well on his retirement.

Centenial, like his "aunt" Burmese, is kept in London for periods of each year and used by the Metropolitan Police so that he, like the black mare, will remain familiar with the sights and sounds of the London streets. He is, however, often stabled at Windsor Castle, to be available as a recreational horse for the royal family. Sometimes both he and Burmese are stabled there, so that Queen Elizabeth and her special guests may ride them in Windsor Park, as she and U.S. President Ronald Reagan did when he visited Queen Elizabeth in 1982.

Centenial's increasing experience as a royal mount in various ceremonial parades, together with his experience as a police patrol horse in London, make him an obvious choice to succeed Burmese as the Queen's mount during the annual Sovereign's Birthday Parade. Perhaps then the RCMP will provide a third black horse which will eventually succeed Centenial. It seems likely that the RCMP has started a tradition of supplying a black mount for the British monarch to ride in prestigious military parades.

BIBLIOGRAPHY

Archer, John A. *Saskatchewan: A History.* Saskatoon: Western Producer Books,1980.
Atkin, Ronald. *Maintain the Right.* Toronto: Macmillan, 1973.
Berton, Pierre. *Hollywood Canada.* Toronto: McClelland and Stewart, 1975.
Braider, D. *The Life, History and Image of the Horse.* New York: Madison Square Press, 1973.
Campbell, Judith. *Royal Horses.* London: New English Library, 1981.
Carruthers, H. B. C. "Mounted Police and Motion Pictures". RCMP *Quarterly* (July 1940).
Caulkin, T. B. "Siberia, 1918-1919". RCMP *Quarterly* (October 1941).
Charters, Dean. *Mountie.* Toronto: Collier-Macmillan, 1973.
D'Artigue, J. *Six Years in the North West.* Belleville: Mika, 1973.
Dempsey, Hugh A. *Jerry Potts.* Calgary: Glenbow Foundation, 1966.
Denny, C. E. *The Law Marches West.* Toronto: J.M. Dent, 1939.
Dick, W. "RCMP Musical Ride (1948)". RCMP *Quarterly* (July 1949).
Duncan, Andrew, *The Reality of Monarchy.* London: Heinemann, 1970.
Dwight, Charles P. *Life in the North-West Mounted Police and Other Sketches.* Toronto: The National Publishing Co., 1892.
Ensminger, M. E. *Horses and Tack.* Boston: Houghton-Mifflin, 1977.
Fahie, J. M. "Gymkhana at Rockcliffe". RCMP *Quarterly* (January 1950).
Geddes, Candida, ed. *The Horse.* London: Peerage Books, 1978.
Goldring, Philip. *The First Contingent: The North-West Mounted Police, 1873-74.* Canadian Historic Sites Paper. Ottawa: Parks Canada, 1979.
Goodall, D. M. *Horses of the New World.* London: David and Charles, 1973.
Greenfield, T. E. "The 'Osses Et Em". RCMP *Quarterly* (Fall 1982).
Harvison, C. W. *The Horsemen.* Toronto: McClelland and Stewart, 1967.
Horrall, S. W. "Veteran of the March West". RCMP *Quarterly* (October 1971).
———. "Lady Dewdney's Own". RCMP *Quarterly* (Summer 1984).
———. *The Pictorial History of the Royal Canadian Mounted Police.* Toronto: McGraw-Hill Ryerson, 1973.

Kelly, Nora. *The Men of the Mounted.* Toronto: J. M. Dent, 1949.

______. and Kelly, William. *The Royal Canadian Mounted Police: A Century of History.* Edmonton: Hurtig, 1973.

Kemp, Vernon A. W. *Without Fear, Favour or Affection.* Toronto: Longmans Green, 1958.

______. *Scarlet and Stetson.* Toronto: Ryerson, 1964.

Kidston, R. J. "Coronation Contingent". RCMP *Quarterly* (October 1937).

Loew, F. M. and Wood, E. H. *Vet in the Saddle.* Saskatoon: Western Producer Books, 1979.

Longstreth, T. M. *The Silent Force.* New York: The Century Co., 1927.

Maunsell, E. H. "Maunsell's Story". RCMP *Quarterly* (Winter 1983).

Munday, L. "Mounts of the Force". RCMP *Quarterly* (July 1949).

North-West Mounted Police. *Annual Reports,* 1874-1904.

Pope, J. *Royal Tour of Canada.* Ottawa: King's Printer, 1901.

Radcliffe, H. H. "The Premiere of the North-West Mounted Police". RCMP *Quarterly* (January 1941).

Royal Canadian Mounted Police. *A Brief Outline of the History and Organization of the RCMP Musical Ride,* 1978.

______. *Annual Reports,* 1920 to present.

______. *Equitation Branch Policy Manual: Remount Training,* 1978.

______. *North-West Mounted Police Saddlery, 1874-1904.* Unpublished booklet, 1978.

______. *Outline of the RCMP Breeding Program,* 1977.

Royal North-West Mounted Police. *Annual Reports,* 1905-20.

Steele, S. B. *Forty Years in Canada.* Toronto: McClelland and Stewart, 1915.

Turner, C. Frank. *Across the Medicine Line.* Toronto: McClelland and Stewart, 1973.

Turner, J. P. *The North-West Mounted Police.* 2 vols. Ottawa: King's Printer, 1950.

Van Patten, R. C. "Police Remounts". RCMP *Quarterly* (April 1951).

Walker, C. "L'Esprit Cavalier". RCMP *Quarterly* (October 1948).

Yuill, A. "Recruit Training". RCMP *Quarterly* (October 1954).

Index

636.108
K295h Kelly, William, 1911-
The horses of the Royal Canadian Mounted Police : a pictorial history / William and Nora Kelly. -- [1st ed.]. -- Toronto, Ont. : Doubleday Canada Ltd. ; Garden City, N.Y. : Doubleday, 1984.
288 p. : ill. (some col.) ; 26 cm.
Bibliography: p. 282-283.
Includes index.
ISBN 0-385-19544-3

c-1
CCL

1. Police horses--Canada--History. 2. Royal Canadian Mounted Police--History. I. Kelly, Nora (Nora Hickson) II. Title

PJo JOCCxc 84-10344